'Austerity is a self-defeating economic policy which has taken an ugly toll in Greece. The silver lining is that, along with the mass unemployment and the rise of Nazism that it engendered, austerity also occasioned a cultural renaissance. This volume of multilingual poetry is a splendid example: living proof that the Greek crisis is of global significance. It deserves an international audience. Now!'
Yanis Varoufakis

'"Wherever I go, Greece wounds me," said George Seferis, the Nobel prize-winning poet born in 1900. There have been wonderful generations of Greek poets since his day. Ancient Greek poems, the Classics, are the basis of Western poetry. For Anglophone readers, they need re-voicing in every generation: brilliant English versions of Homer, from James Joyce to Derek Walcott and Alice Oswald, help us re-hear them. Today's Greek poets, however, have a special relationship, of a peculiarly charged and conflicted intimacy, with these founding texts. The light these poets work in, and the language they speak, are still the light and the language of Homer and the great tragedians. *Austerity Measures*, appearing as Greece faces new difficulties and suffering, offers a newly poignant, imaginative and resonant body of work. The wonderfully inventive translations reveal a different Greece to English readers: one that does not cancel the past but builds upon it'
Ruth Padel

'One of the few benefits of turbulent historical moments is that they tend to give rise to a new cultural efflorescence. Nowhere is this more obvious than in this fascinating anthology, which gathers together a remarkably rich, resourceful range of poetic idioms in response to a common sense of moral and political emergency'
Terry Eagleton

'Karen Van Dyck has collected an extraordinary group of poets and translators who are bound to put Greek poetry on the map again. I've seen it happen twice in my life: with the Generation of the Thirties that included Cavafy, Seferis, Elytes and Ritsos, and that reached world recognition; and again, during the Dictatorship of the Colonels, when the group that appeared in the Harvard anthology *Eighteen Texts* (1972) and others living under censorship earned international recognition with the help of accomplished translators. Now, during another crisis in the country, we find exciting new voices emerging, and I am convinced that they are once again saying something no one else is saying. Call it the knowledge that emerges from the underside of devastation and the creative illumination that comes with tragedy, but something is going on in Greece that we aren't seeing in the news. I give this anthology my strongest support'

Edmund Keeley

'Karen Van Dyck's *Austerity Measures* is a timely trove of new Greek voices that reverberates with urgency and authority, girded with hard-earned truth and a deep seeing necessary for our twenty-first century. Here's a language that goes for the gut and the heart, an earthy sonority. It holds us accountable for what we witness and feel in a time of globalism. This marvellous compendium of lived imagery speaks freely'

Yusef Komunyakaa

ABOUT THE EDITOR

Karen Van Dyck is the Kimon A. Doukas Professor of Modern Greek Literature in the Classics Department at Columbia University. She writes on Modern Greek and Greek Diaspora literature, and gender and translation theory. Her translations include her edited and co-edited collections: *The Rehearsal of Misunderstanding: Three Collections by Contemporary Greek Women Poets* (Wesleyan, 1998); *A Century of Greek Poetry* (Cosmos, 2004); *The Scattered Papers of Penelope: New and Selected Poems by Katerina Anghelaki-Rooke* (Graywolf, 2009), a Lannan Translation selection; and *The Greek Poets: Homer to the Present* (Norton, 2010). Her translations of this new generation of writers from Greece have appeared in *Brooklyn Rail*, *Asymptote*, and *The Baffler*.

AUSTERITY MEASURES

The New Greek Poetry

Edited by Karen Van Dyck

PENGUIN BOOKS

PENGUIN BOOKS

UK | USA | Canada | Ireland | Australia
India | New Zealand | South Africa

Penguin Books is part of the Penguin Random House group of companies
whose addresses can be found at global.penguinrandomhouse.com.

First published 2016

001

Set in 9/12 pt Palatino Linotype
Text design by Claire Mason
Typeset by Jouve (UK), Milton Keynes
Printed in Great Britain by Clays Ltd, St Ives plc

A CIP catalogue record for this book is available from the British Library

ISBN: 978–0–241–25062–4

www.greenpenguin.co.uk

For Jacob, Benjamin, and Leander

It is difficult
to get the news from poems
          yet men die miserably every day
          for lack
of what is found there.

William Carlos Williams

CONTENTS

II
MYTH AND MEDICINE
DIY and Small Press Poets

III
UNJUST PUNISHMENT
Poets Online

IV
STORYTELLING
Poets in Performance and across the Arts

VI
BORDER ZONES
Poets between Cultures and Languages

HIVA PANAHI

INTRODUCTION

When there is less to go around, people fight, grab, get tough. Lately, Greece and the Balkans have been living with more than their share of less. Hunger, unemployment, slashed pensions, and ruined businesses draw chalk circles around victims daily in Athens. Electricity and water shortages reach levels associated with countries at war. More than 27 per cent of Greeks are unemployed. Fifty-five per cent of young people, particularly those in the areas of technology and education, have left Greece to find work elsewhere. Forty per cent of children were living in poverty in 2014, and the number is now approaching 50 per cent. Public debt is the highest in Europe, over 180 per cent of GDP, while austerity measures make staying in the euro zone as difficult as a Grexit. The need for fast answers pushes voters to political extremes. Broken promises and corruption on all sides breed unfounded accusations and fatalism. Hardly anyone keeps money in the bank any more. News of murders and robberies shares equal airtime with ads for high-tech security systems. Meanwhile, refugees fleeing Syria, Afghanistan, and Iraq arrive on islands like Lesvos in their hundreds, and at times in their thousands, not wanting to be in Greece, but unable to get to countries with better social services. And where the refugee boats go, local fishermen follow, lining up on shore to jockey for their engines, hoping to resell them at a profit. More people, less to go around.

Poetry, though, is one thing there is more of. Much more. Poets writing graffiti on walls, poets reading in public squares, theaters, and empty lots, poets performing in slams, chanting slogans, and singing songs at rallies, poets blogging and posting on the internet, poets teaming up with artists and musicians, poets teaching workshops to schoolchildren and migrants. In all of the misery and mess, new poetry is everywhere, too large and too various a body of writing to fit neatly on either side of any ideological rift. Even with bookshops closing and publishers unsure of paper supplies for the next book, poets are getting their poems out there. Established literary magazines are flourishing; small presses and new periodicals abound. And if poetry production is defying economic recession, it is also overleaping the divisions of nation, class, and gender. Greek poetry – poetry written in the Greek language – can be written inside or outside of Greece, by Greeks or non-Greeks, rich or poor, women or men, young or old. Not since the Colonels' Dictatorship in the early 1970s, when poets such as Katerina Anghelaki-Rooke, Jenny Mastoraki, and Pavlina Pampoudi first appeared, has there been such an abundance of poetry being written, nor such a multitude of projects undertaken. Indeed, the historical affinity does not stop there: it is those same poets of the Dictatorship who are doing the lion's share of mentoring in the new generation.

The present anthology samples this living tradition, bearing witness not only to the hard lives being led in Greece and the Balkans today, but also to what poetry does best: offering new ways to imagine what can be radically different realities. From the lyrical dream fragments of Anna Griva to the apocalyptic neo-realism of Stathis Antoniou to Thomas Tsalapatis's wry postmodern prose poems, nothing here is as one might expect, even from the Greek poetry of the recent past. Not many statues; not much myth, at least in the classical sense; no patriotism; not even the very intense light or references to the sea we know from the Nobel Laureates George Seferis and Odysseas Elytis.

What most distinguishes the poetry of this new millennium from what came before it is, on the one hand, its diversity – there are no clear-cut schools or factions – and, on the other hand, the cultural conditions that it takes for granted. Loosely connected, living in Athens, Thessaloniki, and smaller places like Patras, Ksanthi, and Syros as well as outside Greece in Nicosia, Bergen, Paris, and New York, many of these poets have had ready access to computers and the internet since childhood. The reality they seek to represent – here most obviously in poems with titles like 'Empty Inbox' and 'Txt Message' – is infiltrated by, and includes, the virtual. They have grown up with the under-standing that vast stores of information and a wide range of different languages are only ever a click away. Even those who have not been exposed to a mixture of languages in their own cities, towns, and villages, even those who have somehow missed it on the radio and television, have inevi-tably found it on their computer screens; and mother tongue, as such, often doesn't determine the language they choose to write in. Some publish in two or more languages; some self-translate. There are more women writing than at any time in the intervening decades since the Dictatorship, as if by placing almost everyone on the front line once again the hard times have levelled other inequalities.

All of this variety, of course, poses problems for the editor of an anthology such as this. Although the criteria for inclu-sion are roughly language (Greek), age (under fifty), and date of publication (in the last decade), there are exceptions. A few poets write first in English, then in Greek, translating their own work. Some began writing elsewhere but went relatively unrecognized, or turned to Greek only after start-ing careers in Bulgarian, Serbian, and other languages, and are therefore suitable for inclusion despite their greater age: whether linguistically or geographically, they remain com-paratively new to Greek poetry, if not to poetry as a whole. A handful of poems that anticipate the present mood and times, although published on the cusp of the new millen-nium, are also here. Literature often tells us what will happen before history has time to unfold.

Then there are the many possible ways of organizing a survey of this lively and fragmented scene. Should the poets be ordered alphabetically or chronologically? Around themes, or around poetic influences from previous generations? It is clear that some kind of organization is required, not least because many of the poets are making their first appearance in English and will be unknown to most of this book's imaginable readership. Ultimately, division into different venues of poetic activity has seemed to make the most sense. From the magazines and small presses to the blogs and performance spaces, in Athens, in the provinces, and abroad, it is the scenes and their internal variety that shape what this poetry is doing. Poets don't, of course, publish only with one magazine or in one place – there is fluidity and crossover – but the fact that they tend, in my experience, to be most aware of the work of contemporaries associated with their own sphere of production suggests to me that this kind of mapping does serve a real purpose. The underlying hope is that it will help to render an unfamiliar landscape significantly more legible, more navigable, and perhaps even more alive for the reader.

In the end, these poets are worth grouping together because they pose the question of what it can mean for poetry to be political, or to be apolitical, in times of social and economic crisis. They live within the limits of capital controls and unrepresentative referenda; if they live abroad, they are invested in the news of family and friends living within those limits; but, in every case, they write through it. Even in the work of poets who began publishing earlier than the past decade, austerity and an uncertain future are unavoidable presences, whether front and center or peripheral to their vision. But what is the relationship of poetry to the world it inhabits? If, as William Carlos Williams says in the lines which I have made the epigraph to this book, 'men die miserably every day / for lack / of what is found' in poetry, then what is in this writing that could have made those lives less miserable, or even saved them? What *is* found there? If it's *'difficult* to get the news from poems', doesn't this mean that it is nonetheless somehow possible – especially if we come at poems 'at a slight angle to the universe', as E. M. Forster described the Greek Diaspora poet C. P. Cavafy?

There have been other anthologies of poetry about the Greek crisis. By expanding its purview to the whole of contemporary Greek poetry, however, and including a much greater proportion of work which *doesn't* directly address the political situation, this survey aims to provide deeper and more various answers. The poets associated with φρμκ (*Farmakon*) magazine (the title means both 'poison' and 'medicine' in Greek) and grouped here under 'Myth and Medicine' seek to create symbolic worlds that deal obliquely, almost homeopathically, with society's suffering and bafflement. The internet poets in 'Unjust Punishment' – the most explicitly political of those collected here – mix pop culture and micro-level current events into poems which read like dispatches from the streets of inner-city Athens and elsewhere. Those in the 'Storytelling' section are more apt to use narrative and historical fact to place the present in its context; and the sixth and final section, 'Border Zones', moves the focus outside Greece altogether, connecting migrants from the Balkans and Middle East as well as Diaspora Greeks who write in Greek with the double vision of another culture and language.

One approach runs throughout the anthology. These are the 'measures' of the title, which refers not only to courses of state action, but also to the poetic strategies employed in response. Austerity measures call both for cutting back and for turning limited resources to new and creative ends. In poetic terms, this often involves rhyme and syllabic count. In the opening poem, A. E. Stallings dramatizes this resourcefulness by repurposing a news headline, 'Greece downgraded deeper into junk', and using that headline's last word as one of the two repeating rhymes of a villanelle embedded in a prose poem. Similarly, the traditional fifteen-syllable line of the folksong, not coincidentally called 'political verse' (πολιτικός στίχος), winds its way through much of the original Greek in this anthology, surfacing at the most unexpected moments. Yiannis Efthymiades's meditation on the final moments of a jumper from the World Trade Center, *9/11 or Falling Man*, takes still another inventive approach, following the spirit of its long 27-syllable lines by expanding the brevity of a ten-second descent into a series of poems that runs for twenty-seven pages.

This question of resourcefulness can also point to a more general ethos of recycling, reminiscent of the empty shopping cart, put to an imaginative range of uses, that shows up with growing frequency in contemporary Greek film, art, and even a promotional video for Piraeus Bank. More often than not, in this poetry, it is the icons of the everyday that bring the crisis home: IKEA cartons for a roof in Jazra Khaleed's 'Words', for instance, or a caterpillar eaten alive in the center of Athens in Iana Boukova's 'Black *Haiku*'. In 'Mama's a Poet', meanwhile, Glykeria Basdeki turns household chores into a grammar lesson ('all day she cooks up commas / sweeps tenses under the rug') and, in so doing, makes poetry about the everyday political: 'comma', in Greek, means both the punctuation mark and a political party. These poets' relationships to history and current events are a mixed bag, sometimes in-your-face, at other times told at a slant, but always pulling at the corners of language, asking it to take in more, to be more open. The times are an invitation to speak out against dogma, division, and monolingualism – and also, often equally importantly, simply to register the lived experience of Greeks today, the news that stays new when headlines move on to cover other parts of the world.

As for the translators who have contributed to this anthology, many have linguistic identities as mixed as the poets they translate. Like Olga Broumas, Diamanda Galas, and other Greek Diaspora writers and performance artists, Stephanos Papadopoulos lives and works in English, while his poetry often channels Greek with its preponderance of vowels, loanwords, and calques. The same can be said of the poetry of Rachel Hadas and Stallings, although they learned Greek as translators and scholars. Often translators take their diverse affiliations as a cue to experiment with their own language, to stretch readers' expectations in all sorts of new directions, as when Peter Constantine's version of Stathis Baroutsos's 'Speed Dating' finds an analogue for the poet's direct style in the lexicon of the gay online hook-up scene. This is particularly obvious when translators take on the same poet. Krystalli Glyniadakis translates her own poem, 'The Next Hundred Years', with a post-Black Mountain School use of enjambment that fits right into a dominant contemporary American idiom of lyric poetry. Chloe Haralambous ratchets up the register in her translation of Glyniadakis's 'National Hymn' – perhaps to keep postcapitalist readers tuned in to feminism? – translating 'αυνανίζονται' (masturbate) as 'accessorize their wanks'. Stathis Gourgouris, in contrast, imagines Greek and English as one: in a move reminiscent of Richmond Lattimore's translations of Homer, he retains the definite articles and adheres at times to the word order of the Greek when he translates Phoebe Giannisi's poem about Thetis. My efforts place Giannisi in a trans-Atlantic experimental tradition of visual poetics recalling not only her own concrete punctuationless poems, but also those of the late twentieth-century American L=A=N=G=U=A=G=E poets. Her poem about Penelope swimming laps takes the shape of a pool in the English version. Other examples of experimental translation abound, and when possible they are indicated in translators' notes and biographies. For readers and students of Greek, this anthology can provide

the additional pleasure and interest of seeing how transla-
tors relish the problems posed by the macaronic layers of
myth, history, and language that contemporary Greek poetry
exposes.

The translations chosen, for the most part, view constraints
as enabling, rather than limiting: not as a cause for conster-
nation, but as the basis for invention. What is lost in translation
is found again, otherwise and elsewhere. The goal is not to
reproduce the source text – you can't – but to learn from it
so as to make something else possible in the new linguistic
context, acknowledging the linguistic and cultural differ-
ences that translation is summoned to resolve but always
winds up proliferating. Although this anthology maps out
a particular segment of the poetry landscape in Europe, we
must remember that what it discloses is always seen and
heard through the English language. What can be conjured,
woken up, written, and addressed in English? Editorial
weight was consistently placed on the strongest translations,
even at the expense of some very strong original poems.
This anthology of new Greek poetry is representative, then,
not only of a cross-section of Greek poetry now, but also,
simultaneously, of that poetry as it stands in relation to
other places and languages.

My goal has been to deepen and thereby alter the way
readers think of poetry in Europe, especially at its edges
where East and West blur, and to uncover the dilemma of
learning to live with less amid the expectation of more:
what in her last collection the poet and translator Katerina
Anghelaki-Rooke called 'the anorexia of existence'. In post-
crisis Greece, questions of blame and recrimination multiply
in the face of rising suicide rates and hunger strikes. Did
we do this to ourselves, Greeks ask, or was it done to us?
The poems and translations collected here demonstrate
that the impasse Greeks are now facing is not only theirs,
but all of ours, as we struggle to live in a faster, more

culturally heterogeneous world with tools from a slower, more homogeneous past. To recast these poems in the rhythms and multilingual idioms of English with an emphasis on the translated text is to view the crisis cross-culturally, and to treat *Austerity Measures* as a project as much ours as theirs.

Syros, August 2015

NOTE ON TITLES

Throughout this anthology, English translations of Greek book titles are provided so that the reader may get a sense of the larger body of work to which a poem belongs. Only a few poets in the final section have had any collections translated into English yet; these are indicated in bold.

Austerity Measures

If you believe the headlines, then we're sunk. The dateline
oracle, giddy with dread: *Greece downgraded deeper into junk*.
Stash cash beneath the mattress, pack the trunk. Will drach-
mas creep where euros fear to tread? If you believe the
headlines, then we're sunk. A crisis that lasts for years? – call
it a funk. Austerity starves the more its maw is fed, and
downgrades all our deepest bonds to junk.

Every politician is a punk: the right, the left; the blue, the
green, the red; ministers in cahoots with the odd monk.
We've lost our marbles – Elgin took a chunk – Caryatids,
gone on strike, sit down instead. Tear gas lingers like a whiff
of skunk. Weep, Pericles, or maybe just get drunk. We'll
hawk the Parthenon to buy our bread. If you believe
the headlines, then we're sunk, *Greece downgraded deeper
into junk.*

A. E. Stallings

I
TRADITION AND THE INDIVIDUAL TALENT
Poets in Literary Magazines

In the 1980s and 1990s, Greek poetry was going through a dry period. Haris Vlavianos responded by beginning a bi-annual book-length magazine of critical essays and verse, known first as *Ποίηση* (*Poetry*) (1993–2007) and then as *Ποιητική* (*Poetics*) (2008–present). Publication in these magazines is a key common denominator among the poets in this section; another is their prominence. The most established are cultural editors for Greece's oldest newspapers, or hosts of poetry shows on the radio. Unlike the rest of the groups in this anthology, they are predominantly men. Poetically, the focus is on form, on what is classical and what will last. Yiannis Doukas puts rhyme and the poem's shape to work in structuring the dark parts of history. Yannis Stiggas's and Yiannis Efthymiades's verse is more metaphysical, and Efthymiades's more vicious, but both are equally interested in poetic form. Doukas Kapantaïs draws on his grounding in the Classics, as does Dimitra Kotoula, whose work combines the traditional rigour and formality of that literature with the next section's approach to poetry as a healing art.

Poetics is defined, too, by its internationalism, offering emerging poets the chance to read and be read alongside not only the Greek post-war poets, but also the likes of John Ashbery, Anne Carson, Paul Celan, Zbigniew Herbert, Paul Muldoon, and Giuseppe Ungaretti. Accordingly, this section's poets are the likeliest to translate from and have their own poetry translated into English, French, and German. Panayotis Ioannidis's wry, plain style takes something from both Seamus Heaney and Robert Creeley, whom he translates; Dimitris Athinakis, more elegiac and playful, is equally at home with the Anglo-Saxon tradition.

1

PANAYOTIS IOANNIDIS

(Born Athens, Greece, 1967)

To read Panayotis Ioannidis's work is often to be put in mind of the central role poets have historically played in Greece, especially during difficult times, and to find oneself asking what the task of the poet ought to be today. Both his poems and his translations of a variety of English-language poets, among them Seamus Heaney and Robert Creeley, have been appearing in Greek literary journals since 1995. In 2011 he began curating Με τα λόγια [γίνεται] (Words [can] do it), a series of monthly poetry readings at which Greek poets of different generations perform their own poems alongside foreign-language poetry, delivered in the original as well as in translation.

Το Σωσίβιο (*The Lifesaver*), Kastaniotis, 2008;
Ακάλυπτος (*Unsheltered*), Kastaniotis, 2013;
Πολωνία (*Poland*), Kastaniotis, 2016.

Κουνούπι

Εχθές τη νύχτα καθώς διάβαζα
με δυνατό φως στο κρεβάτι
ποίηση γραμμένη υπό συνθήκες καταπίεσης
ένα κουνούπι
με κύκλωνε απειλώντας
και απόλαυση και ύπνο

Το σκότωσα ξανάπιασα το διάβασμα
ώσπου κουράστηκα
κι έσβησα το φως

Ο ποιητής στον διάδρομο

Πηγαίνοντας για τις τουαλέτες
είδα τον ποιητή στο πάτωμα
Ξεπρόβαλε το ογκώδες στήθος του
πάνω στα πλαστικά πλακάκια
Μπροστά πυροσβεστήρας
δίπλα σταχτοδοχείο – πιο κει
ένα καρότσι αχρηστευμένο

Στωικά κοιτάζει
τον απέναντι τοίχο
τα γόνατα των βιαστικών περαστικών

Mosquito

Last night as I was reading
with a bright light in bed
poetry written under the conditions of oppression
a mosquito
circled me, menacing
both enjoyment and sleep

I killed it and took up my reading again,
until I got tired
and turned off the light.

A. E. Stallings

The Poet in the Hallway

As I was headed to the bathroom,
I saw the poet on the floor
His massive chest was emerging
from the linoleum tiles
In front of him, the fire extinguisher,
next to him, the standing ashtray – and there
an abandoned handcart

Stoically he is looking
at the wall opposite,
at the knees of the hurried passers-by.

A. E. Stallings

DIMITRIS ATHINAKIS

(Born Drama, Greece, 1981)

The influence of post-war poets such as Manolis Anagnosta-kis and Tasos Leivaditis informs Dimitris Athinakis's conversational tone and unexpected bendings of the possible. He studied Theology, Philosophy and Philosophy of Science in Athens, Thessaloniki, and Amsterdam, respectively. Today, as Cultural Editor at *Kathimerini*, Greece's most established newspaper, and Creative Director for the social media company medianeras.gr, he is a central figure in the Athens cultural scene. He also translates British and American poetry and fiction.

χωρίσεμεις (*withoutus*), Koinonia ton (de)katon, 2009; Δωμάτιο μικρών διακοπών (*The Short Vacation Room*), Kedros, 2012.

Η επίφαση της τάξης

Ένα συμμαζεμένο σπίτι μου 'χει μείνει.
Στις τσέπες ρούχων
που 'ναι καιρό αφόρετα
βρίσκω εισιτήρια από λεωφορεία –

στο σπίτι ακόμα αναζητώ τον ιδρώτα
που μάλλον ξέχασαν κάποιοι επιβάτες.
Μπερδεύομαι.

Συνεχίζω με τις γωνίες. Τις σκάβω.
Κοιτάζω κάτω απ' τα κρεβάτια
κι από τα πιάτα κάτω
που σωριάζονται με την επίφαση της τάξης.
Πρώτα τα βαθιά, μετά τα ρηχά.
Δεν πάω πουθενά· μόνο λυπάμαι.

Γλείφω το νερό που τρέχει από σπασμένες σωληνώσεις
βάζω τη γλώσσα μου στα λάστιχα του θερμοσίφωνα.
Την απλώνω μέχρι να τεντωθεί όσο μπορεί.
Επιμένω.

Όποτε θυμάμαι, ράβω κάποιες τσέπες
σάμπως να φυλακίσω ό,τι προλάβω.

Κι έχω όλη νύχτα τη γλώσσα τεντωμένη.

A Semblance of Order

A tidy house is what I have left.
In my pockets,
in those unwearable clothes,
I find wet tickets from busses
that carted sweat by the ton –

in the house I'm still seeking the sweat
that some passengers must have left behind.
         I'm perplexed.

I continue with the corners of the house. I forage in them.
   I look under
the beds, under the plates piled
in a semblance of order. First the deep plates, then the
   shallow ones.
I don't go anywhere – I'm just sad.

I lick the water dribbling from decaying pipes,
I stick my tongue into the tube of the boiler.
I stretch it as far as it'll go – I keep stretching.

Whenever I remember to, I sew some pockets shut
– as if to lock up whatever I can.

And my tongue is stretched out all night.

                                        Peter Constantine

Παραλήρημα για τα τέσσερα πόδια μιας αγάπης

Βλέπω τα ναι σου να έρχονται από μακριά
και τα δικά μου, σαν κεριά,
κραδαίνουν,
καίνε
τους αιώνες περιμένοντας

Φύσα δυνατά
μου φεύγει το καπέλο τα γυαλιά το τατουάζ το χέρι μου
       μου φεύγει
το πόδι κι ένα μάτι

       [Μένω έτσι να χαμογελώ εμπρός σε πίδακες
               που η χαρά του τίποτα αναβλύζει]

η χαρά –
μόνη κι αυτή

Μείνε εσύ, αν θέλεις, παραδίπλα
– κι ας μη μας καταλαβαίνει κανείς

       [Δε χρειάζεται κι ετούτο να μας πνίξει]

Μόνο να ρέει
ο καιρός
το κρασί
ο καπνός
να ρέει

Delirium for the Four Legs of a Love

I see your *yesses* coming from afar
and my own, like candles,
brandish
and burn
awaiting the centuries

A strong wind
carries off my hat my glasses my tattoo my arm
    carries off
my leg and an eye

    [I'm left there smiling before jets
      gushing the joy of nothingness]

joy –
it too alone

Stay, if you want, by my side
– even if no one understands us

    [Why let that, too, smother us]

Just let it flow
let time
the wine
the smoke
flow

Karen Emmerich

Αδυναμία

Μα πού πάνε όλοι αυτοί οι νεκροί;
Πού πάνε οι νεκροί όταν πεθαίνουν, μπαμπά;

Τα μάτια του με κοιτάζουν.
     Όμορφα μάτια.
Καμιά φορά θέλω κάτι να γράψω γι' αυτά,
     να τα ρωτήσω γιατί δεν μ' αφήνει ακόμα να καπνίσω.

     Γιατί δεν μ' αφήνεις ακόμα να καπνίσω;

αδυναμία
Φόρεσα σήμερα όλα μου τα ρούχα να μη φαίνονται τα
     κιλά που έχασα,
          οι τρίχες που έχασα,
               η κοιλιά μου που έδειχνε αφιλόξενη.
               Παπούτσια δεν έχω άλλα.

     Σ' τα 'βαλα, αν θυμάσαι, όλα στο τελευταίο δέμα.
Χωρούσες, είπες, μες σ' αυτά, ολόκληρος. Μα πώς χωρούσες;
                         Εσύ ήσουν πάντοτε ψηλός.
Θυμάμαι ακόμα τα χαμόγελα που σχημάτιζαν τα κορδόνια.
     Απ' την πολλή χαρά που θα σε συναντούσαν.

αδυναμία
Θυμάμαι ακόμα τα χαμόγελα που σχημάτιζαν τα
     ρούχα μου –
          αυτά που έβαλα για να βγω έξω.
Πτυχές και τσαλακώματα πολλά, κι εκείνη η καμπύλη
     που κάνουν
          στη μασχάλη μου
          απ' την πολλή αδυναμία.

Weakness

But where do all those dead people go?
Where do dead people go when they die, Dad?

His eyes watch me.
   Beautiful eyes.
Sometimes I want to write about them,
   to ask why they still won't let me smoke.

Why will you still not let me smoke?

weakness
Today I put on all my clothes so no one would see the
   weight I've lost,
      the hair I've lost, so no one would see
         my belly, inhospitable.
            These are my only shoes.

Don't you remember I put the others in your last package?
You said you could fit in them, entire. But how?
You were always tall.
I still remember the smiles the laces made.
Out of joy that they'd be seeing you.

weakness
I still remember the smiles my clothes made –
   the ones I wore to go out.
All creases and folds, those wide curves
   at my armpit
      because of how weak I am, how thin.

Τα πουκάμισα δεν μου κάνουν πια –
    γι' αυτό φόρεσα δυο τρία μαζί.
Οι μπλούζες και τα μάλλινα πουλόβερ με σφίγγουν
    στον λαιμό
αλλά δεν με νοιάζει, γιατί άφησα όλα μου τα κασκόλ
    στο ταχυδρομείο.

> *Ήταν να τα βάλω κι αυτά σε κείνο το δέμα,*
> *αλλ' άρεσαν σ' έναν υπάλληλο*
> *και του τα χάρισα.*
> *Όλα μου τα κασκόλ, για φαντάσου.*

αδυναμία

Δεν έγραψα τίποτε άλλο ύστερα από κείνη την ημέρα.
Μόνο κάθισα μόνος σε κείνη την καρέκλα του
    γραφείου
        και θύμωνα που δεν μ' άφηνε να καπνίζω.
Καπνός έγινα εγώ.
Ανέβαινα στο ταβάνι και γύριζα πίσω στην καρέκλα
    και ξανά στο ταβάνι και ξανά στην καρέκλα.
Βγήκα λίγο στο μπαλκόνι.
    Όσο το σπίτι τόσο το μπαλκόνι.
Στη μια του άκρη τα ρούχα απλωμένα.
    Στην άλλη απλωμένος εγώ.
Συναγωνιζόμασταν ποιος κρέμεται καλύτερα.

αδυναμία

Τα μάτια του.
Τα μάτια του είναι όμορφα.
    Όταν φορούν τ' αγαπημένα μου παπούτσια,
        γίνονται άλλα.
Τα μάτια του είναι λέξεις που δεν χωρούν σε ποίημα.
    Τα μάτια τού μπαμπά.

My shirts don't fit me any more
    so I put on two or three at once.
The button-downs and wool sweaters are tight at my
  neck
but it's fine, since I left all my scarves at the post
  office.

                    I meant to put them in the package too,
                        but one of the clerks liked them
                              so I gave them to him.
                    All of my scarves, just imagine.

weakness
I never wrote after that day.
I just sat alone in the desk chair,
    mad because he wouldn't let me smoke.
So I became smoke.
I rose to the ceiling and came back down to the
  chair,
    and again to the ceiling and again to the chair.
I went out on to the balcony for a while.
    It was as big as the house, or as small.
At one end was the laundry.
    At the other, me.
A kind of contest, to see who was better at hanging.

weakness
His eyes.
His eyes are beautiful.
    When they put on my favorite shoes they
      change.
His eyes are words that won't fit into any poem.
    My father's eyes.

αδυναμία
Μου ήρθε πίσω το δέμα.

> – Άλλη φορά να μη μας ειρωνεύεστε, κύριε.
> – Μα γιατί; Τα χαμογελαστά κορδόνια είναι ωραία.

> Θέλω να ξαναδώ εκείνα σου τα μάτια.

αδυναμία
Κατέβηκα το πρωί στη λεωφόρο.
Σοροί σωριασμένες σωρηδόν.
   Τις βάζανε μια μια σ' ένα φορτηγό. Μεγάλο
   φορτηγό, με ρόδες μεγάλες.
Ετοιμάζονται, φαίνεται, για μεγάλο ταξίδι.

> Μα πού πάνε όλοι αυτοί οι νεκροί;
> Πού πάνε οι νεκροί όταν πεθαίνουν, μπαμπά;

αδυναμία
Τον μπαμπά μου κατάφερα να τον βάλω σε ποίημα.
   Το κάπνισμα δεν κατάφερα ποτέ να το κόψω,
      όμως κάθε φορά που δένω τα κορδόνια μου
      σωριάζομαι μπρος στον καθρέφτη
      και με κοιτώ για ώρες.

Ετοιμάζομαι για τις καινούργιες μέρες.
   Φορώ ό,τι βρω μπροστά μου και πάω στο
   ταχυδρομείο συχνά.

Μ' αρέσουν τα γραμματόσημα –
   έχω πάντα κάπου ν' ακουμπώ τη γλώσσα μου.

weakness
The package was returned.

> – *Next time don't make fun of us, sir.*
> – *What do you mean? Smiling laces are nice.*

> *I want to see your eyes again.*

weakness
This morning I went down to the avenue.
Corpses heaped high in hills.
    We put them on a truck one by one. A big truck, with
        big wheels.
They're preparing, it seems, for a big journey.

> *But where do all those dead people go?*
> *Where do dead people go when they die, Dad?*

weakness
I managed to put my father in a poem.
    I never managed to quit smoking,
        but every time I tie my laces
            I fall in a heap in front of the mirror
                and look at me for hours.

I'm preparing for the new days.
    I put on whatever I find and go to the post office
        often.

I like stamps –
    I always have somewhere to rest my tongue.

Karen Emmerich

YIANNIS EFTHYMIADES

(Born Piraeus, Greece, 1969)

Coming to the Athens poetry world from the outside, both geographically (he still lives in Piraeus) and in terms of his artistic eclecticism (he is an artist and songwriter as well as a poet), Yiannis Efthymiades's formal reworkings of the Greek literary tradition from Dionysis Solomos to Jenny Mastoraki have nonetheless gained him a place at the center. In his 2012 collection about the Twin Towers attack he succeeds in turning an American tragedy into something both global and very Greek. His poems and translations of English and American poetry appear regularly in *Poetics* and other literary magazines. He makes a living writing textbooks and teaching Ancient and Modern Greek at the Piraeus Greek–French Lycée, and also hosts an interview show on poetry and music on web radio, metadeftero.gr.

ΣΤΙΓΜΑ (*Stigmata*), Self-published, 2004; *Καινός διαιρέτης* (*New Division*), Nefeli, 2007; *Γράμματα στον Πρίγκιπα* (*Letters to the Prince*), Mikri Arktos, 2009; *27 ή ο άνθρωπος που πέφτει* (*9/11 or Falling Man*), Mikri Arktos, 2012; *Πατρείδα* (*O Say Can You See*), Kihli, 2016.

από Καινό διαιρέτη

Έρχομαι από το φως,
βαδίζω προς το φως,
ο σκοτεινός διάδρομος τελειώνει.
Περνάω την ιερή βαλβίδα.

από 27 ή ο άνθρωπος που πέφτει

1.2

Όλοι νομίζετε ότι φοβήθηκα και πως γι' αυτό έπεσα
    πανικόβλητος στο κενό
Θε μου, τι βλάκες! Επιτέλους, πήρα για μια μόνη φορά
    όλη μου τη ζωή στα χέρια μου
Προκλητικά, πέφτοντας μπροστά σε τρομαγμένα
    τεράστια μάτια, σας βγάζω τη γλώσσα μου
Την τελευταία στιγμή διέκρινα μέσα στο πλήθος το
    κορίτσι με τη θλίψη στα μάτια
Δεν είχε τίποτα ξεχωριστό να θυμάμαι, μόνο πως ήταν
    ένα κορίτσι θλιμμένο
Θα μπορούσαμε να είχαμε αγαπηθεί δύο καλοκαίρια
    πριν, δύο μετά – θα μπορούσαμε –
Δεν επαληθεύτηκε αυτή η πιθανότητα – πόσες να
    προλάβουν να φτάσουν στο τέρμα;
Κι έτσι εγώ δεν θα είμαι εδώ, ενώ το κορίτσι θα είναι
    εδώ – τι απλή λογική! –
Η δική σας απλή λογική που για κάμποσα χρόνια την
    επαναλάμβανα περίφημα

from New Division

I come from the light,
I walk towards the light,
the dark hallway ends.
I pass the sacred starting line.

Karen Van Dyck

from 9/11 or Falling Man

1.2

all of you think I was scared shitless that's why I dove
  head first into the abyss
god what idiots for once I took my life into my own hands
  and let myself
drop provocative like in front of their eyes immense
  ghoulish I stick my tongue out
then in that last moment I see a girl with a sad look in the
  midst of the crowd
nothing special to remember about her just that she was
  a sad girl that's all
two summers ago or two years after we could've fallen in
  love yeah could've
though this chance in a lifetime didn't come to fruition
  how many ever do
and so in the end I won't be here but the girl sure will
  what simple logic yours
the kind of logic I repeated proudly ad nauseam for so
  many years

2.1

Τις νύχτες όπως πέφτεις μέσα σ' όνειρο, έτσι μπορείς να
καταλάβεις πώς αλήθεια πέφτω
Μετεωρίζομαι, στριφογυρνώ σε ίλιγγο, άλλοτε όρθιος
πάνω σ' ένα κατάστρωμα
Πότε ανάποδα – να που κοιτάζω τον κόσμο σας
ανάποδα και δεν το βρίσκετε κακό –
Πότε με το κεφάλι μες στα πόδια μου, πότε τα χέρια
σαν πουλιού φτερούγες, στριφογυρνώ
Μέσα σε ίλιγγο και, οπ, γίνομαι τέσσερα και τρώω
παγωτό, οπ, είμαι τριάντα πια
Εικοσιοκτώ και βλέπω το παιδί να βγαίνει, γίνομαι
δεκατέσσερα κι η νύχτα όλο αργεί
Εικοσιένα μ' έναν κόσμο να με περιμένει – μα όπως
φάνηκε μονάχα στη στροφή
Είμαι πενήντα, κι είμαι εκατό, είμαι ο χρόνος όλος και
ολόκληρος, κι είναι αυτό αρκετό
Σε μια στιγμή να πυκνωθεί όλος ο αιώνας, να ξανοιχτεί,
επιτέλους, τέταρτη διάσταση

3.3

Πονάνε τα μάτια μου καθώς πέφτω, ο αέρας ορμάει σαν
για να μου τα ξεριζώσει
Πονάνε και οι τρίχες στα μπράτσα μου, είναι η μανία
αυτή της αντίστασής μου για ζωή
Της λαχτάρας της ύλης, που πια φθίνει, να κρατηθεί
ακέραιη απέναντι στην ιδέα
Πονάνε τα μάτια μου απέναντι στη φρίκη, όμως τα
κρατάω ανοιχτά συνέχεια

2.1

those nights when you fall when you're dreaming that's
    how you know I'm really falling I twist
and turn like a meteor in a dizzying spin sometimes right
    side up on deck
other times upside down see how I'm looking at your
    world upside down it's not bad
sometimes with my head between my legs, other times
    with hands like birdwings I twist and
turn in a dizzying spin and bingo I'm four years old
    eating an ice cream cone
then bingo thirty the kid comes out when I'm twenty
    eight at fourteen the day is
endless twenty one the world is new but then it's only a
    bend in the road
and I'm fifty then a hundred I'm all time and time eternal
    and that's enough
in one moment all time seizes up opens again at last the
    fourth dimension

3.3

my eyes hurt as I fall the air accosts me as if to tear them
    out uproot them
they hurt so does the hair on my arms it is mania this
    resistance of mine
this desire for matter to appear as if whole even as it
    disintegrates
my eyes hurt when confronted with the horror but I keep
    them wide open to see

Ο άνθρωπος που πέφτει θέλει να βλέπει, θέλει να ξέρει,
  η γνώση αυτή τον δικαιώνει
Ο άνθρωπος που πέφτει πρέπει πάντα – και τώρα
  πρέπει – να ξέρει ακόμα και την πτώση του
Αυτό είναι το τίμημα: γνώση αντί για αίσθηση, εμπειρία
  αντί για διαίσθηση
Σιγά σιγά εθίζεται και στο τέλος η φρίκη γίνεται εικόνα
  σαν όλες τις άλλες
Και η εικόνα αυτή γιγαντώνεται, ώσπου παίρνει τη
  μορφή ενός κόσμου ολόκληρου

6.1

Πήρε επιτέλους τη ζωή στα χέρια του και έγιναν τα
  χέρια του φτερά του, ναι φτερά του
Για να πετάξει σ' έναν καινούργιο ουρανό, αφώτιστο,
  αδιαίρετο, καλά κρυμμένο
Όπως μικρός στα όνειρα έξω από τα κελιά της κάθε
  μέρας του έλυνε τα δεσμά του
Τότε έμπαινε σε μια χαμένη επικράτεια που χρόνια
  αργότερα θα έβρισκε μπροστά του
Το πιο παράξενο: ήταν πολίτης κι αυτοκράτορας,
  υποτασσότανε και κυβερνούσε
Πότε ξανοίγονταν σε πέλαγα ματιών, πότε σε όρη
  όμορφων φιλιών, χωρίς ανάσα
Και διαπερνούσε το κορμί του ρίγος σαν κληματίδα
  όταν κλυδωνίζεται απ' τον άνεμο
Το μέγα πάθος γίνονταν τεράστιο κύτταρο και μέσα
  του χτυπούσε σαν καρδιά η ζωή του
Έμπαινε κι έβγαινε ανενόχλητος κάθε πρωί, πότε έξω
  απ' τη ζωή, πότε μες στο κορμί της

the man who falls wants to see and wants to know
  knowledge is his justification
the man who falls must always know his own fall even as
  he is falling this is
his punishment knowledge instead of feeling experience
  not intuition
slowly addiction sets in and the horror becomes an image
  like the others
and this image becomes gigantic until it takes the shape
  of a complete world

6.1

finally he took his life in his own hands and his hands
  became wings yes his wings
so he could fly in a new sky with no light indivisible
  hidden from sight
like when he was small in his dreams and untied his
  bonds far from the prison cells of
everyday he'd enter a lost dominion where he'd find
  himself years later shocked
by his predicament both citizen and emperor obeying
  and obeyed
sometimes open to eye seas other times to mountains of
  kisses so exquisite
breath by breath and he'd pass by the shivering center
  like grapevines trimmed by the wind
the great passion would become a giant cell and inside
  life would beat like a heart
in and out undisturbed each morning sometimes outside
  life sometimes in her body

Karen Van Dyck

από Πατρείδα

Ποιος οργισμένος ουρανός μάς γύρισε την πλάτη;
Ποιος κλέφτης άκαρδος καιρός μάς έριξε αλάτι πάνω
   στις πιο βαθιές πληγές;

Στο μεταξύ γεννοβολάμε αισθήματα κι αισθήσεις,
   πνιγόμαστε μέσα σε παραισθήσεις
Κι ο ποταμός χόρτασε αίμα, λάσπη και χολή
Εμείς ρουφάμε ώσπου να σκάσουμε, ρουφάμε όπως το
   αίμα από τρύπημα βελόνας που την έφαγε σκουριά
Βαδίζουμε χωλοί, τα πόδια μας βαριά, τα λες δεμένα,
   τριγύρω σφίγγει το σχοινί της βουλιμίας, ο κάβος της
   πιο σκάρτης ηδονής κι επιθυμίας
Πληθαίνουν οι αγύρτες, ανασαίνουν τον αέρα γύρω
   μου, φωνάζω όπως στα όνειρα, βουβά
Το τέλος το 'χω δει και κάνω πια πως αγαπώ, παίζω τον
   σκύλο τον γρυπό, που γλείφει ξερό κόκκαλο, ή βγάζω
   γλώσσα δηλητήριο, μα εκείνη στρέφεται εντός μου
Ίλιγγος, κι η πέτρα ορίζει πια τον στόχο, σπάστε την
   επιφάνεια του νερού, αυτό το αποτρόπαιο
   κρυστάλλινο απόστημα της πλάνης
Εσάς σας πρέπει ο βυθός της αναβύθισης, κι η κόλαση
   που εγγυάται αγιότητα
Ραντεβού στο κορδόνι . . .

from O Say Can You See

What heated heaven turned her back on us?
What thieving heartless time rubbed salt in our deepest
    wounds?

And meanwhile we spawn senses and sensations, drown
    in delusions
And the river, sated with blood and mud and bile
We suck it up bursting in air, we suck it like blood from a
    puncture by a rust-eaten needle
We walk crippled, our feet leaden, bound by ropes of
    greed, the cable of defective pleasure and desire to
    succeed
Charlatans multiply, they breathe the land of the brave
    around me, I scream as if in dreams, dumb
I've seen the end and still pretend I love, I play the
    limping dog that licks dry bones, or I attack with the
    poison tongue that circulates inside me
Vertigo, and now the stone decides its throw ahead of
    time, go on, break the water's surface, that repellent
    crystalline abscess of illusion
You, you deserve the depths of desolation, the hell that
    guarantees the saint
The hangman's rendez-vous . . .

Karen Van Dyck

YANNIS STIGGAS

(Born Athens, Greece, 1977)

Yannis Stiggas's visual poetics and his intertextual refer-
ences to Paul Celan and Katerina Anghelaki-Rooke make
his poems particularly interesting to British and American
readers, who may know these poets in translation. It is no
coincidence that he is also probably the best known and
most translated of the poets in this section, the languages
into which his work has been translated including French,
German, Serbian, Bulgarian, and Swedish. He studied Medi-
cine in Athens, and still works there as a doctor.

Η αλητεία του αίματος (*The Vagrancy of Blood*), Gavrielides, 2004;
Η όραση θ' αρχίσει ξανά (*Vision Will Start Again*), Kedros, 2006;
Ισόπαλο τραύμα (*An Even Wound*), Kedros, 2009; *Ο δρόμος μέχρι
το περίπτερο* (*Towards the Booth*), Mikri Arktos, 2012; *Βλέπω τον
κύβο Ρούμπικ φαγωμένο* (*I Saw the Gnawed
Rubik's Cube*), Mikri Arktos, 2014.

Απλά μαθηματικά

Φτάνοντας στο τέταρτο χιλιόμετρο της σιωπής,
μου έπεσαν τα καρφιά για Θεό και για ήλιο.
Έκτοτε, περιφέρομαι με το μεγάλο μηδέν υπό μάλης.
Αρχικά, ήταν ένας κοινός υπνόσακος
– ξέρετε, μπαίνεις, δηλαδή ονειρεύεσαι.
Τώρα, είναι ένα πελώριο οικοτροφείο
για τους ψυχικά άφλεκτους.

Αφού έγιναν όλα αυτά με το μηδέν
φανταστείτε τι θα μπορούσε να συμβεί με το Ένα.

Simple Math

Reaching the fourth kilometer of silence
I dropped the nails I had for God and the sun.
Since then I've been going around with the great
zero under my arm.

To start with, it was an ordinary sleeping-bag
– you know, you get in, which means you start dreaming.
Now it is a huge boarding school
for the psychologically inflammable.

Since all this has happened with zero
imagine what might occur with One.

Katerina Anghelaki-Rooke

Ασκήσεις αναπνοής

Γύρισα ανάποδα την ψυχή μου
κι είδα πώς μεγαλώνουν οι πέτρες

(με λίγο φως)
σκληραίνει η τύχη και γίνεται

ν' ανεβαίνουν ψηλά τα πουλιά
κι έπειτα
τα ξεκουρδίζει ο ήλιος

Προσπάθησε ν' αναπνέεις κανονικά
μέσα γαλάζιο – έξω γαλάζιο
σε μια πνοή ξανασυμβαίνουν όλα
Οι πέτρες έλεγα
– τα πάντα δίνονται σαν ξυράφι
κι άμα τα θέλεις πιο βαθιά
μέσα γαλάζιο – έξω γαλάζιο
άμα τα θέλεις πιο βαθιά

καλό κουράγιο

Αυτός ο κόσμος
είναι η πιο σπλαχνική μορφή του ποτέ

Ποτέ ο ιδρώτας
τόσο πολύ με το αίμα

Breathing Exercises

I turned my soul upside down
and I saw how stones grow
(with a little bit of light)
luck hardens and happens

So that birds can rise high
and then
the sun unwinds them

Try to breathe normally
sky-blue in – sky-blue out
in one breath everything happens again.
Stones I was saying –
everything that comes to you is like a razor
and if you want it even deeper
sky-blue in – sky-blue out

Keep it up

This world
is the most compassionate form of never

Never was sweating
                   so bloody

Katerina Anghelaki-Rooke

Οπλισμένο με τρυφερότητα

Για την Κατερίνα Αγγελάκη-Ρουκ

Γεμάτο πούπουλα
το στήθος της
ο ίσκιος της
και το βαθύ της χέρι

γιατί από πολύ μικρή
παίζει το μ' αγαπά
                δεν μ' αγαπά
με το φτέρωμα των αγγέλων

Δεν το κάνει για την απάντηση

το κάνει για να μη φύγουν

Armed with Tenderness

For Katerina Anghelaki-Rooke

Feather-filled
her chest
her shadow
her deep hand,

because since childhood
she's been playing *he loves me,*
                    he loves me not
with the feather-down of angels.

She doesn't do it for the answer,

she does it to keep them near.

Stephanos Papadopoulos

Ο αδερφός μου ο Παύλος
ο σκαφτιάς του Σηκουάνα

«O du gräbst und ich grab
und ich grab mich dir zu»
Paul Celan

Έτσι όπως έσκαβε
μια μέρα έφτασε
στο χιονισμένο στόμα της μητέρας του
στις μακριές πλεξούδες των προγόνων του
μια μέρα πέρασε
τις ρίζες του νερού

τα πέτρινα

τα πύρινα

τα πάνδεινα που πέρασε

έκτοτε του 'μεινε
ένα καμένο σύννεφο στο βλέμμα

μια δυσκολία με τον άνεμο

    Jiskor
Kaddisch

ένα τρελό λαχάνιασμα

«το βάθος» έλεγε
«το βάθος σε σημείο εξάντλησης
και γλώσσα είναι
και πατρίδα μου»

My Brother Paul,
the Digger of the Seine

'O you dig and I dig
            and I dig inside myself towards you'
                                    Paul Celan

One day as he was digging,
he reached
      his mother's snowy mouth,
      the long braids of his ancestors.
Another day he passed
      the water's roots

the stones

the flames

the trials he endured

left him
      with a scorched cloud in his gaze,

a trouble with the wind

      Jiskor
            Kaddisch

a manic breathlessness

'the depth' he said
'the depth to the point of exhaustion
is my language
      and my country.'

Και τότε βγήκε σ' ένα μέρος
γεμάτο δέντρα και ποτάμια και πουλιά

και έμεινε εκστατικός

μέχρι που ακούστηκε στρατιωτικό παράγγελμα:
«να στοιχηθούν ολοταχώς
κάλεσμα για συσσίτιο»

και φύγανε τα δέντρα
        τα ποτάμια
τα πουλιά

Μονάχα ο Σηκουάνας έμεινε
να τον κοιτά στα μάτια.

And then he emerged into a place
full of trees and rivers and birds

and he was ecstatic

until a military command was heard:
'Quick – fall into position,
report to the mess hall'

and the trees
    and rivers
        and birds disappeared.

Only the Seine remained
looking into his eyes.

Stephanos Papadopoulos

Αυτό κουρδίζει μόνο του

Τόσα πολλά γρανάζια
που δεν θα βρω ποτέ
πώς μάτωσε η Άνοιξη
     και φτύνω
το παιδικό μου πράσινο
το τελευταίο κουμπί του ονείρου

Γυμνά τα πράγματα
     συμβαίνουν γρηγορότερα
με το που κάνεις την αρχή
     σ' οσμίζεται το τέλος

είναι μια μαύρη λιτανεία η Άνοιξη
και με κλοτσάει να γίνω

ολόκληρη η δίψα μου

– κι ας πουν ότι πρόκειται για παρένδυση –

Δεν θέλω πια να με λένε Γιάννη

θέλω δυο δράμια
κάτασπρη τύχη
     ας είναι έστω

και κάθε Τετάρτη

Self-Winding

There are so many cogs
I'll never find
how the Spring was bloodied
          and so I spit
on my childhood green,
the dream's last button.

Naked, things
happen faster.
By the time you begin
you can already smell the end.

Springtime is a black litany
kicking me to become

my entire thirst.

(let them say it's about masquerade)

I don't want to be called Yannis any more

I want two drams
of blind-white luck
          even if it's only

every Wednesday.

Stephanos Papadopoulos

Η τέλεια ακουστική του λαβύρινθου

I.

Επειδή
δεν μπόρεσα να πνίξω τον ουρανό
– τόσο γαλάζιο που στο τέλος ελπίζεις –
ένας άγγελος
μου ψιθυρίζει τρυφερά

χτίσε με
σ' ετούτες τις πέτρες

II.

Επειδή
όσο κι αν κάπνισα
δεν βρήκα το μίτο μου

    τόσες αγάπες
    τόσο λαχάνιασμα

και ο Μινώταυρος
        τι βιολιστής, Θεέ μου

III.

Ξέμεινα
με τον ουρανό και το Λόγο

κανείς τους δεν ξέρει να μ' αγαπήσει
(φταίνε λιγάκι κι οι εποχές
τα δόντια μου που 'ναι στραβά
    φταίει
        το έσω σκιάχτρο)

The Labyrinth's Perfect Acoustics

I.

Because
I wasn't able to choke the sky
(so blue that in the end you begin to hope)
an angel
whispers to me tenderly.

Build me
with these stones

II.

Because
as much as I smoked
I never found my inner thread

so many loves
so much breathlessness

and the Minotaur,
        my God, what a fiddler

III.

I was left
with the sky and the word,

none of them knows how to love me.
(the seasons are partly to blame,
my crooked teeth,
      the scarecrow inside
          is to blame.)

IV.

Είμαι τόσο πρόθυμος για συντέλεια
ώσπου να γράψω «λουλούδι»
έχει ήδη χάσει δυο πέταλα
δεν ξέρω αν το φως
είναι τέχνασμα σκότους
      ή ανάποδα

      εγώ

μόνο να βασανίζω τις πεταλούδες
– καμιά τους δεν ξέρει να μ' αγαπήσει

V.

Κι άλλωστε
τούτος ο κόσμος δεν άναψε ποτέ
θέλει να δέσεις κόμπο το κενό

– αν είναι ναυτικός καλύτερα

να κεντήσεις την ψυχή σου καταιγίδες

VI.

τόσες φωνές για σφάξιμο
τόσες φωνές για γδάρσιμο

πού να σου μείνει μία
      λεϊμονιά
      λεϊμονιά
      εδώ που μ' άφησες ριζώνω

IV.

I'm so eager for the ending
that by the time I've written 'flower'
it has already lost two petals.
I don't know if the light
is a trick of darkness
        or the reverse.

        I

only know to torture butterflies
(none of them knows how to love me)

V.

And anyway
this world was never lit
it wants you to tie the void into a knot

– If he's a sailor, better to

stitch your soul with squalls of rain.

VI.

So many voices for slaughter
so many voices for scraping

how do you expect to find one last
        lemon tree
        lemon tree
        I'll root here where you left me.

Stephanos Papadopoulos

από Την αλητεία του αίματος

Εγώ δεν μοιάζω μ' εσάς.
Κάθε βράδυ προσεύχομαι
στην αιώνια σφύρα
και τ' όνειρο μου
έχει μόνο ένα σπόνδυλο

*

Αδημονώ
να γίνει η Ανταρκτική
επιδημία οράσεως.
Να μοιραστεί επιτέλους ο υπόγειος άρτος
ανάλογα με την πίστη στο θαύμα.

Θαύμα είναι να μπορείς να γελάς
κρατώντας την ανία σου,
αυτόν τον μαύρο κύκνο,
στα χέρια.

Θαύμα είναι απλά να γελάς.

*

Φυτεύω το δίκαιο θηρίο
στα ρουθούνια του κόσμου

Σέρνω το γέλιο μου
        ζώο
με μυρίζει και τρέχει
στους στραβούς μήνες

*

from *The Vagrancy of Blood*

I am not like the rest of you.
Each night I pray
to the eternal hammer
and my dream
has only one vertebra.

*

I am impatient
for the Antarctic to become
an epidemic of sight.
For the underground bread to be shared at last
according to each one's faith in the miracle.

Miracle, to be able to laugh
while holding your boredom,
a black swan,
in your arms.

Miracle, simply to laugh.

*

I plant the judicious beast
in the nostrils of the world

I drag my laugh
        animal
it smells me and runs
through the crooked months

*

Το κεφάλι μου
με όλα του τα θηρία τακτοποιημένα
στο πάνω διάζωμα

Το στόμα αντιδρά
με ψεύτικους ουρανούς.
Αντιδρά; Αυτό το ρημάδι;

Άμα τραβήξεις τα δοκάρια του
θα πέσουν λόγια και κάρβουνα λόγια
θα πέσει
       ο τυφλός άγγελος

*

Τα λόγια μας
θα καταλήξουν στη μεγάλη λευκότητα
εκεί που το σώμα
αποποιείται το σώμα του
      είναι διπλός ο λύκος
να μην επιστρέψεις

Σανίδια η μνήμη
όσο την ψάχνεις τρίζει
Με σέρνουν πάλι φθινόπωρα
κρατώ το τελευταίο άνθος
κίτρινος μέσα στο κίτρινο
      θνητός
μέχρι την Αλεξάνδρεια
– πού μοίρασα την πνοή μου; –
και δεν έχω δέντρα για αύριο
      δεν έχω άλλο τσιγάρο
Μεγάλη μεγάλη λευκότητα
σπασμένο σκυλί μέσα

*

My head
all its beasts in a row
on the upper tier

The mouth reacts
with false skies.
Reacts? That old mess?

If you knock down its beams
what will fall are words and charcoal words
what will fall is
                    the blind angel

*

Our words
will end up in the vast whiteness
where the body
renounces its body
        the wolf is double
so you won't return

Give memory some plank
that creaks as you search for it
They drag me again in fall
I hold the last blossom
yellow within the yellow
        mortal
as far as Alexandria
– where did I give my breath? –
and I have no trees for tomorrow
        I have no more cigarettes
Vast vast whiteness
broken dog within

*

Θα σου χαρίσω
    όλα τα σύνεργα της πνοής –
μια επιστροφή στη γελαστή ύλη
για να μάθεις φαρσί τα πουλιά
και να μετράς τον έρωτα
           ποτάμι ποτάμι
Ο χρόνος θα ξαναγίνει απλός
με κοντά παντελόνια
κι εγώ κρεμάμενος επί ξύλου
με την έγνοια μου στη φτερούγα
    Αυτή: το μέγα ατόπημα

*

Φτερούγα είναι ό,τι κόβεται σύρριζα

*

Τα μάτια σου
τέλεια συμφορά των πουλιών

*

Μια αρμονία η φύση με τις λευκότητες

της σελίδας
του χιονιού
των οστών

*

Σώμα είναι η πέτρα που πίστεψε

*

I'll give you
        all the paraphernalia of breath –
a return to laughing matter
so you can learn the birds well
and count eros
            river by river
Time will become simple again
with short pants
and I hanging on the wood
my worry under my wing
        It: the great impropriety

*

Wing, whatever is cut close

*

Your eyes
perfect disaster of birds

*

A harmony, nature with the whitenesses

of the page
of the snow
of the bones

*

Body, the stone that believed

*

Ξέρω ότι δεν προκάλεσα καμία θηριωδία
από αυτές που λατρεύετε
μόνο ξεγύμνωσα τα δόντια μου
στον ίλιγγο που μαστίζει τις πεταλούδες

Άνοιξα τρύπες στη μοίρα
κι έχωσα τη λύπη μου σα ρούχο.
Η μνήμη δεν ξέρει πως να χειριστεί
τα ψαλίδια της
αλλά ο χρόνος δεν αιμάσσει ξανά
γι' αυτό δεν λαξεύω το όνειρο –
το δέχομαι σαν άπληστο κλαδί στο λαιμό
να μου αντλεί μουγγό το ύδωρ

Ποιος πούστης μ' έταξε στο φεγγάρι
κι έχω γίνει η κερκόπορτα της σφαγής;
Να αντιμάχεσαι με στίχους τα στοιχεία σου
    – αυτό θα πει όλεθρος! –
κι η όραση μπερδεύει τις ρίζες της
Βλέπω τον κόσμο παράλυτη ομπρέλα
κι αν ανοίξει
            να πάει στο διάολο

Το φως δεν αντιμετωπίζεται πια χωρίς γάντια
πώς να σφραγίσω το λόγο μου
τώρα που βγάζει τη γενετήσια χλόη;

Σιγά σιγά
    μοιάζουμε με τις πέτρες

Το τέλος είναι ήδη γνωστό:
Εγώ
Εσύ
και τα ρόδα

Η ομορφιά   μπαλτάς στον αυχένα

I know I provoked no brutality
of the sort you all adore
I just bared my teeth
at the vertigo that plagues the butterflies
I opened holes in fate
and shoved my sadness in like a piece of clothing.
Memory doesn't know how to use
its scissors
but time won't bleed again
which is why I don't sculpt the dream –
I accept it like a greedy branch in my throat
dumbly drawing away my water

What fucker promised me to the moon
and I've become the gate that opens onto slaughter?
To fight your elements with poetry
       – that's what devastation means! –
And sight confuses its roots
I see the world as a paralyzed umbrella
and if it opens
          it can go to hell
The light can't be faced any more without gloves
how can I seal my speech
now that it's sprouting genital grass?
Slowly, slowly we resemble stones

The end is already known:
You
Me
and the rose
Beauty   an axe to the nape

Karen Emmerich

YIANNIS DOUKAS

(Born Athens, Greece, 1981)

Yiannis Doukas is one of the most metrically accomplished poets of his generation, having learned from immediate precursors such as Nasos Vayanas. His work also draws on Greek and Anglo-Saxon prosody, mingled with a healthy dose of the news. *The Stendhal Syndrome* (2013) received the Academy of Athens Prize for the best collection by a young poet. The son of Maro Douka, one of Greece's finest novelists, he studied Classics at the University of Athens and Digital Humanities at the University of London. He currently lives in Ireland.

Ο κόσμος όπως ήρθα και τον βρήκα (*The World as I Came and Found It*), Kedros, 2001; *Στα μέσα σύνορα* (*Inner Borders*), Polis, 2011; *Το σύνδρομο Σταντάλ* (*The Stendhal Syndrome*), Polis, 2013.

Τα παιδιά του Άβελ

Παίρνει τους δρόμους η νταλίκα
Ότι το χνάρι της το βρήκα
Εδώ τελειώνει τ' οξυγόνο
Θα ξεμακραίνω, θα ζυγώνω

Η τίγρη θ' ανασάνει για λίγο πριν πεθάνει
Κι ας έχει κιόλας φύγει για το μακρύ κυνήγι

Το Danny F για τη Συρία
Σαν κιβωτός· για τα σφαγεία
Μα με τα κύματα βουλιάζει
Της θάλασσας που δεν ξεβγάζει

Και πάνω στον αφρό της, αρχαίος ταξιδιώτης
Θα βόσκει το κοπάδι σ' υδάτινο λιβάδι

Είναι καιρός για τη θυσία
Κόβει βαθιά την αρτηρία
Αυτό το σώμα το δικό σου
Σαν γιατρικό της μαύρης νόσου

Δεν θα μπορέσω να σου πω
Κι είμαι κοντά, σ' ακολουθώ
Μα δεν το πήρες μυρωδιά
Κι άλλος μαζεύει τη σοδειά

Θαλασσινή μεταφορά
Τη ζωντανή φέρνει βορά
Μες στα νερά και τη σιωπή
Κηλίδα κόκκινη νωπή

Και το μαχαίρι σιωπηλό
Και σου πουλά με το κιλό
Το μεσημέρι να γευτείς
Και σαν φαρμάκι της γιορτής

The Children of Abel

The truck takes the road
That I found its tracks
Here, the oxygen depleted,
I will retreat, I will approach

I won't be able to tell you
And I am close, I follow you
But you haven't caught scent of it
And another gathers the harvest

The tiger will sigh for a while before dying
Even as it has set off already for the long hunt

The Danny F bound for Syria
Like an arc; for slaughterhouses
But it flounders with the waves
Of the sea that does not wash out

Transport by sea
Bearing the live prey
In the water and the silence
A fresh, red blemish

And on its foam, an ancient traveler
Will graze his flock in amphibian fields

It is time for oblation
It cuts deep in the lode
This body of yours
As the remedy of the plague

And the knife is placid
And sells you by the kilo
For you to taste at noon
And as the poison of the party

Chloe Haralambous and Moira Egan

Στον αστερισμό του καρκίνου

Η παρακέντηση στον άσπρο σου λαιμό
Σαν τη δαντέλα που σκεπάζει το τραπέζι
Είδες ατάραχος να φτάνει στον γκρεμό
Βήμα το βήμα η γενιά μας και να παίζει

Στη λεπτομέρεια, ζωή, σε μια πλευρά
Σαν φωτοσκίαση φλαμανδικού πορτρέτου
Φυλακισμένοι, ισοβίτες του μετά
Το περιμένουμε, δεν έρχεται ποτέ του

Σπουργίτια τρέχουνε στις έρημες αυλές
Στον ουρανό οι γλάροι, κρώζουν, του Δουβλίνου
Όλο πληθαίνουν όσα θέλεις κι όσα λες
Τα ερωτήματα σαν κύτταρα καρκίνου

Τώρα που έγινε ο κόσμος διαφανής
Θέλεις εσύ με τη σιωπή να του μιλήσεις
Να μη σ' ακούει άλλος άνθρωπος κανείς
Να κοιμηθείς και την ψυχή σου να κοιμίσεις

Μα κάθε νύχτα θα ξυπνάς με το πονώ
Με δύο οθόνες για μητέρα και ερωμένη
Πως ν' αρθρωθεί ένα συναίσθημα γυμνό
Και μια θερμότητα των λέξεων χαμένη;

On the Constellation of Cancer

The perforation on your white neck
Like lace that covers the table
You watched coolly as our generation
Reached the cliff, step by step, splitting

Hairs, life, on one side,
Like chiaroscuro in Flemish portraits
Imprisoned, lifers of *later*
We wait for it, it never comes

Sparrows run in vacant gardens
In the sky Dublin's gulls caw
The things you want and the things you say
Multiply questions like cancerous cells

Now that the world has become transparent
You want to speak with it in silence
So no one else will hear you
So you can sleep and tuck in your soul

But every night you will waken with *it hurts*
With two screens for mother and lover
How can a bare sentiment be pronounced
And what of the lost warmth of words?

Chloe Haralambous and Moira Egan

DOUKAS KAPANTAÏS

(Born Athens, Greece, 1971)

Doukas Kapantaïs's classical training shows through in his finely crafted shifts of register, drawing on the rich history of the Greek language from Ancient to Modern times. He is not interested in poetry as social commentary. The poem included here is from his first collection and, he notes, should not be read as political allegory as it predates the crisis. He has two doctorates: one from the Sorbonne, in Ancient Greek Philosophy, and the other from Bern, in Logic. He is an Associate Research Professor in the Centre for Greek Philosophy at the Academy of Athens, which administers literary prizes and supports literary translation among its many other activities.

Αγοράκια Κοριτσάκια (*Boys and Girls*), Nefeli, 2004;
Η αυτοκράτειρα (*The Empress*), Nefeli, 2012.

Εξοχικές κατοικίες το χειμώνα

Νύσταζα, και χωρίς να το ζητήσω
τη σφαίρα που μας δείχνει τον καιρό
τον μέσα μας, μου δώσαν να κρατήσω
και μέσα της φοβόμουν να ιδωθώ:

Από το θόλο πέφτανε σεντόνια,
αστραφτερά, κατάλευκα, μεγάλα,
σκεπάζοντας σαν έπιπλα σε σάλα
τα σπίτια μας – μαμούθ κατ' απ' τα χιόνια.

Εν τέλει, όταν απλώθηκαν παντού,
ανέτειλ' ένα κάτασπρο φεγγάρι
στον ουρανό – σημάδι παγετού;
Σε λίγο θα 'ρθει πούλμαν να μας πάρει –

σκεπτόμουν, δίχως ίχνος προσμονής
ή πανικού – άβουλους, προσηνείς.

Country Houses in Winter

I was drowsy. Without asking
anyone for anything I was handed
the crystal ball that shows the weather
inside us. I was scared to see myself in it:

From the vault fell sheets – laundered,
milk-white, large – covering our houses
like living-room furniture kept clean
for guests – mammoth under the snow.

Finally, when they had spread out
everywhere, a milky moon rose
in the sky – the first frost? *In a while
a coach will come to pick us up* –

I thought, without a trace of anticipation
or panic. Spineless, docile.

Karen Van Dyck

DIMITRA KOTOULA

(Born Komotini, Greece, 1974)

Writing in dialogue with the famous twentieth-century poets of ancient myth (George Seferis and Angelos Sike-lianos among them), Dimitra Kotoula brings fresh language and a feminist edge to familiar themes. She studied Archae-ology and History of Art at the University of Ioannina and the Courtauld Institute of Art. Her poetry, essays, and trans-lations have appeared online as well as in poetry anthologies and journals in Greece, Europe, and the Balkans. She works as an archaeologist and lives in Athens.

Τρεις νότες για μια μουσική (*Three Notes for a Melody*),
Nefeli, 2004.

Κεφάλι σατύρου

«Έκανα όλο Σατύρους. Ήθελα να σταματήσω το
σαρκαστικό τους γέλιο που με τρέλαινε»
                                    Γ. Χαλεπάς, 1878

Έχω κάθε δικαίωμα να μείνω μόνος
– ένα ελάχιστο πρόσωπο –
έχω κάθε δικαίωμα μόνος
να παρατηρώ
τους επιτήδειους όγκους
τα μαυρισμένα σκέρτσα πάνω σ' αυτό το μάρμαρο.
Θέλω να καταλάβω
(προσπαθώ να καταλάβω)
ό,τι βιάζεται να δώσει στο μυαλό την ελευθερία του
ό,τι – σε ακραία εκλέπτυνση –
ζητάει από το μυαλό πίσω την ελευθερία του
ολόκληρη την ιστορία
το σενάριο και το μαχαίρι.

                    *

Ο καλλιτέχνης το προσπάθησε.
Είμαστε στα 1878.
Η Ακρόπολη υπάρχει.
Η πατρίδα αυτή υπάρχει (υπάρχει;)
«υπό φρουράν» – έστω –
και «βαίνοντας επί τα χείρω»
το πρόσωπο διυλισμένο μέσα απ' τις πτυχές
(μπορεί σχεδόν να μαντεύει τις κινήσεις να περνούν
ακατάπαυστα βιαστικές
τα ολογράμματα πάνω σ' αυτό το μάρμαρο)

DIMITRA KOTOULA

Head of a Satyr

'I made only Satyrs. I wanted to stop their sarcastic
laughter that was driving me mad.'
G. Chalepas, 1878

I have every right to be alone
– just a face –
I alone have every right
to observe
their clever bulk
the blackened scribbles on this marble.
I want to understand
(I try to understand)
that which hurries to give the mind its freedom
that which, at the heights of refinement,
asks the mind for its freedom back
the whole of history
the script and the knife.

*

The artist attempted it.
We are in 1878.
The Acropolis exists.
This country exists (does it?)
'under observation' – so be it –
and 'going from bad to worse'
the face disintegrated into its folds,
it can almost guess the fleeting movements
that pass unceasingly,
holograms over this marble.

Ό,τι υπάρχει θα καταλυθεί

το κάθε ένα πήλινο εκτύπωμα
το κάθε σχήμα
η ψυχή να εκτίθεται βάναυσα
στην ξαφνική αυτή επανάληψη
κατακλύζοντας τον κενό αέρα (κενό;)
τον αέρα γεμάτο κενό νόημα
μην στρέψεις/ μην το πιστέψεις/
μην ξεγελάς με τα φαντάσματα αυτά το μυαλό σου

*

Έχω κάθε δικαίωμα να μείνω μόνος
Έχω κάθε δικαίωμα μόνος
να παρατηρώ
αυτό το πρόσωπο
το γέλιο πάνω σ' αυτό το πρόσωπο
διαβρώνοντας τη συνείδηση
προβάλλοντας ελαστικό
ολόκληρο αυτό το γέλιο – Πρώτο Πρόσωπο –
βρέχοντας/ χρόνια/ το μυαλό/ να κάμπεται
στο σημείο της έσχατης αντίστασης
που μόνο ο άνεμος μπορεί να το κάμψει.
Ο κόσμος γίνεται ολοένα και μικρότερος – σχεδόν
    άδειος.
(ποια είναι η άκτιστη η πρωταρχική ουσία των
    πραγμάτων)
Το μυαλό παύει ν' αντιστέκεται.
Τα χέρια αναπαύονται χαμηλωμένα.
Έχω κάθε δικαίωμα να μείνω μόνος.
Θέλω να σταματήσω αυτό το γέλιο.
Θέλω ν' ακούσω πίσω απ' αυτό.

DIMITRA KOTOULA

That which exists will be destroyed,

every single clay cast
every single figure
the soul to expose the vulgarities
to this sudden repetition
flooding the empty air (empty?)
The air full of empty meaning
don't turn around/ don't believe it/
don't delude your mind with these phantoms.

*

I have every right to be alone.
I alone have the right
to observe
this face
the laugh on this face
disintegrating its consciousness
offering this elastic, complete
laugh – First Person –
raining/ years/ the mind/ to be bowed
to the point of utmost resistance
where only the wind can bend it.
The world becomes increasingly smaller – almost
    empty
(*which is the uncreated or primordial essence of
    things*)
The mind stops resisting.
The hands lowered in repose.
I have every right to be alone.
I want to stop this laughter.
I want to hear what's behind it.

A. E. Stallings

Ο Ποιητής

δεν μπορεί παρά να κοιτάξει προς τα εκεί –

*

τώρα
ο ποιητής σκίζει
σαν ισχνό κουρασμένο δέρμα
τις προϋποθέσεις που στην ποίησή του
υπερθεματίζει.
Κάτι λιγότερο από άγγιγμα
στον τόνο εκείνου του προτελευταίου *ντο*
(ή μάλλον σε αντίθεση με αυτόν)
τον πείθει πια να μην αναβάλλει.
Η μουσική
– είχε διαβάσει κάποτε –
δεν είναι παρά μια διαδοχή
οπλισμένων και παροπλισμένων ήχων
που ο νους σε απόγνωση
και χωρίς να έχει ακριβώς πεισθεί
επιχειρεί να αναλάβει.

*

δεν μπορεί παρά να κοιτάξει προς τα εκεί –
φρέσκια χλόη συλλαβών σαλεύει κιόλας
στην ατμόσφαιρα φτιάχνοντας νέο δέρμα
ο χυμός του φρούτου χύνεται άτσαλα
ζαλίζοντας ό,τι απελπίζει το μάτι
κι ενώ εξακολουθεί να μην καταλαβαίνει
αν κάτι μέσα στον καθαρό αέρα του Μαΐου
τον αναζητεί
θέλει να σου διηγηθεί την ιστορία του
για κείνη – λέει – τη συνάντηση
ότι έβρεχε
πόσο κοντά η αναπνοή σου βρέθηκε στο χέρι του

The Poet

he's forced to look –

*

now
the poet rips up
the conditions his poetry
advocates
like thin worn-out skin.
Being almost touched
by the pitch of that penultimate *A*
(or rather, resisting it)
persuades him not to wait.
Music
– he read once –
is nothing more than a succession
of armed and disarmed sounds
which a despairing,
doubting mind
might commit to.

*

he's forced to look
at the fresh syllable-grass swaying slightly
in the air, weaving a new skin –
fruit essences spill everywhere
blurring what the eye longs for
and while he still doesn't understand
whether something in the clean May air
is after him
he wants to tell you his story
about that meeting, he says,
how it rained
how your breath touched his hand intimately

πόσο γλυκά   η βροχή
(λάθος)
πόσο γλυκά εκείνη η παράφορη βροχή
οι αιχμηρές φτερούγες της
για πόσο λίγο
όλα (όλα;) όσα με βία συνωστίζονται
χωρίς ειρμό
ραγίζοντας την κρούστα της διήγησης
αιφνιδιάζοντας την έκβαση της ιστορίας

*

    τώρα
    ο ποιητής σχίζει
    σαν ισχνό κουρασμένο δέρμα
    τις προϋποθέσεις που στην ποίησή του
    υπερθεματίζει
    συλλογίζεται το βανδαλισμό που θα
       επακολουθήσει
    το τέλος αυτής του κιόλας της πρότασης
    και –
    τί θλίψη
    να 'ναι το πέρασμα έξω από το τοπίο
    το ελάχιστο ανάμεσα στη λέξη και το μύθο της
       λέξης
    που

– χορεύει
η καρδιά του μέσα στα χέρια του
κι αυτός χορεύει –

η μουσική
κάτι απογεύματα σαν κι αυτό εδώ
τώρα
κρατάει νωπό
χωρίς καμία γλώσσα να 'χει ποτέ διασχίσει.

how tenderly   the rain
(wrong)
how that furious rain tenderly
its sharp wings
for how short a time
all (all?) that is violently contested
out of order
breaking the surface of the narrative
surprising the end of the story

*

now
the poet rips up
the conditions his poetry
advocates
like thin worn-out skin
he considers the vandalism which will follow
when this sentence ends
and –
there's a certain fatalism
in walking across this landscape
in just standing between the word, its myth
and

– he dances,
his heart in his hands
he dances –

what the music
on evenings like this
right now
keeps fresh
and uncaptured by language

Fiona Sampson and Socrates Kambouropoulos

II
MYTH AND MEDICINE
DIY and Small Press Poets

The largely Athens-based poets in this section continue a
strong tradition of surrealism in Greek verse, stretching
from the 1930s through the post-war poems of Miltos
Sachtouris and the later paralogical turn which Yannis
Ritsos, Jenny Mastoraki, and others adopted under the
Colonels' censorship in the 1970s. The aesthetic is semi-DIY:
some self-publish, or turn to Gavrielides, a mass-market
publisher which welcomes first collections; some gravitate
toward distinguished small presses; some take poetry
night classes at the Takis Sinopoulos Foundation; and,
crucially, they form collectives and make their own magazines –
most notably φρμκ (*Farmakon*). In Greek, 'farmakon' is both
poison and medicine, that which hurts and that which
heals. An unstated belief in poetry's ability to work medici-
nally, as a way of managing and living with pain and
uncertainty, unites the raw, documentary-style poems of
Stathis Antoniou with the more polished, mystical medita-
tions of Katerina Iliopoulou. In Anna Griva and Eftychia
Panayiotou, myth-creation slides into an interest in the
magical, whether it is animating strange animal worlds or
opening windows with words. And, like the poets of the
'Storytelling' section, Phoebe Giannisi and Eva Stefani work
in other genres – architecture and experimental film, respect-
ively – but their position here is secured by their mentorship
of the younger poets in this mostly female *parea* (gang). The
attention is repaid. Krystalli Glyniadakis's poem 'National
Anthem, 2008, Redux' upgrades post-Dictatorship femi-
nism for a new generation; and more generally – and
impressively – these younger poets have created an arena
through their writing in which the important work of
their mentors can finally find a place.

KATERINA ILIOPOULOU

(Born Athens, Greece, 1967)

As a creature who understands her own excess in an age in which the cultural capital of nature and myth are at an all-time low, the fox in Katerina Iliopoulou's eponymous poem is this group's mascot. And Iliopoulou is definitely their leading force, both in terms of her poetics and in her pursuit of the self-made project. She is Editor in Chief of *φρμκ* (*Farmakon*) and co-edits *Greek Poetry Now* (greek poetrynow.com). She also writes essays and reviews, works extensively with visual artists, and has translated Sylvia Plath, Mina Loy, Robert Hass, and Ted Hughes.

Ο κύριος Ταυ (*Mister Tau*), Melani, 2007; *Άσυλο* (*Asylum*), Melani, 2008; *Το βιβλίο του χώματος* (*The Book of Soil*), Melani, 2011; *Gestus*, Alfeios/Farmakon, 2014; *Μια φορά κάθε τοπίο και ολότελα* (*Every Place, Once, and Completely*), Melani, 2015.

Η αλεπού

Μέσα στη δέσμη του φωτός εμφανίστηκε
Διέσχισε το δρόμο
Μια μικρή καφέ αλεπού.
Και ξανά το επόμενο βράδυ
Πίσω από έναν θάμνο φευγαλέα
Και μια άλλη φορά η ουρά της μόνο
Σκούπισε το σκοτάδι
Και από τότε πάλι
Τις πατούσες της να βηματίζουν στο βλέμμα σου
Το ζεστό γούνινο σώμα της
Ανάμεσά μας να σκιρτά
Πάντα σε πέρασμα ποτέ σε στάση
«Μα ποιά είσαι;» τη ρωτήσαμε
«Είμαι», είπε, «αυτό που περισσεύει».

The Fox

In the beam of the headlights she appeared
Crossing the road,
A small brown fox.
And again the next night
Flitting behind a bush.
And another time only her tail
Brushed the darkness.
And from then on
Her footprints padded across your sight,
Her warm furry body
Skittering between us.
Always in passing, never staying still.
'But who are you?' we asked her.
'I am,' she said, 'what's superfluous.'

A. E. Stallings

Πενθεσίλεια

I.

Συχνά λένε τη σκιά πανωφόρι
Όμως εγώ κάτω από τα δέντρα είμαι γυμνή
Η σκιά μακραίνει κι απλώνεται σαν φίδι
Μείνε εκεί και μπορεί να σε δαγκώσει
Όπως δαγκώνει το μάρμαρο δαγκώνει το νερό
Όχι όμως οι πευκοβελόνες ούτε η άμμος
Αυτά είναι άλλου είδους φωλιές
Είναι του ανέμου έρμαια σχήματα του τυχαίου.
Να εμπιστευθείς τη δαγκωνιά

II.

Στη χώρα της σκιάς υπάρχουν πράγματα
που περιμένουν
Δεν είναι εύκολο να παραβιάσεις την επικράτειά τους
Παρόλο που δεν μπορούν να σου ορμήξουν
Έχουν τον τρόπο τους να σε καταρρακώνουν
Πρόκειται για ένα είδος διάβρωσης
Με τις πιο ανεπαίσθητες κινήσεις
Με τους πιο αδιόρατους ήχους
Σε κατοικούν
Σε μαθαίνουν τόσο καλά που γίνεσαι πέρασμα
Εσύ δεν μπορείς ποτέ να περάσεις
Η ανωνυμία τους είναι το πραγματικό δηλητήριο του
    κόσμου
Εγώ έμαθα να μπαίνω εδώ
Έγινα θηριοδαμαστής ακίνητων θηρίων

Penthesilea

I.

They can call shadows an overcoat
but still I am naked under the tree
whose own shadow slithers
like a snake. Stay and it will bite
like water, bite like marble but not
like pine needles or sand. Those
are different nests. They are chance
drifting like strands in air.

II.

In the land of shadows
naked things wait.
Not to jump you or rush you.
They have softer ways
to break and tatter you.
With indiscernible sounds,
imperceptible movements
they inhabit you.
They learn you so well
you become a passage
you will never be able to pass.
Their anonymity is the poison of this world.
I have learned how to enter.
I have become a tamer of still beasts.

Δεν είμαι εγώ καμιά καλόγρια
Να τρώω φύλλα
Να πληγιάζω τα χείλια μου στην άγρια φλούδα
Να υψώνω δεήσεις σ' αόρατο ουρανό
Εγώ μασάω το βοτάνι της σιωπής
Στήνω παγίδα από ψάθα και την πνίγω τη σκιά
Ρουφάω την ανάσα της
Αφήνω το τραγούδι της από υδράργυρο να σταλάξει
    στ' αυτιά μου

I am no nun
I don't eat leaves
I don't rub my lips on hard bark
Or raise my eyes to an invisible sky
I chew on the plant of silence
I set a snare of bulrush for the shadow and strangle it
I suck its breath
I let its song of mercury drip into my ears.

Ryan Van Winkle

Ο κύριος Ταυ σε θαλασσινό τοπίο

Μαζεύει ένα βότσαλο απ' την ακροθαλασσιά
Παρατηρεί πως το βότσαλο έχει την αξιοσημείωτη
    ιδιότητα
Να μη διαθέτει εσωτερικό και εξωτερικό.
Τα δύο ταυτίζονται.
Επειδή δεν μπορεί να σκεφτεί τίποτε άλλο,
αποφασίζει πως το βότσαλο είναι εχθρός του κόσμου
και το πετάει μακριά.
Το βότσαλο πέφτοντας δημιουργεί αυτό που λέμε
«τρύπα στο νερό»

Ο κύριος Ταυ αισθάνεται τρομερή έλξη
και ανεξήγητη ζήλια για το βότσαλο.
Παίρνει λοιπόν ένα άλλο και το βάζει στο στόμα του.
Στην αρχή είναι αλμυρό.
Είναι ένα θαλασσινό πράγμα.
Λίγο μετά δεν είναι τίποτα.
Ένας σκληρός όγκος σιωπής μέσα στο στόμα του,
που ρουφάει τη φωνή του.

Με έκπληξή του όμως διαπιστώνει
Πως και χωρίς φωνή μπορεί να μιλάει.
Προφανώς οι επικλήσεις του εισακούγονται.
Ένα σμάρι θαλασσοπούλια προσγειώνεται στα
    πόδια του.
Όταν φεύγουν αφήνουν πίσω τους ένα δυσανάγνωστο
    κείμενο.
Ο κύριος Ταυ σκύβει κι αρχίζει ευθύς να το μελετάει.

Mister Tau in a Seascape

He is picking up a pebble from the seashore
He observes that the pebble has the noteworthy
    attribute
That it does not have an inside and an outside
The two are one and the same.
Then, because he cannot think of anything else
He decides the pebble is the enemy of the world
And hurls it far away.
The fallen pebble creates what we call
A 'hole in the water'

Mister Tau feels a terrific attraction
An inexplicable envy for the pebble.
Therefore he takes another one and puts it in his mouth.
At first it is salty.
It is a sea thing.
A little bit later it isn't anything.
A hard mass of silence inside his mouth
That swallows his voice.

To his surprise, however, he discovers
That even without a voice he is able to speak.
Evidently his appeals have been granted.
A flock of seabirds lands at his feet.
When they fly off, they leave behind them an
    unreadable text.
Mister Tau stoops down and starts immediately to
    study it.

A. E. Stallings

Η σειρήνα

Τα σεντόνια είναι λευκές σελίδες
Κάθε βράδυ γράφει ακούραστα
Τις γεμίζει πυρετωδώς
Όπως λένε πως κάνουν οι ποιητές
Μα το πρωί τα σεντόνια είναι ζώα παράφορα
Είναι κύματα θάλασσα άγρια που αναδιπλώνεται

Και από εκεί αναδύεται συχνά μία μικρή σειρήνα
Τον κοιτάζει απαλά κι έπειτα
Βγάζει τα μάτια της και του τα προσφέρει
Δυο γυάλινους βόλους πράσινους
Ο Κύριος Ταυ δεν τολμά να απλώσει τα χέρια
Μα πώς ποθεί τη δροσιά τους και πώς σαλεύουν τα
    δάχτυλά του σαν φύκια
Να τ᾽ αγγίξουν

Τα μάτια της θα ρούφαγαν όλη τη σκόνη
Που είναι η κλεψύδρα του καιρού
Θα έκαναν το αίμα νερό
Και τον ασβέστη κρύσταλλο
Η προσφορά εκκρεμεί
Μα ο Κύριος Ταυ όλο το αναβάλλει
Ποιος αντέχει να ζει σ᾽ ένα διάφανο σπίτι;

The Siren

The bed sheets are white pages
Every night he writes tirelessly
He fills them feverishly
As they say the poets do
But in the morning the sheets are raging animals
They are waves, a wild sea folding on itself

And from there a tiny siren often rises
Who looks at him softly and then
Takes out her eyes and offers them to him,
Two glass marbles, green
Mister Tau does not dare stretch out his hands
But how he longs for their coolness and how his fingers
    quiver like seaweed
To touch them

Her eyes would suck down all the dust
Which is the hourglass of time
They would turn blood into water
And the silica into crystal
Her offer stands
But Mister Tau keeps putting the whole thing off.
Who can bear to live in a transparent house?

A. E. Stallings

STATHIS ANTONIOU

(Born Athens, Greece, 1982)

A cross between neorealism and melodrama marks Stathis Antoniou's offbeat narrative poems. He studied Mathematics, and now works as both a researcher in Applied Mathematics at the National Technical University of Athens and a business consultant for Avon Cosmetics. Poetically, he is very much self-taught; his bricolage approach includes night classes at the Takis Sinopoulos Foundation in Athens and at the Shakespeare and Co. bookshop in Paris. Though he is yet to publish even a chapbook, his poems, short stories, and travel writing have recently begun to appear in the magazines *Tetradia tou Elpinora (Elpenor's Notebooks)*, *(de) kata (nth degree)*, *Teflon*, and *Geotropio*.

Τα σκυλιά

Μια πινακίδα σήμανε ότι πλησιάζει σε κατοικημένη περιοχή. Αναρωτήθηκε γιατί άνθρωποι αποφάσισαν να εγκατασταθούν σε ένα τόσο αποκρουστικό περιβάλλον.

Λίγο πριν το πρώτο σπίτι, οι προβολείς του φώτισαν ένα κόκκινο ύφασμα πιασμένο στα κλαδιά· ένα φόρεμα που κυμάτιζε λες και τα δέντρα έγδυσαν μια γυναίκα και τώρα επιδείκνυαν το κατόρθωμά τους.

Χαμήλωσε ταχύτητα.

Άγρια χόρτα έπνιγαν τις αυλές. Πιτσιρικάδες τον κοιτούσαν σαν να ζύγιζαν την αξία του σε λεφτά. Αντί για παράθυρα, τζάμια σπασμένα ή ραγισμένα.

Μια μυρωδιά καμένου κρέατος σκέπαζε τα κενά ανάμεσα στα αραιοκατοικημένα σπίτια. Οι τοίχοι ήταν γεμάτοι κακογραμμένα συνθήματα. Η πιο χαρούμενη εικόνα ήταν δυο μεσήλικες που έπαιζαν κάποιο επιτραπέζιο παιχνίδι, καθισμένοι πάνω σε μπιντόνια μπογιάς.

Αν και δεν υπήρχαν σκουπίδια, οι δρόμοι ήταν βρόμικοι. Τα σπίτια φέγγονταν από παλιές λάμπες που κρέμονταν σαν ξεριζωμένα μάτια από τα ταβάνια.

Τι αίσθηση του «ωραίου» μπορεί να είχε κάποιος που μεγάλωσε εδώ;

Παρότι χάρηκε που τα μάτια του είδαν αυτό το μέρος, ένιωσε ανακούφιση όταν τα σπίτια άρχισαν ν' αραιώνουν.

The Dogs

A road sign indicated that he was entering an inhabited region. He wondered how people would choose to settle in such a repulsive place.

Just before the first house, his headlights lit on a red cloth caught in branches, a dress that dangled as if the trees had taken a woman and were now showing their exploit.

He lowered his speed.

Wild grasses choked the yards. Teenagers looked at him, weighing his worth in change. Instead of windows, broken glass everywhere.

The smell of burnt meat wafted in the emptiness between the houses. The walls were scrawled with slogans. The happiest sight: two middle-aged men playing a board game, sitting on paint cans.

Although there was no garbage, the roads were dirty. The houses were lit by old lamps that hung like gouged eyes from the beams.

What sense of beauty could somebody have growing up here?

Although he was glad that he had seen this place, he felt relief when the houses began to thin out.

Τρία σκυλιά άρχισαν να γαβγίζουν, τρέχοντας πλάι στις ρόδες του. Παρόλο που αυτό τού είχε ξανατύχει πολλές φορές, κάτι ήταν διαφορετικό εδώ, κάτι στο γαβγισμά τους. Ενώ πάντα νόμιζε πως τ᾽ αδέσποτα σκυλιά τον διώχνουν, τούτα δω έλεγαν αυτό που οι κάτοικοι ντρέπονταν να ζητήσουν, τον παρακαλούσαν να μείνει μαζί τους, να μοιραστεί τη μοναξιά τους.

Three dogs started to bark, running beside the wheels of his car. This had happened many times before, but something was different now, something in their bark. While he always had the feeling that stray dogs were after him, these were demanding what the inhabitants were too embarrassed to say. They were begging him to stay, to share their loneliness.

- Karen Van Dyck

ANNA GRIVA

(Born Athens, Greece, 1985)

Anna Griva's inventive animal poems reflect the paralogical and elliptical influence of the Dictatorship generation of poets – Jenny Mastoraki, but also Maria Laina, who, when asked if art imitates life, replied: 'Isn't one reality enough?' Griva is a well-respected translator from the Italian, and actively engaged in initiating her own translation projects, mostly of women's poetry and usually of poetry less well known than the work generally chosen for translation by the *Poetics* group of the first section. She is also involved in the translation project Workshop Gamma, run by Marios Spiliopoulos at the Athens School of the Arts; see the *Novelty Within or Beyond Language* anthology, listed in this book's Further Reading, for the work which has emerged from this exciting collaboration between young poets and artists. Like many trained philologists of her generation, she makes a living as a tutor for the Greek university exams.

Η φωνή του σκοτωμένου (*The Voice of the Dead*), Charamada, 2010; *Οι μέρες που ήμασταν άγριοι* (*Our Wild Days*), Gavrielides, 2012; *Έτσι είναι τα πουλιά* (*Birds Are That Way*), Gavrielides, 2015.

Δοκιμή

Το αυτί μου
αρπάζεται
από αναίτιους θορύβους
και στην καρδιά
φουσκώνει
το συναπάντημα
ενός γκρεμού

έλξη αντιλάλου
άδειο φορτίο
με ρουφά
και με γεμίζει
μια κάθοδος
όπως βυθίζονται
τα σύννεφα
στην πτώση
του νερού τους

μένω πρηνής
και ανερμήνευτος
και δοκιμάζω
αναδιπλώσεις
μέχρι ν' αντέξω
ακίνδυνα
του ποιήματος

την αναχώρηση
στα μάτια των αλόγων
σαν τα καρφιά
σφηνώνονται
οι πεδιάδες

Attempt

My ear is
seized by
random
sounds and in
my heart
a precipice
unfolds

an echo
pulls an
empty
load draws
me and
a descent
fills me
as clouds
sink in
their water's
fall

I lie
prone
unread
attempt
retreat until
I can endure
the poem's
leaving

prairies drive
like nails

και της ταχύτητας
η πρόκληση
μετριέται μονάχα
στην έκταση
των πληγών.

από *Βυθός*

Μπορεί το κολύμπι να είναι μια έκταση ερήμου
φοίνικες πλήττουν τη γαλήνη της
και δεν αφήνουν τη ζωή να κυλήσει
όπως ο αναβάτης στην πλάτη του σκύλου
που έλεγε μη με συγκρίνεις με ιππότη
γιατί δεν έχω στη ζώνη μου φλουριά και ξίφος
και μέχρι τότε δεν το είχα φανταστεί έτσι
αυτό που του έλειπε.

into galloping
horses' eyes

wounds
the only
measure of
their speed's
defiance.

Maria Margaronis

from *Depths*

Swimming could be an extension of the desert
palm trees exasperate her calm
and stop life from moving on
like the rider on the dog
who said don't compare me to the rider on the horse
because I haven't a sword or sheath, not in my belt
and up til now I hadn't considered it
as something he was missing

Karen Van Dyck

Οι τρόποι να μη λυπάστε

Προσέχτε τα βήματά σας
κάτω απ' τις φυλλωσιές των δέντρων κρύβεται
το σώμα σας ντυμένο τα φτερά της νυχτερίδας
και τα τυφλά της μάτια
αν σκοντάψετε ξεγλιστρά πάνω σας
κρέμεται ανάποδα απ' το σαγόνι σας
όπως απ' της σπηλιάς τα εξογκώματα
και τα νύχια που χρόνια μεγάλωναν
κι ελίσσονταν στα κλαδιά
βρίσκουν επιτέλους μια θέση στο μυαλό σας

προσέχτε τη μήτρα σας αν είστε γυναίκες
το καρύδι που μεγαλώνει το λαιμό σας αν είστε άντρες
και παιδιά αν μείνατε βρείτε επιτέλους έναν τρόπο
να πεθάνετε ανώδυνα χωρίς να χρειαστεί ούτε άντρες
ούτε γυναίκες να φανείτε

προσέχτε τον κίνδυνο που ανατέλλει κάθε πρωί απ' το
    βουνό
σταθείτε μακριά και δώστε του ονόματα να τον ξορκίσετε
κόψη ξυράφι
φλοιό ανθρώπου λιωμένη ύλη
μες στα χέρια
κάποτε σύσπαση σιωπή
νύχτα πουλιά που τρόμαξαν
των κυνηγών το βόρβορο

και τις βαριές πατημασιές τους
ταίρι
προπάντων ταίρι
που οσφραίνεται το αίμα μας

Ways to Avoid Sadness

Be careful where you tread
under the trees' foliage lurks
your body clothed in bats' wings
and blind eyes
if you trip it slithers on to you
hangs upside down from your chin
as if from a cave's protrusions
and the claws that have grown for years
winding around the branches
find a home at last inside your brain

Be careful of your womb if you are women
of the Adam's apple swelling your throat if you are men
and if you are still children find a way at last
to die painlessly without needing to appear
either men or women

Be careful of the danger that rises every morning from
    the mountain
keep your distance and give it names to exorcize it
razor cut
human peel melted material
in your hands
sometimes spasm silence
night startled birds
the hunters' swamp

and heavy footsteps
mate
above all mate
who scents our blood.

Maria Margaronis

Ο πόλεμος με τα ζώα μου

Οταν οι αρθρώσεις θωρακίζουνε
θυμό και κίνηση στα οστά μου
απλώνω τα χέρια ανοίγομαι
στον κίνδυνο να υπάρχω
τρέφεται άνεμο η ουρά
ανάμεσα στα πόδια
και μια παλιά ισορροπία
– τη θυμάμαι –
χτυπά στις πέτρες
και σηκώνεται
πιο μαλακή στο βάρος της

τα ζώα
με κρατούν
δεμένη
στο ένστικτό τους

τρέμω γρυλίζω σαν σκυλί
στην πόρτα του σφαγείου
και αμολιέται η μύτη μου
υγρή για λίγο αίμα
η νοστιμιά αναπάντεχη
η έλξη φρέσκια
μέχρι να γίνει ο θάνατος
ένα ξερό υφάδι
κι όσο κι αν γλείφω απαλά
η γλώσσα να πετρώνει

χαιδεύω ακόμη
ανθούς στο λαιμό μου
περιβόλια αντίστροφα
στη δύναμη των φόνων.

The War with My Animals

When my articulations shield
anger and movement in my bones
I stretch out my arms I open
to the danger that I exist
wind feeds the tail
between my legs
and an old balance
– I remember it –
strikes the stones
and rises
softer in its weight

the animals
hold me
bound
to their instinct

I tremble I growl like a dog
at the door of the slaughterhouse
my nose darts forward
damp for a little blood
irresistible saltiness
fresh desire
till death dries
to a barren weave
and though I lick it gently
my tongue turns to stone

Still I caress
blossoms at my throat
gardens against
the power of murders

Maria Margaronis

Το μάθημα των μυρμηγκιών

Στην επικράτεια των μυρμηγκιών
η σκέψη είναι δύσκολη
όχι πως φταίει το κεφάλι τους
ή των κινήσεων οι αυτοματισμοί
μα πιο πολύ είναι που σέρνονται
κάτω απ' τις γέφυρες των σπόρων
και σταματούν αν μυριστούν βροχή ή χιόνι
αυτή όλη η έγνοια τους
και πώς μετά ξανά στο γύρισμα του ήλιου
θα στρώσουν τα φαγώσιμα
σαν τη μπουγάδα της γριάς
μια πιθαμή απ' το μούχλιασμα μακριά
να 'χουν να τρων και να διηγούνται
μόνο νεράκι δίσεχτο και των τρελών τρεχάλα
και τη μπουκιά στο στόμα τους βρεγμένη
μα όλο λαχτάρα να γευτούν
όχι δεν πρέπει!
η σωτηρία τόσο πάντα απείχε απ' την πέψη
όσο κι από τον κίνδυνο πνιγμού

κι ούτε το καλοκαίρι δε γίνεται εύκολη η σκέψη
γιατί οι βροχές παραμονεύουν
ακόμη κι αν στάζουν ιδρώτες των ζώων
κι ανάσες καυτές μες στη φωλιά τους
γι' αυτό οι εποχές όλες περνούν με μία έγνοια
και δίχως άλλη πλοκή

μόνο οι κεραίες γλιτώνουν
χωρίς καθόλου να σκέπτονται
και μπλέκονται ωραία
σαν της μουσικής
το τύλιγμα

The Ants' Lesson

In the empire of the ants
thinking is difficult
it's not the fault of their heads
or their automatic movements
it's more that they drag themselves
under bridges of seeds
and stop if they scent rain or snow
that's all they care about
and then at the sun's return
how to spread out their food
like an old woman's washing
on the verge of going mouldy
so they can eat and tell their tales
all unlucky trickling and crazy caravans
and the bite in their mouth damp
but all eagerness to taste
no you musn't!
Salvation always was just that distance from digestion
and from the risk of drowning

and thinking isn't any easier in summer
because the rains lie in wait
even if there's animal sweat dripping
and breath burning in their nest
so all the seasons pass with one preoccupation
and no other plot

only their antennae get away
without thinking altogether
tangling beautifully
like music's
winding

τις βλέπεις και λες
αυτή είναι η κίνηση όλη του κόσμου
μακριά απ'τα παιδιαρίσματα
που στήνει ο καιρός
όταν μαθαίνουμε και κοινωνούμε
ο ένας τον άλλο
ακουμπώντας τ' αυτιά
στο πιο μαύρο σημείο τους

όσοι ξεχνάνε να σκεφτούν
καλύτερα χορεύουν
όπως σκαρίφημα
κάτω απ΄ το γέλιο
πικρής απόγνωσης.

you see them and say
this is the movement of the world
far away from the childishness
that time throws up
when we learn to communicate
one with another
touching our ears together
at their blackest point

those who forget to think
dance better
a sketch
under the laughter
of bitter desolation.

Maria Margaronis

Επίνικος

Τις νύχτες σκοτώνω την ώρα μου
πάνω στα έπιπλα
με ένα θερμόμετρο στη μασχάλη ταξιδεύω
απ' το ένα δωμάτιο στ᾽ άλλο
και μαγειρεύω στο μπρίκι μου
το ταρακούνημα της κουρτίνας
η πόρτα κλειδώνει μόνη της πια:
δεν έχω τίποτα να δώσω
σε τόσους επισκέπτες
– γιατί έρχεστε; Γιατί έρχεστε ακόμη
και σπαταλάτε τ᾽ αστέρια πάνω μου;

Τόσα παιχνίδια γύρω μου
τόσες αφύλακτες χαρές

κάποτε τρεφόμουν με νερό μόνο
και είχα γίνει βαριά σαν πέτρα
με φυσούσες κι έμενα ακίνητη
στις πλαγιές των λόφων
τώρα βαδίζω κρυφά στα κοπάδια των ζώων
τα κάνω κομμάτια με τα δόντια μου
και δε χορταίνω δε χορταίνω το αίμα τους
(η ίδια δεν είμαι;)
κάποτε γυρόφερνα το θάνατο
σαν κουτσή γριά
που καθαρίζει την κουζίνα της
τώρα τον φυτεύω με τα χέρια μου
ανάμεσα στα λουλούδια
και τον βλέπω να μεγαλώνει
και να μαθαίνει το περπάτημα

ANNA GRIVA

Triumphal Ode

Nights I kill time
against the furniture
with a thermometer under my arm I sail
from one room to another
cook up in my coffee pot
the stirring of the curtain
the door locks itself now:
I have nothing to offer
all these visitors
– why do you come? why do you still come
and waste the stars on me?

so much play around me
so many unguarded joys

once I was nourished by water
and I grew stone heavy
if you blew I'd still be motionless
up there on the hillside
now I secretly stalk herds of animals
tear them to pieces with my teeth
never get enough never enough of their blood
(aren't I the same?)
once I circled death
like a lame crone
cleaning her kitchen
now I plant him with my own hands
among the flowers
and watch him grow
and learn to walk

τραβώ στα νύχια μου
τον κομπασμό της άνοιξης
κι αποκοιμιέμαι
πουλί εν πτήσει:
η ανακούφιση
θα μοιάζει πάντοτε
με το θυμίαμα
των ηφαιστείων

I drag spring's swagger
with my fingernails
and sleep
a bird in flight:
relief
always resembles
the incense
of volcanoes

Maria Margaronis

PHOEBE GIANNISI

(Born Athens, Greece, 1964)

In the 1980s Phoebe Giannisi and some other artists created the fanzine *Mavro Mouseio* (*Black Museum*). Although she went on to publish her poetry in established venues like *Poetics*, her work continues to be featured in alternative magazines, *Farmakon* among them. Her poetry reflects a visual and classical background, gained through studies in Architecture in Athens and later a Ph.D. in Classics in Lyon. She was a member of *Urban Void*, a group of architects and artists who organized and performed on issues of ecology and urban landscape. Her audiovisual poetry installation *Tettix* showed at the National Museum of Contemporary Art in 2012. Giannisi has translated Ancient lyric poetry and work by Hélène Cixous, Gerhard Falkner, Andrew Maxwell, and others. She teaches at the University of Thessaly in Volos.

Αχινοί (*Sea Urchins*), Mavro Mouseio, 1995;
Ραμαζάνι (*Ramadan*), Mavro Mouseio, 1997;
Θηλιές (*Loops*), Nefeli, 2005; *Ομηρικά* (*Homerica*),
Kedros, 2009; *Τέττιξ* (*Tettix*), Gavrielides, 2012.

(Πηνελόπη – I am addicted to you)

έχει πάθος με την πισίνα
κάθε μέρα στην πισίνα πάνω-κάτω
την ίδια διαδρομή ξανά και ξανά
η πισίνα την κρατά στη ζωή
το κολύμπι στην πισίνα την συντηρεί
το συνεχές πηγαινέλα
η ρυθμική αναπνοή
ο συντονισμός χεριών ποδιών
με το κεφάλι
μέσα έξω μέσα έξω
στο νερό
το κεφάλι
επαναλαμβανόμενα μπαίνει και βγαίνει
φυσά μέσα ρουφά έξω τον αέρα
οι παύσεις κάθε λίγο στο διάδρομο
τα πλακάκια κάτω από την επιφάνεια μέσα
στο φως
τα ξένα σώματα απειλητικά
με σκουφιά ή με πέδιλα
το νερό μες στο χλώριο
ο ουρανός πάνω από κυπαρίσσια
η πισίνα με κρατά στη ζωή
το συνεχές τραγούδι
το μέτρημα
ένα δύο τρία τέσσερα πέντε
έξι επτά οκτώ εννιά δεκαπέντε
δεκαεννιά χτυπήματα περιστροφές
το τραγούδι του μετρήματος η επανάληψη απολιθώνει
το τραγούδι της πισίνας με σώζει
με σώζει από τη γνώση πως
δε μ' αγαπά

(Penelope – Ἔχω πάθος για σένα)

She is passionate about swimming every day in the pool up and down the same lane over and over the pool keeps her alive swimming in the pool sustains her the continual back and forth the rhythmic breathing the hands and feet synchronized with the head going in and out of the water the head repeatedly going up and down for air breathing in and out resting sometimes in the lane the tiles under the surface in the light the foreign bodies monsters with their caps and flippers the chlorine water the sky over the cypresses the pool keeps her alive the continual song the counting one two three four five six seven eight nine fifteen nineteen kicks to a lap and turn the song of counting the repetition turns the pool song to stone saves me saves me from the knowledge that he doesn't love me

Karen Van Dyck

(Θέτις)

Θέτις
αυτή που τίθεται
ίσως
πάντα αυτή που θέτει
όπως γνωρίζουμε ακόμα αυτή
που αρνήθηκε να τεθεί
στον άνδρα να παραδοθεί
γενόμενη
φωτιά άνεμος νερό
δέντρο πτηνό όρνιθα τίγρη
γενόμενη
λιοντάρι φίδι σουπιά
ώσπου κάποτε στο ακρωτήριο Σηπιάς ο θνητός
την έθεσε γερά κρατώντας
με σταθερή λαβή την λεία κατέκτησε
και την έφαγε μέσα στον έρωτα
άφησε μόνο το λευκό κόκαλό της
το κόκαλο της σουπιάς στην παραλία
καθαρό πλυμένο από το κύμα
η Θέτις δεν είναι πια εκεί
φυσά μια ντουντούκα από τα βάθη
της θάλασσας
ένα χωνί ένα μεγάλο κοχύλι αντηχεί
τα λόγια που λένε
«παρ' όλα τα μελάνια που αμόλησα
ο άνδρας με καταβρόχθισε
εγώ θεά αυτός θνητός»
ο πολεμιστής πάντοτε επιστρέφει νεκρός

(Thetis)

Thetis
the one in position
perhaps
always the one who posits
as we know even she
who refused to be placed
to a man to surrender
becoming
fire wind water
tree bird fowl tiger
becoming
lion snake cuttlefish
until once at the Sepia peninsula the mortal
steadfastly held her in place gripping
the conquered prey in a stronghold
and ate her in the act of love
leaving behind only her white bone
the sepia bone on the shore
washed clean by the waves
Thetis is no longer there
she blows a conch from the depths
of the sea
a funnel a large seashell echoes
the words that call
'for all the ink I spewed
the man swallowed me whole
I a goddess, he a mortal'
the warrior always returns dead

Stathis Gourgouris

(Λωτοφάγοι II)

θα μείνω εδώ στην στροφή του δρόμου στο γύρισμα
του κόλπου στην άκρη του ακρωτηρίου στην κορυφή
του υψηλού βουνού στις ανοιχτές της θάλασσας
   αγκάλες
στην εκβολή του ποταμού
θα μείνω εδώ
τα μήλα κόκκινα τα αχλάδια ζουμερά οι πάτοι
των παπουτσιών δεν φθείρονται
ξυπόλυτος περπατάς με ρούχα ελαφριά
τέλος καλοκαιριού μα ο χειμώνας δεν έρχεται
μπορείς έξω να κάθεσαι την ώρα που νυχτώνει
αηδόνια ακούγονται τα φώτα ανάβουν
εμπρός στα μεγάλα τραπέζια δείπνα μικρά του δειλινού
με νυχτοπεταλούδες δείπνα μεθυσμένα
το φάρμακο το έφαγες
το φάρμακο ένα λουλούδι
το φάρμακο είναι το φάρμακο
η λήθη
το κάθε στιγμή καινούργια αρχή
είναι δεν ξέρω από πού έρχομαι δεν θέλω να γυρίσω
το φάρμακο
το πάντα τώρα πάντα τώρα

(Lotus Eaters II)

I'll stay here at the road's turn at the bend
of the bay the end of the headland the top of
the high mountain in the open arms of the sea at the
mouth of the
river
I'll stay here apples are red pears juicy the soles
of shoes don't wear down
you walk barefoot in light clothing
end of summer
but the winter doesn't come
you're able to sit outside in the dusk at nightfall
nightingales are heard lights come on
over the big tables the small meals of late afternoon
dinners with moths
tipsy
you've already downed the medicine
the medicine a flower
the medicine is the medicine
forgetfulness is every moment a brand new beginning
it's I don't know where I come from I don't want to
    return
the medicine is always now always now.

Angelos Sakkis

EFTYCHIA PANAYIOTOU

(Born Cyprus, 1980)

Eftychia Panayiotou brings another tradition of Greek poetry to the contemporary Athens scene. The influence of the Cypriot Kostas Montis is felt in her short, elliptical poems; so too is that of the Alexandrian Diaspora poet C. P. Cavafy, another who wrote in Greek outside of Greece. She translates Anne Sexton and Anne Carson and writes reviews for the newspaper *Avgi* and other publications. She is currently completing her Ph.D. on the poetry of the Generation of the 1970s at the University of Athens.

Μέγας κηπουρός (*Great Gardener*), Koinonia ton (de)katon, 2007; *Μαύρη Μωραλίνα* (*Black Moralina*), Kedros, 2010; *Χορευτές* (*Dancers*), Kedros, 2014.

Μέγας κηπουρός

Στον Μίλτο

παραλογίζεται τα βράδια ο κηπουρός μου.
σπείρει λέξεις στο χώμα
θάβει λέξεις κάτω απ' το χώμα.
λέξεις λαβωμένες, πρώτα τις χτυπά
τις δένει έπειτα χωρίς φόβο
οίκτο ποτέ του δεν νιώθει γι' αυτές,
κλαίνε σπαράζουν σκούζουν καταριούνται
– λέξεις είναι –
τις βουβαίνει.
το καταφέρνει το αίμα.
δεν είναι ο κηπουρός μου αυτός.

σπείρει το θάνατο.
με σπέρνει θάνατο.
γίνομαι ο θάνατος.

The Great Gardener

For Miltos

in the evenings my gardener raves, delirious.
he sows words in the soil
buries words under the soil.
hurt words, which first he hits
then binds without fear
he never feels compassion for them,
they cry they thrash they shout they curse
– they're words, after all –
but he silences them.
he bludgeons the blood.
this man is not my gardener.

he sows death.
death sows me.
i become death.

Karen Emmerich

η εξοχή του μυαλού μου

ξύπνησα χαράματα ν' αλλάξω
παράθυρο, στράβωσε να κοιτά απέναντι
τη θέα μου κόβοντας.
ανοίγω τα παντζούρια, ατίθασα
από τον αέρα και τ' άλλα κακά, ξεγλιστράνε από
τα δάχτυλά μου – ψεύτες ερωμένοι.
μάταια προσπαθώ ν' ανοίξω διάπλατα
το φως να μπει λίγο, λέω, είπα θέλω φως,
αλλά χαράματα είναι ακόμη, χαράματα άγρια.

γενηθήτω φως είπα σ' ένα παράθυρο αναίτιο.

The Outside of My Mind

I woke at sunrise to change
the window, warped from looking
across, slicing my view.
I open the shutters, wild
from wind and misfortune. They slip
through my fingers – unfaithful lovers.
In vain I try to spread them wide.
To let in the light, I say. I need light, I said.
But it's still sunrise, angry sunrise.

Let there be light, I said, to a no-fault window.

Karen Van Dyck

Λίγο πριν σηκωθείς

Μην πεις πως δεν πόθησες τα φτερά του παγονιού,
ένα φόρεμα να σκουπίζει την πίστα με βαλς.
Κι αν την κορόνα σού έκλεψε τελικά το καρδιοχτύπι
όταν σε κοίταξε στα μάτια ο τολμηρότερος,
μην πεις πως ήτανε κατακτητής·

στα γόνατα είχε πέσει.

Η δικαιοσύνη σου δικαιοσύνη μου

ο άνθρωπος που ξερίζωσε το σπίτι του
δεν ήμουν εγώ· φήμες ήταν πως είμαι προδότης.
γιατί τις ώρες που σηκωνόμουν χαράματα
ν' ανοίξω την πόρτα, εκείνη έκλεινε
ορμητικά, με μίσος,
τα δάχτυλά μου σπάζοντας.
μένοντας μ' ένα χέρι, το «κακό»,
έγραφα επιστολές, απεγνωσμένα,
προς ιερείς και φίλους και συντρόφους.
στα τελευταία, άρχισα να στέλνω απλώς επιστολές:

εξομολογήσεις δίκην δικαιοσύνης.
εξομολογήσεις για δικαιοσύνη.
εξομολογήσεις πνιγμένο δόντι.

Just Before You Stood Up

Don't say you didn't want peacock wings,
a dress that swept across the waltz floor.
And if your tiara stole the show in a heartbeat
when the boldest of all stared you down
don't say he was the conqueror;

he was on his knees.

Karen Van Dyck

Your Justice My Justice

the person who uprooted his house
wasn't me; they were rumors, that i'm a traitor.
because the hours when i'd get up at dawn
to open the door, it would close
with a bang, with hatred,
breaking my fingers.
with just one hand, the 'bad' one,
i would write letters, despairingly,
to priests and friends and comrades.
in the end, i started just to send letters:

confessions of quasi-justice
confessions for justice.
confessions a smothered tooth.

Karen Emmerich

EVA STEFANI

(Born USA, 1964)

The fables in Eva Stefani's prose poems are not about animals; instead, they concern themselves with dysfunctional families and their quirky afterlives. Best known as an experimental documentary filmmaker and visual artist, Stefani was born in America to Greek parents. She studied Cinema and Anthropology in Paris, London, and New York, and teaches Cinema Studies at the University of Athens and the Freie Universität, Berlin. Her films include *Athene* (1995), *Akropolis* (2001), *The Box* (2004), *What Time Is It?* (2007), and *Bathers* (2008), and have been screened at film festivals including IDFA, Cinéma du Réel, FIPA, and Lisboa Docs. She also writes criticism, such as her *10 κείμενα για το ντοκυμαντέρ* (*10 Texts about Documentaries*), published by Patakis in 2007.

Τα μαλλιά του Φιν (*Fin's Hair*), Polis, 2014.

Βυθός

Έχω ένα βάρος στην κοιλιά. Ζητώ να με εγχειρίσουν. Παίρνω ένα λεπίδι και μια κουτάλα να βοηθήσω στην εκσκαφή. Στην αρχή βγάζω λίγη άμμο και άσπρες πέτρες. Προχωράω πιο βαθιά και πέφτω πάνω σε μια μαλακιά μάζα. Ένα βουνό από φύκια. Συνεχίζω να ψάχνω αλλά το λεπίδι και η κουτάλα γλιστράνε δίχως να σκοντάφτουν πουθενά. Θεραπεύτηκα; Μπα. Πετάω τα εργαλεία και βάζω το χέρι μου στο ανοιχτό σώμα που καίει. Πιάνω κάτι. Μια αλυσίδα. Την τραβάω προς τα έξω και ιδού η αιτία του κακού. Το παλιό ρολόι του μπαμπά.

Πλάτη

Έχασα τις μπότες μου και έμεινα μέσα γιατί πού να πάω χωρίς τις μπότες. Όταν ξημέρωσε είχα μια πράσινη καμπούρα. Στον καθρέφτη είδα ότι μια φιστικιά φύτρωσε στην πλάτη μου. Κάτω από το δέντρο ξάπλωναν μητέρες και παιδιά απολαμβάνοντας τη σκιά.

Depths

I have a weight in my belly. I ask them to operate. I hold a scalpel and a ladle to aid the excavation. A little sand and white pebbles at first. I move deeper and stumble upon a soft lump. A mound of seaweed. I keep searching but the scalpel and spoon slide around in vain. All cured? I doubt it. I throw the tools to the side and shove my hands into the burning body. I reach something. A chain. I pull it out. At last, the cause of all the pain. My dad's old watch.

Krystalli Glyniadakis and Chloe Haralambous

Back

I lost my boots and stayed indoors because where could I go without my boots? When dawn broke I had a green humped back. I watched in the mirror as a pistachio tree sprouted between my shoulders. Under the tree mothers and children lay around enjoying the shade.

Krystalli Glyniadakis and Chloe Haralambous

Οικογένεια

Κοιμόμαστε όλοι μαζί στην κουζίνα για να βλέπουμε τηλεόραση. Ξαπλώνουμε ο ένας πάνω στον άλλο. Πρώτα ο μπαμπάς μπρούμυτα. Μετά η μαμά ανάσκελα. Ανάμεσα στον μπαμπά και στη μαμά μπαίνει ο ένας αδερφός. Από πάνω τα δίδυμα. Στην κορυφή η κόρη μπρούμυτα. Κουβέρτες δεν χρειάζονται γιατί ο ένας ζεσταίνει τον άλλο. Στο κρεβάτι μπορούν να μπουν και άλλοι συγγενείς, αρκεί ο καθένας να έχει το δικό του τηλεκοντρόλ.

Πρωτοχρονιά

Πρωτοχρονιά και δεν έχουμε βασιλόπιτα. Είναι όλα κλειστά. Προσφέρω το αριστερό μου στήθος που είναι ζεστό σαν τσουρέκι. Ο μπαμπάς το χαράζει με το μαχαίρι. «Του Χριστού, του φτωχού, του σπιτιού, του μπαμπά, της μαμάς, του αδερφού, της αδερφής. Και του χρόνου να 'μαστε καλά».

Family

We sleep in the kitchen together so we can watch TV. We lie on top of each other. First Dad on his belly. Then Mother on her back. One brother between them. The twins on top. And finally the daughter face down on top of everyone. We don't need blankets because we keep each other warm. More relatives can fit in the bed if they bring their own remote control.

Krystalli Glyniadakis and Chloe Haralambous

New Year's Eve

New Year's and no cake. The shops are shut. I offer my left breast, warm as brioche. My father carves it with a knife: 'one for Christ, one for the poor, one for the house, the father, the mother, the brother, the sister. May next year find us all well.'

Krystalli Glyniadakis and Chloe Haralambous

KRYSTALLI GLYNIADAKIS

(Born Athens, Greece, 1979)

Krystalli Glyniadakis is difficult to categorize. She co-hosts a book show on national television; she publishes in major Greek literary magazines like *Nea Estia*, *Poetics*, and *The Books Journal*; and, like the poets in the final section, she also works between multiple languages, translating and self-translating in Greek, English, and Norwegian. But what makes her work most peculiarly itself is her strong sense – shared with Eva Stefani (p. 129) and with the other poets in the present grouping – of poetry as a healing social project. She studied Philosophy and Political Theory at the London School of Economics and Philosophy of Religion at King's College, London, and also holds an MA in Creative Writing from the University of East Anglia.

Λονδίνο–Ιστανμπούλ (London–Istanbul), Polis, 2009; *Αστικά ερείπια (και αντιπερισπασμοί) (Urban Ruins (And Diversions))*, Polis, 2014.

Εθνικός Ύμνος, 2008, Redux

Για την Εύα Στεφανή

Οι χούντες αυνανίζονται μετ᾽ εθνικών συμβόλων.
    (Ας έρθει κάποιος να μου πει πως είναι λάθος τούτο.)
Κι εσύ τους λες πως η πολλή εθνοφροσύνη
βλάπτει·
                         (τυφλώνει)
κι αυτοί σε πάνε μέσα με νόμο περί ασέμνων.

Για ένα αιδοίο, δηλαδή.

Το βράδυ, σπίτι τους, οι εθνικοί ηγέτες
(οι τωρινοί και οι ευελπιστούντες)
              ανάβουν με την πάρτη τους μπροστά από
              τον καθρέφτη.
Μετ᾽ εθνικών συμβόλων αυνανίζονται οι χούντες.
Κι ούτ᾽ ένας τους δεν έχει ψυλλιαστεί
πως ενα ροδο   ερωτικο και τρυφερό
υποδηλώνει αγάπη
παράδοση κι ελευθερία συνάμα
αντί για βία που ασκούν αυτοί που ακούν
τον ύμνο και καυλώνουν.

Μα έτσι είναι αυτά·
η θηλυκότητα ποτέ δεν έπεισε το Έθνος.

National Anthem, 2008, Redux

For Eva Stefani

Juntas accessorize their wanks with national emblems.
                                        (Am I right?)
You tell them a citizen can be too upstanding
(easily wilted;
                    unhinged)
They lock you up for lewdness.

For saying cunt, that is.

Home at night, national leaders
– incumbent or aspiring –
                    stand stiff and ablaze at the mirror.
Juntas accessorize their wanks with national
    emblems.
None of them catches the scent
of a rose   hot and tender
hinting at love
lore and freedom
in the rumble of those who get hard
listening to the national anthem.

So it goes;
Femininity never satisfied the nation.

                                        Chloe Haralambous

Τα επόμενα εκατό χρόνια

Έπιασα να δω
τι θα 'πρεπε να πρωτομάθω
για να ζωγραφίσω απ' την αρχή τον κόσμο·
κι όλα έβγαζαν άθροισμα ηλεκτρονικό
ούτε πουλιά ούτε ψάρια
ούτε τα ίδια απ' την αρχή
τίποτα όπως ήταν
ή όπως σχεδιάζουν·
μόνο ένα ατέλειωτο πλέγμα πληροφοριών
σ' ένα κόσμο που ζυγίζει τ' ορθολογικό
με το κιλό και το πουλάει χύμα
στα μανάβικα.
Και ξέρεις τι;
Δε φοβήθηκα. Καιρός ν' αλλάξουνε τα πράγματα.
Καιρός να μείνει το νερό για το νερό
τα ψάρια για τα ψάρια
κι ο άυλος, εναργής άνθρωπος
να επιστρέψει στην αστρόσκονη
και να χαθεί· ούτε οίκτος
ούτε περηφάνια
ούτε δικαιοσύνη.
Μια σιωπή μονάχα, κοσμική
κι εμείς αστράκια που ανάβουνε τις νύχτες
στο αιώνιο κι απέραντο σκοτάδι.

The Next Hundred Years

So I sat me down to see
what it is that I should learn
and master in order
to repaint the world anew;
and all figures and all
sums
came up electronic:
no birds or fish
nothing of the same
nothing as it is
nothing as they plan
just an endless net of information
weighed down by science, cut
and sold by the pound
in grocery stores.
And I was not afraid.
It's due time things change
it's time the water be left untouched,
the birds be for the birds,
it's time that Man – spiritual, pellucid –
return to stardust
and be gone; no mercy
and no pride
and no more talk of justice.
Just cosmic stillness.
And we, the little stars that light
up in this eternal darkness.

Self-translated

UNJUST PUNISHMENT
Poets Online

Though Greek poets have been blogging and disseminating their work outside of the usual channels since the late 1990s, it was not until the crisis broke that groups began to form and organize into recognizable entities. Of these, the online magazines *e-poema* (2006–), *Greek Poetry Now* (2009–), and especially *Τέφλον* (*Teflon*, 2009–), with its accompanying print version, are perhaps the most representative. Founded by Jazra Khaleed and Kyoko Kishida and enjoying strong female involvement from the start (Pavlina Marvin, Danae Sioziou), *Teflon* is very much the product of the blog communities that birthed it. It continues their aesthetic of pop culture-influenced 'fast' poetry, turning the language of newspapers, magazines, and advertising to counter-cultural ends; it is angry, full of blood, guts, and frank references to sex, and there are associations, especially on Khaleed's part, with the highly politicized Greek rap scene. Within these horizons, the poets' output is eclectic: what connects them, besides their online presence, is that they all place themselves outside of recognizable traditions, drawing instead on their own personal pantheons. Kishida is influenced by Japanese art and translated in Japan. Danae Sioziou brings influences shared with the poets of 'Myth and Medicine', most notably Miltos Sachtouris and Katerina Anghelaki-Rooke, into the *Teflon* camp. Stathis Baroutsos's queer aesthetic points to another strong current in internet poetry, but, like Yannis Moundelas, he aims to be completely independent, circulating his poems exclusively as a kind of digital samizdat and never putting them in print. Thomas Ioannou may provide the best proof of this medium's reach: far from the traditional image of the activist, he is a neurologist whose political poetry struck a chord and went viral.

KYOKO KISHIDA

(Born Greece, 1983)

Kyoko Kishida (a pen name, taken from the Japanese actress best known for her role in the 1964 film *The Woman in the Dunes*) publishes all of her poetry with *Teflon*, the magazine she founded with Jazra Khaleed (p. 155). The first issue, which included everything from Langston Hughes to Yusef Kumunyakaa, described poetry as food 'witch-cooked, but also served raw'; the formulation could apply just as well to Kishida's own poems, which often read like improvisational, momentary realizations of thoughts and thought-patterns which have long been brewing under the surface. She also writes essays and translates, most recently from the poetry of the African American lesbian poets Pat Parker and Cheryl Clarke.

Οι έκφυλες ήταν φίλες μου

Μ' αρέσει το σπάσιμο της γραμμικότητας
Η τέχνη που ενέχει περισσότερες αισθήσεις
Να μη σταματάς ποτέ να κάνεις ερωτήσεις
Σ' όμορφα ντυμένες για να τραβάς
κουπί με όρεξη θεωρίες
– Τριγύρω χειραγώγηση των κλίσεων
Οδομαχίες, συνθήματα, κυνηγητά
Οι χειρότεροι εχθροί τρυπώνουν μουλωχτά –
Στο βάθος του ορίζοντα το παραπέτασμα σκίζεται
Οι Έκφυλες δε θα σου
πουν ότι ήταν εκεί
Έχουν σαλπάρει σε μπάσους
ωκεανούς καιρό τώρα
Τ' αλατισμένα μάτια τους
διατείνονται φωτοβόλα έχθρητα
Στροβοσκοπικές βροντές
για κακοραμμένα κουστούμια

Degenerate Girls Were My Girlfriends

I like the fracturing of linearity
Art that involves more senses
Asking questions non-stop
To row with gusto
to beautifully dressed scenes
Leading clichés around by the hand
Streetfights, codes, hunts
The worst enemies burrowing in deep
The curtain back in the skyline's coming apart
The Degenerate Girls won't
tell you they were there
They've set sail on shrinking
oceans for some time now
Their salted eyes
tighten luminous hostilities
Strobe-lighten thunderclaps
for poorly tailored outfits

George Economou

Kleine Nachtmusik

Είπα στις μέρες να σταματήσουν να στροβιλίζονται
και φώλιασα μέσα στο βάζο με τη μαρμελάδα
να μη με βρουν οι καταδότες κι οι αμφεταμινικοί
   παλμοί.
Να δω εσύ
για πόσο ακόμα θα κρατάς αυτό το πιστόλι στον
   κρόταφο των ημερών
με την κρυφή λαχτάρα ενός κυκλάμινου στην κάννη.
Οι κόρες των ματιών σου θα μετοικήσουν σύντομα
σε άλλο γαλαξία.
Και τι θα κάνεις τότε μόνος με τους γκιώνηδες
πάνω στη στέγη;

Kleine Nachtmusik

I told the days to stop whirling
and I made myself a nest in the jam jar
so that traitors and amphetamine pulses
    won't find me.
Now let me see
how much longer you'll hold this pistol to the temple of
    the days
with the hidden desire of a cyclamen in its barrel
Soon your pupils will emigrate
to another galaxy
And then what will you do alone
with the screech owls on the roof?

Rachel Hadas

Το βιολί

«Κάθε μήνα το ίδιο βιολί!»
Παλίρροια Λάβα Σκότος Φέξη
Της μήτρας σφίξη και διαστολή
Οι αιώνες ιερουργούν τον κύκλο
Που μας 'μάθαν να φροντίζουμε οι μανάδες
Ως μια ανωμαλία υγιεινής
Εκφυλισμένες μάς συντονίζουν φερομόνες
Των άσηπτων νοικοκυρών εχθροί
Μια μηνιαία νεύρωση
Που πλέον καταστέλλουν με οπιοειδή
    Πες το βιολί ή κόκκινο λουλούδι που ανθεί
    Σε πείσμα των καιρών το μάτι κλείσε στη σελήνη
    Το αίμα από τη μήτρα σου ενώ ρέει ξεσηκώσου
    Νιώσε: ΚΑΙΝΟΥΡΙΑ!
        ΑΣΤΡΑΦΤΕΡΗ!
        ΔΥΝΑΤΗ!

The Violin

'Every month the same plaintive song!'
Tide Lava Darkness Dawn
The womb tightens and dilates
Centuries officiate the cycle
Our mothers taught us to tend
As an anomaly of hygiene
Our degenerate pheromones coordinate us
Enemies of the aseptic housewives
A monthly neurosis
By now controlled with opiates
 Call it a plaintive violin or a red mandarin
 In defiance of time wink at the moon
 Despite the blood that flows from your womb
 Rise up!
 Feel: NEW!
  DAZZLING BRIGHT!
  EXTRA STRONG!

Karen Van Dyck

Λωτοφάγοι

Αυτή η σιωπηλή κατανόηση
δε χωρά στις ντουζίνες χρόνια που μου δόθηκαν.
Φόνευσε τη.
Δηλητηρίασέ τη σταδιακά
όπως μόλυνε κι αυτή εμάς
που πάντα την αποστρεφόμασταν.
Ποιος φύτεψε χαλίκια μέσα στα ζαχαρωτά;
Ποιος έδεσε αμόνια στα φτερά των γλάρων;
Γιατί χρησιμοποιούμε ακόμα το επίρρημα «στωικά»;

Σεβασμό;
Σε ποιους;
Στους λωτοφάγους;

The Lotus Eaters

This unspoken understanding
doesn't fit into the dozens of years I have left.
Murder it.
Poison it piecemeal
just as it contaminated us –
we who had always turned away from here.
Who planted pebbles in the candy?
Who tied anvils to the seagulls' wings?
Why do we still use the adverb 'stoically'?

Respect?
For whom?
For the lotus eaters?

Rachel Hadas

Λίβας ή τα φουσάτα

Η μέρα που θα καούνε τα σπαρτά
πρέπει να σε βρει έτοιμο.
Αν έχουν προλάβει να σου κόψουν τα φτερά
ξαμόλα μια κραυγή
να με προφτάσει εκεί που θα κείμαι
πριν απ' τις φλόγες.
Για τις επόμενες μέρες θα κρύβομαι στις θημωνιές,
να ξέρεις.
Το νου σου:
σιμά θα σπαραχθούν όλα τ' αηδόνια.
Πρέπει να βρούμε γρήγορα
ένα υπόγειο φρέαρ
δροσερό
να σταυρώσουμε τα σώματα μας
το 'να πάνω στ' άλλο.
Θάμβος

ενάντια στο τέλος των ημερών.

Sirocco or Soldiery

The day they burn the crops
you must be ready.
If they've already cut off your wings
let out a scream
to catch me where I'll be lying
before the flames arrive.
The next days I'll be hiding in the haystacks –
just so you know. And bear in mind:
right there all the nightingales will be torn in pieces.
We'll have to find – and quickly –
an underground well
that is cool
to crucify our bodies
one on top of the other.
A murkiness

against the end of days.

Rachel Hadas

JAZRA KHALEED

(Born Chechnya, 1979)

The engaged politics and, in the original Greek, the rhyme schemes of Jazra Khaleed's poetry owe much to the anti-fascist rap scene in Greece. His works are protests against the injustices in contemporary Greece, especially the growing racism; his poetry and performances have been described by the international press as 'possessing the kind of energy that pervades the riots on the streets of Athens'. The film rendition of his poem about the refugee situation, 'The AEGEAN or the Anus of Death', won prizes at the Paris Festival for Different and Experimental Cinema and the Balkans Beyond Borders Short Film Festival. His poems have been widely translated for publications in Europe, the US, and Japan. As a founding co-editor of *Teflon*, and particularly through his own translations published there, he has introduced the works of Amiri Baraka, Keston Sutherland, and many other political and experimental poets to a Greek readership. He also writes on topics as varied as Aborigines and hip hop. He lives in Exarchia, the inner-city Athens neighborhood most associated with protests and police violence. His poetry blog is jazrakhaleed. blogspot.gr.

Wörter

Δεν έχω πατρίδα
Κατοικώ μέσα στις λέξεις
Μαυροφορεμένες
Αιχμάλωτες
Μουσταφά Χαγιάτι, μ' ακούς;
Στη γλώσσα εδρεύει η εξουσία
Μέσα της περιπολεί η αστυνομία
Δε χρειαζόμαστε άλλους ποιητικούς κύκλους
Δε χρειαζόμαστε άλλους σεφέρηδες
Στη γειτονιά μου θυσιάζουν τους παρθένους ποιητές
Ράπερς με σκονισμένα μάτια και φαρδιά παντελόνια
σπρώχνουν ρίμες σε πιτσιρίκια που σνιφάρουν λέξεις
Να πέφτεις και να ξανασηκώνεσαι: η τέχνη του ποιητή
Ζαν Ζενέ, μ' ακούς;
Οι λέξεις μου είναι άστεγες
Κοιμούνται στα παγκάκια της Κλαυθμώνος
σκεπασμένες με χαρτόκουτα από το Ikea
Οι λέξεις μου δεν μιλάνε στις ειδήσεις
Κάνουν πεζοδρόμιο κάθε βράδυ
Οι λέξεις μου είναι προλετάρισσες, σκλάβες όπως εγώ
Δουλεύουν στα φασονάδικα μέρα νύχτα
Δε θέλω άλλα μοιρολόγια
Δε θέλω άλλα ρήματα που ν' ανήκουν στον άμαχο
    πληθυσμό
Χρειάζομαι μια καινούργια γλώσσα, όχι νταβατζιλίκια
Περιμένω μια επανάσταση να με εφεύρει
Ποθώ τη γλώσσα του ταξικού ανταγωνισμού
Μια γλώσσα που έχει γευτεί την εξέγερση
Θα την κατασκευάσω!
Αχ, τι αλαζονεία

Words

I have no fatherland
I live within words
That are shrouded in black
And held hostage
Mustapha Khayati, can you hear me?
The seat of power is in language
Where the police patrol
No more poetry circles!
No more poet laureates!
In my neighborhood virgin poets are sacrificed
Rappers with dust-blown eyes and baggy pants
push rhymes on kids sniffing words
Fall and get back up again: the art of the poet
Jean Genet, can you hear me?
My words are homeless
They sleep on the benches of Klafthmonos Square
covered in IKEA cartons
My words do not speak on the news
They're out hustling every night
My words are proletarian, slaves like me
They work in sweatshops night and day
I want no more dirges
I want no more verbs belonging to the non-combatants
I need a new language, not pimping
I'm waiting for a revolution to invent me
Hungering for the language of class war
A language that has tasted insurgency
I shall create it!
Ah, what arrogance!

Εντάξει, φεύγω
Μα κοίτα, στο πρόσωπό μου χαράζει η αυγή μιας νέας
   ποίησης
Καμιά λέξη δε θα μείνει αιχμάλωτη πίσω
Αναζητώ ένα πέρασμα

Ρεφρέν

Με λένε Γ-Ι-Α-Ζ-Ρ-Α
Γεννήθηκα στης Δύσης το σκοτάδι
Λαθραίος μένω σε πείσμα αριστερών
Όμορφα περνά το βράδυ
τσακίζοντας κεφάλια φασιστών

Κάπου στην Αθήνα

Κάπου στην Αθήνα ο Δεκέμβρης έχει έξι
Το παιδί θα σκοτώσει τον μπάτσο πριν να φέξει
Κάπου στην Αθήνα ο Δεκέμβρης έχει επτά
Στη Σταδίου οι τράπεζες καίγονται στη σειρά
Κάπου στην Αθήνα ο Δεκέμβρης έχει οχτώ
Στα ερείπια της Βουλής ας στήσουμε χορό
Κάπου στην Αθήνα ο Δεκέμβρης έχει εννιά
Οι ποιητές στους δρόμους υμνούνε τη φωτιά
Κάπου στην Αθήνα ο Δεκέμβρης έχει καμιά
Οι αντάρτες σπάσαν τα ρολόγια στα καμπαναριά

OK, I'll be off
But take a look: in my face the dawn of a new poetry is
   breaking
No word will be left behind, held hostage,
I'm seeking a new passage.

Peter Constantine

Refrain

My name is J-A-Z-R-A
I was born in the dark West
Illegal despite the efforts of the Left
At night I have a great time
smashing fascist heads

Karen Van Dyck

Somewhere in Athens

Somewhere in Athens December the Sixth
The kid will kill the cop before sunup
Somewhere in Athens December the Seventh
On the streets the banks are burnt one by one
Somewhere in Athens December the Eighth
Let's cut a rug in Parliament's rubble
Somewhere in Athens December the Ninth
The poets in the streets eulogize fires
Somewhere in Athens December the Naught
Because the rebels shot the bell-tower clocks

Sarah McCann

Μαύρα χείλη

Ακούστε
Εσείς που μασουλάτε τη μοναξιά μου
με την τηλεόραση ανοικτή
Εσείς που έρχεστε στην κηδεία μου
για να ανάψετε ένα κερί
Ακούστε
Ένα ρήμα θα σας σφηνώσω στα μάτια
Ένα μπιτ θα σας φυτέψω στα στήθια

Εγώ δεν έχω μήτε φράγκο στην καρδιά,
ούτε κολακείες και επίθετα κρυμμένα στην τσέπη
Σκορπίζω την ομορφιά μου στο μπετόν
Με τα χέρια βουτηγμένα στο αίμα ποιητών
γράφω τα πάντα στα 9mm
Δεν υπάρχει κανείς να σεβαστώ
Μετανάστης τριάντα ετών
Δεν έχω ευθύνες
Φτύνω ρίμες στα 120 bpm

Εσείς οι μέσοι άνθρωποι!
Τεμαχίζετε τον έρωτα σε ίντσες
Αγοράζετε τον έρωτα με πιστωτικές κάρτες
Καυχιέστε επιδόσεις
Μπροστά σε μια οθόνη κατεβάζετε στύσεις
Εμένα το κορμί μου κανείς σας δεν μπορεί να το αγγίξει
Εγώ κάθε βράδυ βάφω τα χείλη μου μαύρα

Ακούστε με εσείς που φυλλομετράτε τις ήττες μου
Με θέλετε ευθεία γραμμή, άντρα αντί παιδί
Με θέλετε καλοραμμένο σακάκι
Ευγενικό και νουνεχή
Μου δένετε τα χέρια σε δείκτες ρολογιών

Black Lips

Listen
You who chew on my solitude
with your televisions on
You who attend my funeral every morning
to light a candle
Listen
I will drive a verb into your eyes
I will plant a beat in your chests

I don't have a cent in my heart
or smooth talk and epithets hidden in my pocket
I scatter my beauty on concrete streets
I dip my hands in poets' blood
I write everything in 9 mm caliber
There's no one for me to respect
A thirty-year-old Muslim punk
I bear no responsibility
I spit rhymes at 120 B.P.M.

You man in the street!
You portion out love in inches
Purchase love with credit cards
Trumpet your prowess
At your screen you download erections
None of you can touch my body
I paint my lips black every night

Listen to me, you who leaf through my defeats!
You want me to be a straight line, a man and not a boy
You want me to be a well-sewn jacket
Polite and politic
You tie my arms to watch hands

Προσπαθείτε να με σφηνώσετε σ' αυτόν τον κόσμο
Μπορείτε, όπως εγώ,
να κάνετε τις λέξεις πράξεις;
να κυοφορήσετε την άνοιξη;
να καείτε χωρίς να αφήσετε στάχτες;

Ελάτε να σας κάνω ανθρώπους
εσάς αξιότιμε δικαστή που σκουπίζετε τις ενοχές από
    τα γένια σας
εσάς αγαπητέ δημοσιογράφε που διαφημίζετε το θάνατο
εσάς τη φιλάνθρωπη κυρία που χαϊδεύετε κεφαλάκια
    παιδιών χωρίς καν να σκύψετε
κι εσάς που διαβάζετε αυτό το ποίημα σαλιώνοντας το
    δάκτυλο
Προσφέρω σε όλους σας το σώμα μου για προσκύνημα
Πιστέψτε με
μια μέρα θα με λατρέψετε σαν το Χριστό

Όμως λυπάμαι για εσάς κύριε
Δε διαπραγματεύομαι με ορκωτούς λογιστές λέξεων,
με κριτικούς τέχνης που τρώνε από τα χέρια μου
Μπορείτε, αν θέλετε, να μου πλύνετε τα πόδια
Μη το πάρετε προσωπικά

Τι να τις κάνω τις σφαίρες όταν υπάρχουν τόσες λέξεις
πρόθυμες να πεθάνουν για μένα;

You try to jam me into this world
Can you, like me,
turn words into deeds?
Can you carry springtime in your bellies?
Burn without ashes?

Come let me make you human,
you, Your Honor, who wipe guilt from your beard
you, esteemed journalist, who tout death
you, philanthropic lady, who pat children's heads without
    bending down
and you who read this poem, licking your finger –
To all of you I offer my body for genuflection
Believe me
one day you will adore me like Christ

But I'm sorry for you sir –
I do not negotiate with chartered accountants of words,
with art critics who eat from my hand
You may, if you desire, wash my feet
Don't take it personally

Why do I need bullets if there are so many words
prepared to die for me?

Peter Constantine

Νεκρή φύση

Το μεσημέρι είναι ζεστό. Με ακρωτηριάζει
Έχω να φάω δύο μέρες. Εγκυμονώ μια καταιγίδα
Στη γειτονιά μου δεν παίζουνε παιδιά
Οι εραστές φορούν καπέλα τζόκεϊ
Είναι επίπεδοι. Όπως και τα φιλιά τους
Είναι ατσαλάκωτοι
Περπατούν στους δρόμους με τους αγκώνες σε πλήρη
    έκταση
Στη γειτονιά μου τα γεγονότα είναι κολλημένα στους
    τοίχους
Η ευτυχία σαπίζει σαν σφαίρα στο στομάχι μπάτσου
Στο σφαγείο της καθημερινότητας εγώ πουλάω
    μπαλτάδες
Γράφω ένα ποίημα κάθε φορά που πηγαίνω απ' το σπίτι
    μου στο μετρό
Αναμένω μια συγκίνηση

Still Life

Midday is hot. It cripples me
It's been two days since I ate. I'm pregnant with
   tempest
Children don't play in my neighborhood
Lovers don jockey caps
They are flat. Like their kisses
They are unwrinkled
They walk along the streets, elbows jutted out
News gets plastered to the walls in my neighborhood
Glee festers like a bullet in a cop's stomach
I myself sell butcher knives at the abattoir of the
   everyday
I write a poem every time I go from my home to the
   metro
I am waiting to be touched

Sarah McCann

Ο θάνατος απόψε

Απόψε ο θάνατος θα χηρέψει
Τα πολυβόλα δε λένε να ξεκαυλώσουν
Στρατιώτες γυρίζουν πίσω στις πατρίδες τους
Ευνουχισμένοι
Λειψοί
Δεν θα πυροβολήσουν πια
Δεν θα βιάσουν πια
Στα δάχτυλά τους κολλάει ο θάνατος σαν ρετσίνι
Ο δικός τους θάνατος
Οι μέρες σταματάνε σε μπλόκο μπάτσων
Είναι μουσουλμάνες μανάδες
Δεν έχουν χαρτιά, τις απελαύνουν
Απόψε ο θάνατος θα χηρέψει
Είδα την ειρήνη να βγάζει τα φρύδια της
Λίγο πριν ανέβει στη σκηνή
Μασουλώντας ποπκόρν
Το πλήθος στην πλατεία
Χειροκροτεί βομβαρδισμούς αμάχων
Δολοφονίες μεταναστών
Τη νίκη του πολιτισμού
Τον θρίαμβο της δημοκρατίας
Το πρωτοκοσμικό στριπτίζ
Απόψε ο θάνατος θα χηρέψει
Κραυγές ατιμασμένων γυναικών βουβαίνουν τα
    αυτιά μου
Βόμβες διασποράς χουζουρεύουν στο στομάχι μου
Εγώ διαφεντεύω την σελήνη
Εγώ ορίζω τη παλίρροια
Μπάτσοι προσπαθούν να φυλακίσουν την
    αστρολογία μου
Ένας ακόμα ακήρυχτος πόλεμος

Death Tonight

Tonight death will turn widower
Machine guns still lusting in heat
Soldiers return to their countries
Castrated
Maimed
No longer to shoot
No longer to rape
Death sticks to their fingers like resin
Their deaths
The days stop at a checkpoint
The days are Muslim mothers
They don't have papers, they are deported
Tonight death will turn widower
I saw peace pluck her eyebrows
Just before she stepped on stage
Chewing popcorn
The masses on the square
Applaud the bombing of innocents
Murders of immigrants
The victory of civilization
The triumph of democracy
A first-world strip show
Tonight death will turn widower
Shrieks of dishonored women deafen my ears
Cluster bombs burrow into my stomach
I rule the moon
I assign all ebb and flow
The cops try to imprison gravity
Yet another undeclared war

Τα μάτια των παιδιών φέγγουν μαύρα στους προβολείς
    των Apache
Γεμάτα στάχτες
Γεμάτα μίσος
Αμείλικτα
Η λήθη πουλάει ακόμα μια γενοκτονία στο eBay
Το αύριο είναι ήδη μια λέξη δίχως μέλλον
Ο θάνατος απόψε

The children's eyes shine black in the Apache's
    searchlights
Filled with ashes
Filled with hatred
Remorseless
Oblivion is selling one more genocide on eBay
Tomorrow is already a word without future
Death tonight

Peter Constantine

Γάμα την αποκάλυψη

γάμα την αποκάλυψη. ρίμες στη μεσολογγίου ψάχνουνε
για κάλυψη. μπάτσοι μπουκάρουν στην κατάληψη. το
ίδιο έργο κάθε βράδυ σε επανάληψη. ψηλά αγνάντευε μα
χαμηλά πολέμα. βάλε μέγκα, η αστυνομία μιλάει με το
στόμα του πρετεντέρη. στη φόδρα ράψε ένα μαχαίρι.
μπράβοι την πέφτουν μέρα μεσημέρι.

χούντα. ο στρατός στους δρόμους. τα παιδιά παίζουν
μπάτσους κι αστυνόμους. στη βουλή τ' αφεντικά διατάσσουν
νόμους. οι εργάτες στο μαντρί, εργασία και τιβί. γκλάμουρ
και γκαβλί, οι νεολαίοι μοιάζουνε μέλισσες δίχως κεντρί.
οι αντάρτες φυλακή, θηρία στο κλουβί. κι οι ποιητές; οι
ποιητές στη σιωπή. λεωφόρος δίχως βοή.

ποιητάδες, μείνετε σπίτι. εύθραυστοι σαν κυκλάμινα, μια
ζωή στην ήττα και την άμυνα. ξοφλημένοι αριστεροί,
μπουρζουάδες του ποιείν. στο μακελειό σκορπάτε σαν τα
ποντίκια απ' το σάμινα. νεκρά φύση. εγώ εκπαιδεύω λέξεις
φενταγίν. δεν γράφω ποίηση, γράφω προκηρύξεις. να
δούμε πού θα είστε όταν το αίμα στο δρόμο πήξει.

Fuck Armageddon

Fuck Armageddon. The cops get it on. Writhing and fucking
dead on top of the poems, who redden. The poems blush
their own blood into Messolonghi Street. The poems: fulsome
plankton. Blenderized in the French-kissing maws of the
armored Megaladon-shark policemen. Who have their heads
so far up their ass the police can't even fit an arm in there?
The pretenders! Angels of TV! Tarry, pretenders, with
smiles unscary! Come visit Messolonghi! They murder in
broad daylight here – (you should be so lucky!)

Junta: army in the streets. Toy boots on every Caligula
kiddy's feet. Mobsters larding the laws to pure pork-fat – no
bone, no meat. The labor is sleepily grunting in their pens:
doing Miley Mohawks and Masturbating to the QVC TV
gems. Our youth are milk powder when I fucking asked for
cayenne. The rebels are truncheoned by the Megaladon
policemen. The leopards are caged like KFC hens. And the
poets? The poets are quiet again. Messolonghi Street: silent
as Danny Boy's Glenn.

Fuck off, flower poets. Fragile as your amaryllis. Blinding
and bloating yourself with silk: constantly eating and shitting
a chrysalis. The doddering leftists toast with milk the stinking
rats on the sinking Samina, who flee too fast to let the cheese
curdle. My words are Fayadeen: verbal, fatal, fertile – where
will you be when the blood begins to burble?

Max Ritvo

171

Re: Λωτοφάγοι

Η ζωή δε μετριέται σε χρόνια
Μετριέται σε ανάσες και μπιτ
Ο πόνος σε βατ
Η αγάπη σε λεύγες

Σε ποιον πρόσφεραν κρασί και δε μέθυσε;
Σε ποιον υποσχέθηκαν ήλιο και φόρεσε μαύρα
   γυαλιά;
Σε ποιον χάρισαν δέντρο και δεν αποκοιμήθηκε
   στη σκιά του;

Μη λυπάσαι αυτούς που μένουν
Να λυπάσαι αυτούς που φεύγουν
Φύλαξε τον οίκτο σου για τον Οδυσσέα
Ενώσου με τους Λωτοφάγους

Re: Lotus Eaters

Life is not to be counted in years
But in breaths and beats
Pain in watts
Love in leagues

Who has been offered wine and did not get drunk?
Who has been promised sunshine and then wore
   dark glasses?
Who has been given a tree as a gift and did not sleep
   in its shadow?

Do not grieve for those who remain
Grieve for those who depart
Save your sympathy for Odysseus
Unite with the lotus eaters.

Peter Constantine

STATHIS BAROUTSOS

(Born Germany, 1980)

The blog poet Stathis Baroutsos was put on the map in English by an interview with the translator Peter Constantine in the online magazine *Words Without Borders*. Despite being widely translated into English, Spanish, Kapampangan, Tagalog, and Japanese, he has never been published in Greece, where he grew up.

Τα παιδιά μου

Τα παιδιά μου ζούνε κάτω απο σανίδες βρόμικες μέσα
σε παραπήγματα.
Δεν τα βλέπει ο ήλιος που καίει τα πατώματα, δεν
αναπνέουν τον αέρα που μπαίνει μέσα από τα
σπασμένα τζάμια.
Τα παιδιά μου βρίσκονται ακόμα σε μια κυοφορία,
κουκουλωμένα μέσα σε μεγάλα πράσινα φύλλα.
Δεν είναι έτοιμα να βγουν στον κόσμο.
Τα αγκαλιάζουν μεγάλα πράσινα φύλλα κάτω απο τις
βρώμικες σανίδες, που τις χτυπά ο ανελέητος ήλιος
μέσα στα παραπήγματα.
Ακούνε μονάχα Chopin και τρίζουν μέσα στα
κουκούλια τους.
Μέσα στα μεγάλα πράσινα φύλλα κάτω από τις
σανίδες των παραπηγμάτων δεν φτάνει ο αέρας ούτε
ο ήλιος, παρά μόνο ο Chopin.
Περιμένουν υπομονετικά να γεννηθούν.

My Children

My children live in shacks beneath the filthy planks.
They cannot see the light that burns upon them; they
    cannot breathe the broken window air.
My children live like insects, hooded blind in large
    green leaves.
Their exit is not safe.
The large green arms do hold them dear beneath the
    cage of wood the sun impales.
Within their nests they whisper answers only to
    Chopin.
While burning suns attack with beams like knives,
    their green embrace
Does hold them safer still beneath the barrack floors
    where
They answer only to Chopin.
And so like this they measure time in nectar's dark
    until the waltz begins.

Karen Van Dyck

Speed Dating

Βρίσκομαι στο επίκεντρο ατελείωτων αναζητήσεων.
Αναλώνομαι σε κρεβάτια περαστικών.
Κάνω βόλτες με αμάξια,
πάντα από την ίδια θέση του συνοδηγού,
με το χέρι στην ίδια θέση, του ποδιού σου.
Τα δωμάτια μοιάζουν τόσο ίδια
και τα μπάνια κάθε πρωί καθόλου διαφορετικά.
Δεν θυμάμαι πουθενά έναν διαφορετικό ήχο από τους
    ήχους
στα μπαλκόνια και ο καφές τα πρωινά έχει πάντα την
    ίδια γεύση.
Γυρεύω να ξεφύγω από κείνα τα κρεβάτια
μετά από κάθε πρόωρη εκσπερμάτωση.
Οι αγκαλιές δεν προφέρουν τίποτε το διαφορετικό
και ότι τολμά να μοιάζει το βάζει στα πόδια.
Από κείνους άλλοι μοιάζουν στον μπαμπά μου
κι άλλοι στη μαμά μου. Άλλοι με θέλουν πολύ
και άλλοι λίγο και εγώ
τριγυρνώ στους δρόμους με επιφύλαξη στα μάτια
και όνειρα αποκαμωμένα.
Δεν έχω επιλέξει κανέναν.
Τώρα θα σ' το πω πώς γίνομαι σαν τον μπαμπά μου και
    τη μαμά μου.
Φοβάμαι όπως αυτοί, για εμένα.
Αν γκρεμίζω φυλακές, αν προσπαθώ να παραδεχθώ
πως δεν με αφορούν οι γοητευτικοί κατά τα άλλα
    δεσμώτες,
τόσο περισσότερο βυθίζομαι στο κρεβάτι με τα καρφιά
    μου.
Όσο κι αν μετράω κάθε μέρα μέχρι το τρία να ξεφύγω
απο εμένα, εσένα και αυτόν,
ξέρω πως είναι ατελέσφορο.

Speed Dating

I'm in an endless search.
I burn out in the beds of strangers,
I ride in cars,
always in the same passenger seat,
my hand always in the same place on your thigh.
The rooms all seem the same,
same showers every morning,
same sounds on all the balconies
where morning cups of coffee always taste the same.
I try to escape those beds after every premature
    ejaculation.
The embraces whisper what they always whisper
and anyone resembling those closest to me abandons me –
some resemble my father,
others my mother. Some want me a lot,
some just a bit, and I
walk the streets with careful eyes
and unsure dreams.
I haven't picked anyone.
But let me tell you how I've turned into my father and my
    mother:
Like them, I worry about myself –
the more I knock down prison walls
and accept that siren sadists mean nothing to me
the more I sink into my bed of nails.
Though every day I count to three and run
from myself, from you, from him.
I know it's futile.

Μετά από την τόση επινοημένη στέρηση
συρρικνώνω το χρόνο μονάχα σε δυο μέρες,
να σου δείξω, να προσπαθήσω, να πλασθώ,
να σε εξερευνήσω,
να σε χαρτογραφήσω.
Πια είμαι κενός, έγινα καθρέφτης,
αντικρίζω το παραπληγικό μου σώμα.
Ξέρεις είναι τρομακτικό έστω και για μια στιγμή
να σηκώσεις τα μάτια στην ευθεία.
Όχι ψηλά μα στην ευθεία, εκεί που κοιτάς κατάματα
εμένα εσένα αυτόν.

I give myself only two days
to roam you,
to map you,
to prove that you're not for me.
I'm empty now, a mirror,
I face my impotent body.
You see it's frightening to raise your eyes
even for a moment, and look straight before you,
not up, but straight before you, looking
me, you, and him
in the eye.

Peter Constantine

SMS

– megali nixta apopse

– nai megali, to proi oi efialtes tha exoun aftoktonhsei

– arkei na mhn paroun kai mena mazi tous

– avrio einai h afethria sou

– thn afethria mou thn exo kapsei, eixa ola ta kalokairia
  tou kosmou kai ta kana fotografies

– liose ta asteria se ena koutali

– den thelo na zhso ksaplomenos, thelo na troo me ta
  xeria, allios ti ta thelo ta xeria mou

– tis kores ton mation sou sygkrato mh spasoun, ta
  kalokairia sou pos tha sta gyriso piso na ta pareis
  zontana?

– kourastika leo na koimitho

Txt Message

– Big night 2nite

– Yep, by morning all nightmares will have committed
  suicide

– As long as they don't take me with them too

– Ur turning a new leaf tomorrow

– I've burnt my new leaf, I had all the summers of the
  world & turned them into pics

– Dissolve the stars in a spoon

– I don't want to live lying down, I want to eat with my
  hands, otherwise what do I need my hands 4.

– I'm restraining the pupils of ur eyes so they won't
  shatter, how can I return ur summers to you alive?

– I'm tired, I'm off to bed

Peter Constantine

Birdsong

Ο κύριος με το ροζ πουκάμισο κάθισε δίπλα μου στο μπαρ. Φορούσε ροζ πουκάμισο και ροζ πουλόβερ. Έπινε το ποτό του προσεκτικά μη λερωθεί και άναβε κάθε τσιγάρο του αργά και σταθερά. Όταν τελείωνε το κάπνισμα πατούσε εφτά φορές το αποτσίγαρο στο τασάκι για να σβήσει καλά. Ακουμπούσε το ποτό με το ένα χέρι και με το άλλο σχημάτιζε τους αριθμούς των φίλων του στο κινητό.

Αλήθεια δεν έδωσα σημασία ποτέ τι ήχο κάνει το 9 ή το 1 πάνω στο πληκτρολόγιο ενός τηλεφώνου.

Με κοιτούσε με βλέμμα εξονυχιστικό και άκουγε με προσοχή την κάθε μου λέξη. Ο κύριος με το ροζ πουκάμισο και το ροζ πουλόβερ τελείωσε το ποτό του, σηκώθηκε και αποχαιρέτησε ευγενικά. Θα πήγαινε στην εξοχή την άλλη μέρα είπε, για να ακούσει τα πουλιά. Θα τραγουδούσε ένα τραγούδι και το βράδυ θα αποκοιμιόταν δίπλα στο ραδιόφωνο.

Birdsong

The guy in the pink shirt sat down next to me at the bar. He was wearing a pink shirt and a pink vest. He sipped his drink carefully, not spilling a drop, and lit each cigarette slowly and steadily. When he finished a smoke, he stubbed it out seven times in the ashtray to make sure. He rested one hand on his drink, and his other hand entered friends' numbers into his cell phone.

To be honest, I'd never paid attention to the sound a 9 or a 1 makes on the keypad.

He watched me carefully and listened closely to my every word. The guy in the pink shirt and the pink vest finished his drink, got up, and politely said his goodbyes. He was off on a trip to the countryside the next day, he said, so he could hear the birds. He'd sing a song, and fall asleep next to the radio in the evening.

Sarah McCann

DANAE SIOZIOU

(Born Karlsruhe, Germany, 1987)

The poetry of Danae Sioziou typifies an important trend within the *Teflon* group that is also noticeable in the work of Glykeria Basdeki (p. 279) and other women poets living and working outside Athens: the intersection of the fatalistic and the feminist. Like Marvin (p. 203) and Kishida (p. 143) in this section – and, beyond Greece, like Sophie Collins and *tender*, the online 'quarterly journal made by women' she edits with fellow UK poet Rachael Allen – Sioziou presents us with poems that speak for and about women without feeling the need to explain themselves, or to apologize for repeating the complaints of an earlier generation. Raised in Germany and Greece, she studied English Literature and European History at the University of Athens, and Arts Administration at Panteion University. Her poems, translations, and articles have been published in various journals online and off (*Poetics, Teflon, e-poema, The Books Journal, Athens Review of Books, Chronos*). Her blog can be found at danaesioziou.wordpress.com.

Οι φύλακες

Κοιμηθήκαμε δύσκολα εκείνο το βράδυ
με τα σκυλιά μας ν' αλυχτούν όλη τη νύχτα.
Ούτε στιγμή δεν το σκεφτήκαμε πως ήταν
η φωνή τους
αγγελιοφόρος του θανάτου
και πως σαν φύλακες καλοί μάς προειδοποιούσαν
για τη διάρρηξη που θα επιχειρούσε στο σπίτι μας.
Μέσα στην ησυχία του μικρού μας δωματίου
ξαγρυπνούσαμε
με το πείσμα και το παράπονο
παιδιών που τ' αδικήσανε και περιμένουν νηστικά
να μεγαλώσυυνε πολύ σε μία νύχτα
να λάβουν εξήγηση για την άδικη τιμωρία τους
και τον κόσμο.

The Guards

We couldn't sleep
our dogs howling all night.
We didn't think for a second
it was their voice
the messengers of death
warning us like vigilant guards
of a break-in
ready to happen in our house.
We stayed awake
in the quiet of our small room
stubbornly, whining
like children treated unjustly
waiting without dinner
to grow up all at once
in one night
and finally receive
the explanation for their unjust punishment
and the world.

Karen Van Dyck

Βαρύτητα

Παλιά φωτογραφία.
Στο κλικ το οριστικό του φωτογράφου
χαμογελούν πιασμένοι χέρι χέρι
μάνα μου και πατέρας μου αγαπημένοι.
Στο παιδικό καρότσι τα όνειρα σκεπασμένα
πεσμένα σπασμένα στο πεζοδρόμιο
τα νεράντζια που κανείς δε μάζεψε.

Heaviness

Old snapshot.
In the photographer's firm click
they're smiling, hand in hand,
my mother and my father. They're in love.
Dreams in the baby carriage, covered up:
fallen, squashed on the sidewalk,
bitter oranges no one has picked.

Rachel Hadas

Οικιακά

Δεν πρόσεξε
ίσως και να μην το κατάλαβε
απλά συνέχισε να κόβει
πέρα απ' τη φλούδα των αχλαδιών
τα χέρια της.

Το αίμα κύλησε ήσυχα
απ' τις γραμμές της τύχης
της ζωής, του έρωτα
στο νεροχύτη
και στροβιλίστηκε
ανάμεσα στα άπλυτα πιάτα
και τα αποφάγια.

Η γάτα της ανήσυχη
έτρεξε κοντά της
και με συμπόνια ειλικρινή
έγλειψε τα τραύματα της
ενώ εκείνη

για μία σύντομη
μια ακαριαία στιγμή
είδε τον εαυτό της
μέσα απ' τα γυάλινα γατίσια μάτια
ξένο

μες σε βρόμικο κλουβί φυλακισμένο
οροφή δίχως ανατολή
στο πάτωμα μικρά σκαθάρια
στο νεροχύτη η σκοτεινή λίμνη
που μέσα μουλιάζουνε τα χέρια της

Around the House

She wasn't paying attention
maybe she didn't even notice
she simply continued cutting
beyond the pears she was peeling
her hands

Blood ran gently
from the lines of fate
of life of love
and into the sink
and swirled around among the dirty dishes
and the scraps of food

Her cat, uneasy,
ran up to her
and with sincere fellow feeling
licked her wounds
while she

for a split second
saw herself
through its glassy cat eyes
a stranger

imprisoned in a filthy cage
a ceiling without sunrise
little beetles on the floor
in the sink a dark lake
she soaked her hands in

και τώρα αστράφτει στεφανωμένη από
πάχνη λευκή, απολυμαντική.

Απ' το βυθό της
αναδύονται πανσέληνα, ολόασπρα φεγγάρια
σκέφτηκε
να τελειώνει σήμερα τουλάχιστον
με τα πιάτα.

Χαρτογραφώντας τη γεωγραφία της συμπτωματολογίας του βήματος

Άλλοι διαβάζανε φλιτζάνια και χαρτιά
                                        εσύ
τα αποτυπώματα των υποδημάτων σε άσφαλτο
                                        χώμα
                                                νερό και
                                                χιόνι.

Μπορούσες να διαγνώσεις εκεί
                        το ιδεόγραμμα
μιας μέρας καλής ή κακής
                        το ειδικό βάρος
μιας χαράς, μιας λύπης
                        τη συνισταμένη
ενός παραπατήματος,
                        μιας πτώσης
στον υπολογισμό
                                της βαρύτητας
σωμάτων
        σ υ μ π τ ω μ ά τ ω ν
                        ειδικής πυκνότητας.

194

and now it shines, crowned with
the white frost of detergent

From the depths of the sink
rise full moons brilliant white
she thought
let me at least
finish the dishes today

Rachel Hadas

Mapping the Geography of the Symptoms of a Footstep

Others read teacups and cards
                        you
read the imprint of shoes on asphalt
                              earth
                                    water and
                                          snow.
There you could distinguish
                        the signature
of a good day or a bad day
                        the special weight
of a joy, of a sorrow
                        the effect
of a stumble
                  or a fall
on the estimate
                        of the weight
of bodies
        of *symptoms*
                  of a peculiar density.

Rachel Hadas

YANNIS MOUNDELAS

(Born Athens, Greece, 1982)

Resignation breeds new imaginative leaps in Yannis Moundelas's poems, which he publishes exclusively online and under various pseudonyms. Since he began as a poet in the Greek blogging community he has gained an international following, and his work has now been translated into numerous languages, among them Spanish and Japanese. Like Baroutsos (p. 175) and Khaleed (p. 155), his poetry has appeared in English translation in *Words Without Borders*. He has yet to publish a collection, and may never do so: the place to be, he believes, is not on paper.

Ανάδρομος Ερμής

με την άκρη των χεριών του, θαρρώ τα δάχτυλα και
    λίγο τα νύχια,
σχεδιάζει φωτιές, με γλώσσες φιδιών.
ένα παιδί με αδυναμία στις πτώσεις και χάρτινα φτερά
    στην πλάτη,
σκέφτεται συνέχεια πυρκαγιές και βιαιοπραγίες.
ζει, χρόνια, στο ημιυπόγειο του πιο πολύχρωμου
    ονείρου του,
εκεί που πιάνει υγρασία και δηλητήριο μουχλιασμένο
    στάζει από τους τοίχους.
τρώει τις σημειώσεις του και ποτέ δεν πεινάει, μόνο
    γκρινιάζει για το νερό, που το θέλει
χειμωνιάτικα κρύο και όχι παγωμένο.
σβήνει τα τσιγάρα στις παλάμες του και όταν έχει
    καύλες σφυρίζει σαν τρένο, μέχρι
εκτροχιασμού και μετά πουφ . . . καπνός που τον
    εισπνέει και τελειώνει . . .
εδώ στον στολισμένο του τάφο έγινε όσα φοβόταν, όσα
    τον πλήγωσαν
και όσα δεν καταλάβαινε . . . δυνατότερος πια,
    πασαλειμμένος με στάχτες, περιτριγυρισμένος από
    φλόγες,
ανοίγει κάθε τόσο τα χάρτινα φτερά του για να σε
    συναντήσει.
όλα αυτά για σένα, για να τον δεις, για να δεις πως
    μπορεί κι αυτός . . . να φτύνει την βαρύτητα . . . να
    αγνοεί το μέτρο . . . να νικά τον μεγαλύτερό του
    φόβο . . . να είναι καλύτερος από όσο πιστεύει . . .
    χειρότερος από όσο μπορεί . . .

Mercury in Retrograde

With fingers – fingertips and edge of nail –
he plots fires with tongues of snakes,
a child yearning for sheer drops, with paper wings on his
    shoulders,
thinking and thinking of fires and acts of violence.
For years he lives in the basement of his polychrome
    dreams
where dampness lingers and moldy poison drips from
    walls.
He devours his scribblings and is never hungry, but only
    whines for water
which he likes winter-chilled, not frozen.
He stubs out his cigarettes on the palms of his hands, and
    when he is hot and aroused
he whistles to derailment like a train and then, puff! . . .
    he breathes in smoke as he climaxes,
an orgasmic lunge, and then the plunge.
Here on his decked-out tomb all he feared has come to
    pass, all that wounded him,
and all he didn't understand . . . stronger now, smeared in
    ash, encircled by flames,
he spreads from time to time his paper wings to meet you.

Peter Constantine

Ελέφαντας στον αέρα

Ένας ελέφαντας αποφάσισε μια μέρα πως δεν του
    ταιριάζει να είναι ελέφαντας και πως ήρθε η ώρα του
    να πετάξει και να γίνει πεταλούδα. Και ξέρεις γιατί
    ποτέ δεν τα κατάφερε; Γιατί το μόνο που τον ένοιαζε
    ήταν η ιδέα του . . .
Δεν ήθελε να γίνει φανταχτερός
Δεν ήθελε να νικήσει τη βαρύτητα
Δεν ήθελε να ταξιδεύει στις μαργαρίτες

Ήθελε απλά να γίνει πεταλούδα
Και δεν έγινε ποτέ . . .
Και έμεινε εκεί στα χαμηλά . . . πιεσμένος από το
    βάρος του
Να χαζεύει τους άλλους ελέφαντες που έγιναν
    πεταλούδες και δύο φάλαινες που γίνανε παγόνια . . .
Και γέρασε ελέφαντας αφού η ιδέα του ήταν από την
    αρχή απλά μια ιδέα
Χωρίς φως
Χωρίς φτερά
Μόνο ο θάνατος θα του τα χαρίσει πια . . .

Truncated Clouds

An elephant decided one day that being an elephant
    didn't suit him and the time had come for him to fly
    away a butterfly
But do you know why he never succeeded?
The only thing he cared about was the idea –
He didn't want to make a spectacle of himself
He didn't want to fight gravity
He didn't want to fly over to the daisies

He simply wanted to become a butterfly
And never did
And remained grounded . . . weighed by his weight
Staring at other elephants who had become butterflies
    and two whales who had turned into peacocks
And he grew old as an elephant, his idea no more than
    an idea
Without light
Without wings
Which now only death would give him

Peter Constantine

PAVLINA MARVIN

(Born Athens, Greece, 1987)

Pavlina Marvin's topical, close-to-the-bone work is now being recognized by the mainstream, but she began as one of the bloggers who created *Teflon*. Born in Athens, she grew up in the city of Ermoupolis on the island of Syros. She studied History but after studying poetry at the Takis Sinopoulos Foundation decided to make poetry her life. Her poems, book and theatre reviews, and children's literature have been published extensively in print and online.

Τα ζιζάνια

Δεν έπρεπε να βγάλω τα ζιζάνια –
χάσαμε όλο μας το στάχυ.
Τώρα, στις εποχές της στέρησης,
να τι μου σώθηκε:
Το άδειο μας χωράφι,
στη μέση ξόανο εγώ
να ναυαγώ
πουλιά νεκρόφερτα
μαμούνια αιμόφυρτα
και γύρω γύρω λίγες μνήμες των καρπών.

Το απόλυτο απόβλητο

Το μωρό μας, νιώθωντας ανεπιθύμητο τελείως,
    προσεβλήθη
και, λίγο πριν την έκτρωση, άγνωστο πώς, απεβλήθη.
Ξεκάθαρη αυτοκτονία. Τι ειρωνεία!
Το μοναδικό δικό μας πλασματάκι,
ιδιάζον τώρα σκουληκάκι
στα νοσοκομειακά απόβλητα.
Δε λυπάμαι.
Μωρό μου, εσύ;
Έλα τώρα, και πάραυτα παράτα αυτές τις κλάψες.
Αν στην παλάμη μου το έβαζα και σ' το 'δειχνα
το βλέμμα θα 'στρεφες αλλού, από αηδία.
Τι τάχατες ενόμισες πως ήτανε;
Ένας ακόμη θανατούλης, όχι αναξιοπρεπής, αφού,
    χωρίς κηδεία.

The Weeds

I shouldn't have pulled up all the weeds –
there's not a stalk left.
Now, in the season of deprivation,
see what remains:
Our empty field
and me in the middle, a shipwrecked
fetish,
death-dealing birds,
blood-bathed vermin,
and all around, scattered memories of crops.

Karen Emmerich

The Perfect Outcast

Our baby, feeling entirely undesired, took offense
and, shortly before the abortion, mysteriously miscarried.
An unambiguous suicide. What irony!
Our unique little creature,
now a unique little worm
amid hospital waste.
I'm not sad.
What about you, honey?
Come on, brush away those tears.
If I'd put it in my palm and held it out to you
you would have looked away, repulsed.
What did you think it was, anyhow?
Just another little death, not undignified, since there was
   no funeral.

Karen Emmerich

THOMAS IOANNOU

(Born Preveza, Greece, 1979)

With their examinations of modern hubris, the poems of Thomas Ioannou have been circulated widely on the internet as a commentary on the dire straits in which Greece and Europe now find themselves. Ioannou studied Medicine at the University of Athens with a specialty in neurology. He is a practicing physician at the University of Ioannina. Since 2009, he has also served on the editorial board of *Ta Poiitika*, the magazine founded by two of the most influential critics who write about this new generation of poets: Titika Dimitroulia and Kostas Papageorgiou. Ioannou's poems and essays have been published in various literary magazines and newspapers. Unusually for this web-centric group, he has published a collection of his poetry; it received the Greek National Prize for New Writing in 2011.

Ιπποκράτους 15 (*Ippokratous 15*), Shakespearikon, 2011.

Έντιμος συμβιβασμός

Σε πλησιάζουν με το χαμόγελο ακριβείας τους

Με τον ισορροπημένο λόγο τους
Σε χτυπούν στην πλάτη
Με την οικειότητα του εκ του πλησίον μίσους

Μάθανε βλέπεις να οικειοποιούνται
Ακόμα και τους χθεσινούς εχθρούς
Να συμφιλιώνονται με τα πάθη τους
Ληθοβολώντας τη μνήμη
Πετώντας πέτρες στη θάλασσα
Για να σωπάσει η ταραχή της

Όσο κι αν αντιδράσεις στην αρχή
Και θελήσεις τις γωνίες σου
Οξείες να κρατήσεις
Κι αυτό το σπάσιμο στη φωνή να σε προδίδει
Στο τέλος θα συναινέσεις
Να επιμεληθούν άλλοι την εξαφάνισή σου

Θα φτιάξουν αυτοί τον κόμπο στο λαιμό σου
Προσδίδοντας επισημότητα στη λύπη σου
Σα να δένουν τη γραβάτα-γλώσσα τους

Κάθε σύσπαση των χειλιών σου
Και μορφασμός
Θα συντονιστεί με το δημόσιο αίσθημα
Κάθε σου λέξη θα αποζητά επικύρωση
Από μια διευρυμένη
Από μια συντριπτική πλειοψηφία

Honourable Compromise

They approach you with their precise smiles
Their balanced arguments
They slap you on the back
With the familiarity of intimate hatred

They've learned, you see, to take control
Even of yesterday's enemies
To make peace with their passions
Stoning memory
Throwing rocks at the sea
To still its turbulence

However much you react at first
And try to keep your corners
Sharp
Though that break in your voice betrays you
In the end you'll agree
To let others arrange your elimination

They will tighten the knot at your neck
Lending your sorrow formality
As if their tongues were ties

Every twitch of your lips
Every grimace
Will be coordinated with public opinion
Your every word will beg for validation
From a broad
From an overwhelming majority

Κι αν μειοψηφήσει κάποια τύψη
Που δεν πείστηκε για τις προθέσεις σου
Μην απολογηθείς
Δίκη προθέσεων θα κάνουμε τώρα;

Το ουσιώδες είναι
Ότι απέφυγες τα χειρότερα
Συνάπτοντας έναν καθ' όλα
Έντιμο συμβιβασμό

And if some conscience dissents
Unconvinced about your intentions
Don't apologize
Are we judging intentions now?

The key thing is
That you avoided the worst
By agreeing to an eminently
Honourable compromise

Maria Margaronis

IV

STORYTELLING
Poets in Performance and across the Arts

In summer 2015, at a reading organized by the poet Thomas Tsalapatis and the director Theo Terzopoulos at the latter's Theater Attis in Athens, young poets gathered to read poems on the theme of Antigone and the unburied dead. Politically engaged, in keeping with Terzopoulos's own focus on race and the migrant in his avant-garde adaptations of Greek tragedy, there was an electric sense of urgency. History was happening now. The work on show was noteworthy for its performative nature and its tendency to straddle different media and genres. There were poets who worked with composers, others who worked with artists, and even an unpublished shepherd. Many, in fact, were known *primarily* for their artistic output in genres other than poetry. Poets from throughout Greece and elsewhere were present, but what sets this section apart – only two of these writers, Elena Penga and Elena Polygeni, did not read – is its embodiment of the two trends in wider Greek poetry which dominated that evening. First is a narrative drive in which the double sense of the Greek word ιστορία (*istoria*), 'history' and 'story', is foregrounded. So, Apostolos Thivaios tells us the stories the news won't cover; while Z. D. Ainalis and Stamatis Polenakis deploy myth and historical irony, respectively, to rearrange our sense of the present. Second, as already suggested, is multidisciplinarity: Demosthenes Papamarkos is best known as a short-story writer, Penga and Polenakis as playwrights, and Polygeni as a performance artist. Influenced by a strong tradition of the short story – the Greek novel barely exists – prose poetry also plays a big part; and indeed Penga's Kathy Acker-esque non-dramatic work divides its translators, being presented as poetry in France and, until now, as flash fiction everywhere else.

213

THOMAS TSALAPATIS

(Born Athens, Greece, 1984)

The ironic new histories of Thomas Tsalapatis's prose poems make him the key figure in this group. He studied Theater at the University of Athens. His first collection, *Daybreak is Execution, Mr. Krack*, received the National Poetry Prize. His second, *Alba*, was published in 2015 to rave reviews. Known for what critics have called his young and restless take on the crisis, he is a prolific writer of articles and theater and book reviews, and an organizer of events such as the Attis poetry readings. His poems have been translated into English, French, Spanish, and Italian, and he himself has translated from the poetry of W. B. Yeats and W. H. Auden. His writing can be found at *Groucho Marxism*: tsalapatis.blogspot.com.

Το ξημέρωμα είναι σφαγή, κύριε Κρακ (*Daybreak is Execution, Mr. Krack*), Ekati, 2013; *Άλμπα* (*Alba*), Ekati, 2015.

Το κουτί

Έχω ένα μικρό κουτί που πάντα μέσα του κάποιον σφάζουν.

Λίγο πιο μεγάλο από κουτί παπουτσιών. Λίγο πιο άχαρο από κουτί με πούρα. Δεν ξέρω ποιος, δεν ξέρω ποιον, μα κάποιον σφάζουν. Και ήχος δεν ακούγεται (εκτός από τις φορές που ακούγεται). Το τοποθετώ στη βιβλιοθήκη, στο τραπέζι όταν θέλω να περνώ τις ώρες μου κοιτάζοντάς το, μακριά από τα παράθυρα να μην το κιτρινίσει ο ήλιος, κάτω από το κρεβάτι μου όταν θέλω να νιώσω άτακτος. Μέσα του κάποιον σφάζουν, ακόμη και όταν στο σπίτι μας έχουμε γιορτή, ακόμα και την Κυριακή, ακόμα και όταν βρέχει.

Όταν βρήκα το κουτί – δε θα πω πώς, δε θα πω πού – το έφερα με ικανοποίηση σπίτι. Την ώρα εκείνη νόμιζα πως θα άκουγα τον ήχο της θάλασσας. Όμως, εκεί μέσα γίνονται σφαγές.

Άρχισε να με αρρωσταίνει η φασαρία, η γνώση των συμβάντων, τα γεγονότα μέσα στο κουτί. Η παρουσία του άρχισε να με αρρωσταίνει. Έπρεπε να δράσω, να απελευθερωθώ, να ηρεμήσω, να κάνω ένα μπάνιο. Αποφάσεις έπρεπε να παρθούν.

Έτσι, το ταχυδρόμησα σε έναν φίλο· έναν φίλο που έχω μόνο για να του κάνω δώρα. Τύλιξα το κουτί με αθώο πολύχρωμο χαρτόνι, έδεσα το χαρτόνι με αθώα πολύχρωμη κορδέλα. Μέσα στο κουτί με τα γράμματα υπάρχει ένα κουτί και μέσα στο κουτί αυτό κάποιον σφάζουν. Στο γραμματοκιβώτιο περιμένει να φτάσει στα χέρια ενός φίλου. Μια φιλία που συντηρώ απλώς για να κάνω δώρα.

The Box

Inside my small box they're always slaughtering someone.

A little larger than a shoebox. A little plainer than a cigar box. Don't know who, don't know whom, but they're slaughtering someone. Can't hear a sound (except when you can). I place it on the bookshelf, on the table when I want to spend time looking at it, far away from the window so the sun doesn't turn it yellow; under my bed when I'm feeling naughty. They're slaughtering someone inside, even when we're having a party at our house, even on Sunday, even when it's raining.

When I found the box – I won't say how, won't say where – I brought it home, very satisfied with myself. At first I thought I'd be able to hear the sound of the sea. But no, there's an execution going on inside there.

The racket was sickening, my growing awareness of what was happening, the acts inside the box. The box revolted me. I had to do something, to free myself, calm down, take a shower. I needed to take charge.

So, I mailed it to a friend. A friend I keep just for giving presents to. I wrapped the box in innocently colorful cardboard, I wrapped the cardboard in innocently colorful ribbon. Inside the box surrounded by letters there's a box and in that box they're slaughtering someone. Sitting in the mailbox, it's waiting to reach my friend. The friend I keep just to give presents to.

Jacob Moe

Δευτέρα των λέξεων

Ημέρα πρώτη
στις γειτονιές της Άλμπα
Και εκείνος βράζει νερό, όλο βράζει νερό
Στο κοίλο κομμάτι της γλώσσας
Εκεί που λιμνάζουν οι λέξεις
Οι αχειροποίητες, οι τοιχογραφημένες, οι άκαπνες
Στο νερό
Στον ατμό
Και εκείνος
Βράζει νερό, όλο βράζει νερό
Μαθαίνοντας πώς συντάσσεται εκείνο που λιγοστεύει
Μαθαίνοντας το πώς τα Π και τα Τ χάνουν την ευθεία
        της στέγης του
Το πώς τα ζ και τα ξ ξεριζώνονται
Το πώς φονεύονται τα φωνήεντα
Το πώς η γλώσσα κοχλάζει

Προσφορά των σιωπηλών
Σε εκείνους που σιώπησαν

Word Monday

The first day
In Alba's neighborhood
And he is boiling water, always boiling water
In the curved part of language
where words stagnate
The unused ones, the ones on walls,
the non-smoking ones
In the water
In the steam
And he is
Boiling water, always boiling water
Learning that what is scarce is what takes charge
Learning how Π and Τ lose their flat roofs
How ζ and ξ dry up at the roots
How vowels get murdered
How language bubbles up

An offering of the silent
For those who grew silent

                                    Karen Van Dyck

Z. D. AINALIS

(Born Athens, Greece, 1982)

History and storytelling are tightly bound up with one another in Z. D. Ainalis's poems, which, like those of Stamatis Polenakis (p. 229), often call for annotation. Ainalis studied Philology at the University of Ioannina, and is currently pursuing a doctorate in Byzantine History and Philology in Paris, where he lives. He has published on German Romantic poetry, and his Greek translations from the poetry of the Turkish Cypriot Commonwealth poet Mehmet Yashin – whose multilingual poems are included in the last section (p. 403) – were published in ebook by Vakxikon.gr in 2015 under the title *Άγγελοι εκδικητές* (*Angelic Avengers*).

Ηλεκτρογραφία (*Electrography*), Gavrielides, 2006; *Αποσπάσματα* (*Fragments*), Gavrielides, 2008; *Η σιωπή της Σίβας* (*The Silence of Shiva*) [ebook], Vakxikon.gr, 2011; *Μυθολογία* (*Mythology*), Panopticon, 2013.

Τηλέμαχος

Τις παλάμες μου κόψανε λάφυρα στον άλλο πόλεμο
    λαθροκυνηγοί
ό, τι περίσσεψε το χώρεσαν σε σκουριασμένους χαλκάδες
γι' αυτό και τώρα βλέπεις να κρατώ με τα δόντια το
    καλαμάρι
με τη γλώσσα να βάφω
τη σελίδα κατάστικτη
σταγόνες το αίμα μου
τα χείλ' υπολείμματα σάρκες σκισμένες
ούλα σμάλτα σπασμένα δόντια
κλάματα σάλια
και δε μιλώ για τον εαυτό μου
όμως τη μάνα μου τσούλα τη σιχάθηκα
να μπάζει απ' το παράθυρο κατά δεκάδες τους
    πειρασμούς

πρόστυχη
να τους καυλώνει
κι έπειτα σύξυλους στα κρύα του λουτρού
απολαμβάνοντας τη μοναρχική κυριαρχία της στα
    τόσα σερνικά
κι ας τη μαστίγωνε φρικτά η λαίλαπα της σάρκας
κάθε που ξύπναγε τυλιγμένη της αυγής την ικμάδα
νικημένη απ' τα φαντάσματα της νύχτας
κι όμως
δε μιλώ για τον εαυτό μου
γι' αυτό και συλλογίζουμαι τόσο πολύ τούτες τις μέρες
    και τον Νεοπτόλεμο
και τόσους άλλους

καμένη γενιά
γενιά μου

Telemachus

The bounty hunters looted, sliced my hands in that
    other war
and what was left they strung on rusted chain rings
which is why I grip the inkwell with my teeth
and use my tongue to paint
the speckled pages
with drops of my own blood.
My lips are scraps of tattered flesh
gums, enamel, shattered teeth,
spit, tears.
And I'm not talking about myself
but my mother that slut, she disgusts me
letting temptations in through her window by the
    dozen.

She's vile
she gets them off,
then leaves them speechless in the cold bath
reveling in her monarchic rule over so many men
even if she felt the hurricane sting of the flesh
when she woke in the wet dawn
wrapped by the ghosts of night,
and yet
I'm not talking about myself
which is why I mull these days on Neoptolemos
and so many others

burnt generation
my generation.

Stephanos Papadopoulos

3ⁿ Σεπτεμβρίου 1843

Γερνάνε γρήγορα οι μέρες στην Ελλάδα
σβήνει απότομα το φως
τρώνε σκυλιά τα δάκτυλα του ήλιου
παίζουν αδέσποτα παιδιά στα περιθώρια του δρόμου
έρχονται νύχτα μητρικές φωνές κραυγές
για να μαντρώσουν

Κι έπειτα τίποτα
σιωπή
οι μπάτσοι έφιπποι σφυρίζουν
λακέδες με λιβρέα τσακίζονται
φερέφωνα
κυρίες με κρινολίνα κι άμαξες
Νυδραίοι εφοπλιστές κι ευνούχοι Φαναριώτες
καλαμαράδες φραγκοφόρετοι και πένες
    πληρωμένες

στο Φόρο πένητες μασάνε το σκοτάδι

ένα φεγγάρι θάνατος
κόσα στο σβέρκο καρφωμένο

γενιά παρά γενιά εμφύλιος, γενιά παρά γενιά
    εκκαθάριση
και όλο απ' το μηδέν ν' αρχίζω

Παίζουν ακόμα, τραγουδάν, γελάν στους δρόμους τα
    παιδιά μας;

September 3rd 1843

Times turn quickly in Greece
the light goes out abruptly
dogs eat sun rays
stray children play by the side of the road
at night maternal voices, cries
come to shut us in

And then nothing
silence
the cops whistle on horseback
liveried lackeys trip over themselves
sock puppets
ladies in crinolines and coaches
old shipowners from Hydra, Greek eunuchs from the
    Porte
bureaucrats in western dress and paid pen pushers

in the Forum
paupers chew on darkness

a death moon, a scythe
pinning the back of the neck

every other generation civil wars
and purges

and starting again from scratch every time

Do our children still play, still sing, still laugh in the
    streets?

Μαζεύονται τώρ' από παντού φωνές κραυγές
συρρέουν μπρος στ' ανάκτορα αλαλάζουν
βάζουν φωτιά περιδεείς και δέονται
ελπίζουν
σβήνουν απότομα οι φωτιές
διαλύονται
γερνάνε γρήγορα οι μέρες στην Ελλάδα

Voices, cries gather now from all around
streaming before the palace, cheering
setting fires in terror, praying
hoping
the fires go out abruptly
they scatter
times turn quickly in Greece

Maria Margaronis

STAMATIS POLENAKIS

(Born Athens, Greece, 1970)

The surreal direction of some of Stamatis Polenakis's poems puts him in dialogue with *Farmakon* poets like Anna Griva (p. 95). He studied Spanish literature in Madrid, and one feels the influence of Salvador Dalí lurking behind some poems. But his main focuses are on history, and on story-telling that crosses genres. He is best known as a playwright; his plays have been produced at Greece's National Theatre and the more experimental theatre space Fournos. Like those plays, his poems are intensely preoccupied with their world's political and human present. His work has been translated into English, French, Romanian, and German.

Το χέρι του χρόνου (*The Hand of Time*), Omvros, 2002; *Τα γαλάζια άλογα του Φραντς Μαρκ* (*The Blue Horses of Franz Marc*), Odos Panos, 2006; *Νοτρ Νταμ* (*Notre Dame*), Odos Panos, 2008; *Τα σκαλοπάτια της Οδησσού* (*The Odessa Steps*), Mikri Arktos, 2012; *Η ένδοξη πέτρα* (*The Glorious Stone*), Mikri Arktos, 2014.

Η ποίηση δεν αρκεί

Κύριοι, μην αφήνετε να σας ξεγελά
τίποτα και κανένας.
Δεν χρεοκοπήσαμε σήμερα
έχουμε ήδη χρεοκοπήσει
εδώ και πολλά χρόνια.
Σήμερα ο καθένας μπορεί πια εύκολα
να περπατά επί των κυμάτων
άδεια πετάγονται τα μπουκάλια στο νερό
χωρίς να μεταφέρουν κρυμμένα μηνύματα
οι σειρήνες ούτε τραγουδούν ούτε σιωπούν
    μένουν απλώς ακίνητες
σαστισμένες από την ιδιωτικοποίηση
των υδάτων και όχι
η ποίηση δεν αρκεί αφού η θάλασσα γέμισε
σκουπίδια και καπότες
κι ας γράφει όσα σονέτα θέλει για το Φάληρο
ο Λορέντζος Μαβίλης.

Poetry Does Not Suffice

Gentlemen, don't let anything,
anyone, deceive you:
we were not bankrupted today,
we have been bankrupt for a long time now.
Today it's easy enough
for anyone to walk on water:
the empty bottles bob on the surface
without carrying any secret messages.
The sirens don't sing, nor are they silent,
they merely stay motionless,
dumbstruck by the privatization
of the waves and no
poetry doesn't suffice since the sea filled up
with trash and condoms.
Let him write as many sonnets as he wants about Faliro,
that Lorentzos Mavilis.

A. E. Stallings

Ποίηση 2048

Τόσο πολύ εχρεοκοπήσαμε σύντροφοι
που ώς και τα ξενοδοχεία
τα χτισμένα από τα κόκαλα των νεκρών,
τα ωραία παραθαλάσσια ξενοδοχεία
που φτιάξαμε με τα αργύρια
της προδοσίας του Πλουμπίδη,
ώς και αυτά ακόμα, εγκαταλείφθηκαν
και σαπίζουν κάτω από τη λάσπη και τη
βροχή. Ούτε αυτή η εποχή είναι εποχή
για ποίηση: πληρώνουμε ακόμα
με νόμισμα εμφυλίου.

Το μεγάλο αίνιγμα

Αποχαιρέτα την για πάντα αυτή τη σύντομη
εποχή της ελευθερίας.
Αντίο αλησμόνητες μέρες και νύχτες ένδοξες
και φύλλα που τα παίρνει ο άνεμος.
Υπήρξαμε νέοι, σε τίποτα δεν ελπίζαμε
και περιμέναμε το αύριο με το τυφλό πείσμα
του ναυαγού που ρίχνει στο νερό πέτρες.

Poetry 2048

We were so bankrupt, comrades,
that even the hotels,
those built from the bones of the dead,
the lovely seaside hotels
which we made with the silver
from the treason of Ploumbides,
yes even those, were abandoned
and they rot from underneath with the mud and the
rain. Not even this age is an age
for poetry: we are still paying
in the coin of Civil War.

A. E. Stallings

The Great Enigma

Goodbye forever to this brief
age of freedom.
Farewell unforgettable days and glorious nights
and leaves swept away by the wind.
We were young, we hoped for nothing
and we waited for tomorrow with the blind obstinacy
of the castaway who throws stones in the water.

Richard Pierce

Ελεγεία

Τίποτα, ούτε καν ο πνιγμός ενός παιδιού
δεν σταματά τον κόσμο απ' την αιώνια κίνησή του
Ξέρω ότι σήμερα ή χθες κάποιο παιδί πνίγηκε·
ένα παιδί που πνίγηκε σήμερα ή χθες
δεν είναι τίποτα· είναι μια άψυχη μαριονέτα
στα χέρια του Θεού· είναι ένα μικρό ποίημα
ακίνητο μέσα στην αιώνια κίνηση του κόσμου.

Elegy

Nothing, not even the drowning of a child,
stops the perpetual motion of the world.
I know that today or yesterday some child drowned;
a child who drowned today or yesterday
is nothing – an inanimate puppet
in the hands of God, a short motionless poem
in the perpetual motion of the world.

Richard Pierce

ELENA PENGA

(Born Thessaloniki, Greece, 1964)

East Village punk naïveté meets Margarita Karapanou's wise child from *Kassandra and the Wolf* in Elena Penga's theatrical and poetical writing alike. Born in Thessaloniki, she studied Theater and Philosophy at Wesleyan University and Screen and Theater Writing at the University of Southern California in Los Angeles. She is best known for her plays, but has also published three collections of her short prose pieces. The most recent, *Tight Belts and Other Skin* (Agra, 2012), won the Greek Academy Prize and has been translated into Swedish and English. She also wrote the screenplay for Lakis Papastathis's award-winning film about the phenomenal Greek short-story writer Giorgios Vizyenos, *His Only Journey in His Life.*

Σκονώς (*Squash*), Agra, 1997; Αυτή θερινή (*She Summerlike*), Agra, 1986; Σφιχτές ζώνες και άλλα δέρματα (*Tight Belts and Other Skin*), Agra, 2012.

Διάδρομοι

Τα αγάλματα, οι ναοί, τα σπίτια, όλα στην αρχαιότητα ήταν χρωματιστά, ζωγραφισμένα. Η Δήλος ήταν πολύχρωμη. Ακόμη και τώρα, μετά από τόσες εκατοντάδες χρόνια, όταν ανακαλύπτουν ένα άγαλμα, αυτό έχει τα χρώματά του. Το βγάζουν από τη γη, και τα χρώματά του μένουν στο χώμα, σα να βγάζουν το γλυπτό μέσα από γάντι.

Διάδρομοι. Και αρχαιολογία. Διάδρομοι και διαδρομές. Και μνήμη. Και ξενοδοχεία. Ωραία ξενοδοχεία γεμάτα αγάλματα και λουλούδια. Διασχίζεις διαδρόμους αθόρυβα περνάς έξω από πόρτες. Έχει ζέστη. Πολυτέλεια. Εξωτισμό. Μεγάλα σάρκινα λουλούδια σε μεγάλα πορσελάνινα βάζα.

Επιθυμείς να φτιάξεις μια σχέση με τις ωραίες εικόνες. Το προσπαθείς καθώς διασχίζεις διαδρόμους. Η ψυχή έχει τον τρόπο της να μεταβολίζει τις πληροφορίες που της έρχονται από το σώμα και τον έξω κόσμο. Έχω ακούσει πως υπάρχει η περίπτωση να καταστραφεί ολόκληρος ένας ζωντανός οργανισμός, ένα μωρό, ένας ενήλικας, μόνο και μόνο για να διατηρήσει μια παράσταση διαρκούς ηδονής. Απόλυτης ευδαιμονίας.

Διάδρομοι. Επιθυμείς να οδηγήσουν πέρα. Έξω. Να βγεις και εσύ σαν το γλυπτό που βγαίνει από το χώμα στο φως, σα μέσα από γάντι. Χρόνια μετά. Σε απροσδόκητη στιγμή. Θα βγείς άραγε; Στο φως; Εσύ που δεν είσαι πέτρα, αλλά σάρκα, που δεν είσαι νεκρή, αλλά ζωντανή;

Και έπειτα είναι και τόσες άλλες αποστάσεις. Διάδρομοι εκατοντάδων ετών φωτός. Δρόμοι που διασχίζει μία πέτρα για να γίνει κυκλαδίτικο ειδώλιο, για να γίνει μια γυναίκα του Πικάσο. Και να μείνει έτσι. Γλυπτό που εκπέμπει τις συναντήσεις που είχε άλλοτε, όταν ήταν πέτρα, πριν γίνει γλυπτό.

Passages

The statues, the temples, the houses, everything in Antiquity was colored, painted. Delos was multicolored. Even today, after so many thousands of years, when they find a statue, it is covered in paint. They pull it out of the earth, and the colors stay in the dirt like a sculpture coming out of a glove.

Passages. And archaeology. Passages and routes. And memory. And hotels. Beautiful hotels full of statues and flowers. You walk through the corridors silently. You pass by closed doors. It is hot. Luxurious. Exotic. Gigantic fleshy flowers in gigantic porcelain vases.

You want to find a way to relate to the beautiful sights. You try. As you walk through the corridors. The soul has a way of metabolizing information that comes from the body and the outside world. I have heard that it is possible for a living organism, a baby, an adult, to self-destruct just because it is trying to keep the illusion of continuous pleasure alive. Of absolute ecstasy.

Corridors. You want them to take you further. Outside. So you can escape like the sculpture from the dirt. Out into the light. Like coming out of a glove. Years later. Completely unexpectedly. Are you coming? Out into the light? You who aren't stone, but flesh? You who aren't dead, but alive?

And then there are so many other kinds of distance. Passages hundreds of light years away. The roads a stone takes to become a Cycladic figurine, a Picasso woman. The lengths it goes to stay that way. Sculpture that still emits the encounters it had back then, when it was a stone, before it became a sculpture.

Karen Van Dyck

Κεφάλια

Ήμουν πολύ μικρός γύρω στα δέκα. Πηγαίναμε διακοπές σε ένα νησί. Το νησί ήταν η Κάλυμνος. Απέναντί μας έμενε ένας καπετάνιος. Σφουγγαράς. Μαζί του είχε ένα μικρό κορίτσι, την Αννούλα. Συχνά πήγαινα στο σπίτι της και παίζαμε με τις κούκλες της και με άλλα παιχνίδια. Μια μέρα, κάποια στιγμή, βρεθήκαμε στην αποθήκη, κάτω στο υπόγειο που ήταν γεμάτο σφουγγάρια. Αυτό που θυμάμαι ήταν πως δεν είχαμε καμιά αίσθηση των σωμάτων μας. Θυμάμαι χάδια, φιλιά, αγγίζαμε τα μαλλιά ο ένας του άλλου. Δεν είχαμε καμιά αίσθηση πως υπάρχει κάτι άλλο από αυτό.

Δηλαδή μόνο κεφάλια;

Ναι, μόνο κεφάλια. Μαλλιά και πρόσωπο. Τα σώματά μας ήταν χωμένα μέσα στα φουσκωτά σφουγγάρια. Δεν τα νιώθαμε.

Heads

I was very young, about ten. We went on vacation to an island. The island was called Kalymnos. Across from us lived a captain. A sponge-diver. He had a little girl named Annoula. I went to her house often. We played with her dolls and other games. One day at a certain point we found ourselves in the backroom of the cellar. It was full of sponges. What I remember is that we had no sense of our bodies. I remember caresses, kisses, touching each other's hair. We had no sense that anything else existed.

So you were just heads?

Yes, just heads. Hair and faces. Our bodies were buried in puffy sponges. We couldn't feel them.

Karen Van Dyck

Ψάρια

Δες εκεί. Τα ψάρια αλλάζουν χρώμα. Μόλις ερεθιστεί το αρσενικό γίνεται μαύρο. Ανεβαίνουν στην επιφάνεια με το θηλυκό, και μόλις τελειώσει η σεξουαλική πράξη, ξαναγίνεται ασημένιο. Είναι τόσο πολλά και τόσο ερεθισμένα που δίνουν την εντύπωση πως αναβοσβήνουν φώτα. Τα βλέπεις;

Είμαστε τόσο ψηλά. Δεν βλέπω τίποτα.

Τους ψαράδες τούς βλέπεις;

Ναι. Τους μισώ.

Γιατί;

Γιατί πιάνουν ψάρια. Δεν είναι καθόλου φιλικοί.

Έτσι είναι οι ψαράδες. Δεν είναι φιλικοί, γιατί είναι προληπτικοί. Αν σε πάρουνε μαζί τους για ψάρεμα και πιάσουνε πολλά ψάρια, τότε σε ξαναπαίρνουνε μαζί τους. Τότε θέλουν να σε παίρνουν συνέχεια μαζί τους.

Fish

Take a look at that. The fish change color. When the male gets excited he turns black. He rises to the surface with the female, and as soon as they have sex, he turns silver again. There are so many and they're so excited, it looks like lights flickering on and off. See them?

We're so high up. I can't see anything.

Can you see the fishermen?

Yes. I hate them.

Why?

Because they catch fish. They're not at all friendly.

That's the way fishermen are. They're not friendly. They're superstitious. If they take you out fishing and catch a lot of fish, they take you out again. Then they want to take you out all the time.

Karen Van Dyck

Δέρμα

Έχεις πάει στην Αμερική;
  Όχι. Ωραία είναι;
  Ναι.
  Για μένα η Αμερική ειναι ο Μάικλ Τζάκσον. Απο μαύρος θέλησε να γίνει λευκός και κατέστρεψε πάνω του καθετί που του θύμιζε την προέλευσή του. Έγινε αυτός ο δημιουργός του εαυτού του.
  Και οι τραβεστί κάτι παρόμοιο κάνουν.
  Ναι.
  Υπάρχει και η άλλη η Αμερικάνα η Βίλντενσταϊν που ήθελε να μοιάσει με γάτα και το κατάφερε. Μετά από 59 χειρουργικές επεμβάσεις. Την έχεις δει;
  Πού;
  Στα περιοδικά.
  Όχι. Πώς είναι;
  Τρομακτική. Μοιάζει με γάτα.
  Το δέρμα του ανθρώπινου σώματος αν απλωνόταν οριζοντίως θα κάλυπτε ένα διπλό κρεβάτι.
  Το έχεις δει;
  Πού;
  Στα περιοδικά.
  Στα περιοδικά;
  Όλα υπάρχουν στα περιοδικά.

Skin

Ever been to America?
  No. Is it beautiful?
  Yes.
  For me America is Michael Jackson. He wanted to be white but he was born black so he destroyed everything about himself that reminded him of his origins. He became his own creator.
  Trans people do that too.
  Yes.
  And then there's that American woman Wildenstein who wanted to look like a cat and actually succeeded. After 59 surgeries. Ever seen her?
  Where?
  In the tabloids.
  No, how does she look?
  Scary. Like a cat.
  If you were to spread the skin of a human body horizontally it would cover a double bed.
  Ever seen it?
  Where?
  In the tabloids.
  In the tabloids?
  Everything's in the tabloids.

Karen Van Dyck

Ροζ εφιαλτικό

Βρέχει. Εδώ. Και εκεί. Εκεί που εσύ τραγουδάς. Βρέχει πολύ
δυνατά. Κάθομαι μέσα στο νυχτερινό μου σπίτι, μέσα σε
μια βαθιά περιστρεφόμενη πολυθρόνα. Περιστρέφομαι
με την πολυθρόνα και ακούω τη βροχή. Εσύ τραγουδάς.
Η βροχή ακούγεται. Εκείνη ακούω. Τη βροχή. Έρχεται
ένας ακόμη άνθρωπος. Φέρνει ένα καινούργιο ροζ καπέλο
για το φωτιστικό. Σβήνει το φως, ξεβιδώνει τη λάμπα,
βγάζει το μαύρο, βάζει το ροζ καπέλο στο φωτιστικό,
ξανανάβει το φως. Καθόμαστε μέσα στο ροζ φως και
μιλάμε για καπέλα. Καπέλα για φωτιστικά. Ανοίγω τις
μπαλκονόπορτες. Εσύ τραγουδάς. Αλλά η βροχη ακούγεται
πιο δυνατή. Μπαίνει μέσα στο σπίτι. Χτυπά πάνω στα
καπέλα των φωτιστικών. Ρίχνει κάτω τα φωτιστικά. Έρχεται
σε σύγκρουση με την πραγματικότητα. Οι κερασιές στον
κήπο του γείτονα έχουν χρόνια να δώσουν καρπούς.
Μπαίνουν τέσσερις άντρες με βέργες. Μπαίνουν στον
κήπο του γείτονα τώρα μαζί με τη βροχή. Ήρθαν να
πειθαρχήσουν τα δέντρα με σκοπό να τα κόψουν αν δεν
ανθίσουν. Βλέπω τους άντρες να χτυπούν τα δέντρα.
Βλέπω τη βροχή να χτυπά τους άντρες.

Nightmare Pink

It's raining. Here. There. Where you're singing. Raining very hard. I'm sitting in the house in a deep swivel chair. It's nighttime. I spin the chair around and listen to the rain. You're singing. The rain is loud enough to hear. I listen. To the rain. Another person arrives. With a pink lampshade. Brand new. He switches off the light, unscrews the bulb, takes off the black shade, puts on the pink one, then switches the light back on. We sit bathed in pink light and talk about shades. Lampshades. I open the balcony doors. You're singing. But the rain is louder. It comes into the house. Hits the lampshades. Knocks over the lights. Collides with reality. The cherry trees in the neighbor's yard haven't had fruit for years. Four men enter carrying sticks. They enter the neighbor's yard along with the rain. They've come to discipline the trees and chop them down if they don't blossom. I watch the men hit the trees. I watch the rain hit the men.

Karen Van Dyck

APOSTOLOS THIVAIOS

(Born Athens, Greece, 1980)

News and the crisis are central to Apostolos Thivaios's output; indeed, true to the immediate, fleeting nature of the online environments in which his poetry is often published, it even doubles at times as a form of report. He studied Economics in Athens and currently works in the banking sector. His writing has appeared in some literary magazines, most notably the 2009 *Almanac* published by the *Poiein* team (see Further Reading). His writing can be found on their website, as well as at 24grammata.com.

17, Ekati, 2011; *Τα όνειρα της Μάριελ* (*Mariel's Dreams*), 24 Grammata, 2012; *Cubanacan*, 24 Grammata, 2012.

Πραγματικότης

Ελήφθησαν όλες οι αναγκαίες προφυλάξεις.
Απομακρύνθηκαν οι ένοικοι των κτιρίων,
Τα υπέροχα ζώα του βασιλιά.
Το άγαλμα με τα ακίνητα μάτια
Τοποθετήθηκε στο κτίσμα τύπου τολ,
Θα το ανακαλύψουν έπειτα από αιώνες
Οι ζωντανοί μιας άλλης εποχής.
Θα εντοπίσουν τα χέρια,
Τα θραύσματα από το κρανίο,
Τα άδεια μάτια θα εντοπίσουν.
Ύστερα κοιτώντας τις φωτογραφίες
των ευαίσθητων φιλμ,
Θα μνημονεύσουν τους νεκρούς συγγενείς.
Θα προβούν στην παραδοχή πως
ελήφθησαν όλες οι αναγκαίες προφυλάξεις.
θα εξερευνήσουν τα σώματα,
Με όλες τους τις ατέλειες,
Με τους λόφους και τις λίμνες,
Με τη διάχυτη ροπή προς τη φθορά.
Οι άνθρωποι θα μπορέσουν να γεράσουν
Προσμένοντας την απάντηση
Στην έκκληση για βοήθεια.
Μα πάλι οι υπολογισμοί κρίνονται επίφοβοι.
Γιατί κάποιος υπάλληλος του δήμου
Με όψη γελωτοποιού
Μπορεί να υποκλέψει τελικά
τα βιβλία των ληξιαρχείων
Και έτσι κανείς
να μην μπορεί να αποδείξει
Πως υπήρξε κάποτε ζωντανός.
Τώρα όλοι κοιτούν προς τη νύχτα,
Επίμονα,

Reality

All the necessary precautions were taken.
The residents of the buildings went far away,
the splendid royal animals.
The statue with its motionless eyes
was placed in a building like a toll booth
for people living in another age
to discover centuries later.
They'll locate the hands,
the skull fragments,
they'll find the empty eyes.
Later, looking at the photographs
on the hypersensitive film
they'll mention the dead relatives.
In their acknowledgements they'll stress
that all the necessary precautions were taken.
They'll examine the bodies,
with all their imperfections,
with their hills and lakes,
their general tendency to decay.
People are bound to grow old.
waiting for an answer
to their plea for help.
But again such evaluations are risky.
Because some public servant
with a waggish disposition
could, in the end, get hold of
the registry books
so no one
would be able to establish
there was once a living person here.
Now everyone is looking at the night,
insistently,

Το άγαλμα διατηρεί τη θεϊκή ακαμψία του.
Στο στόμα, σωροί από γύψο
Φράζουν τα ουρλιαχτά των αιώνων.
Μάταια, λοιπόν ελήφθησαν
Τόσες προφυλάξεις,
Μάταια διατυπώθηκαν
Τόσοι δισταγμοί,
Τόσα υπονοούμενα.
Οι αγαπημένοι,
Οι παλιοί μας φίλοι,
Δεν θα φανούν πια.

the statue preserves its divine rigidity.
On the mouth, lumps of plaster
block the howling of the ages.
So it was useless to take all those precautions,
pointless to express so many doubts
so many insinuations.
Our loved ones,
our old friends,
won't show up any more.

Gail Holst-Warhaft

Διεθνή

Στη στήλη των «Διεθνών»,
Στις καταχωρήσεις περί παραδόξων,
Καταστροφών φυσικών,
Υπήρξε μια αναφορά,
Μια είδηση με προεκτάσεις θεολογικές.
Ανευρέθη, λέει, ο τάφος του Απόστολου Φιλίππου,
Ανάμεσα στα ερείπια της ξακουστής
Των Φρυγών πόλεως.
Ανάμεσα σε θέατρα, δεξαμενές άλατος,
Μες στις πέτρες των θεάτρων,
Των άλλων των κτιρίων,
Των δημοσίων,
Εντοπίσθηκε ετούτο το περίφημο εύρημα.
Μα σε τούτα τα συντρίμμια,
– δεν αναγραφόταν στην είδηση –
Δεν θα βρεθεί,
Με βεβαιότητα,
Εκείνο το σύμπλεγμα των σωμάτων
Που σύχναζε στις θέρμες,
Εκείνα τα κορμιά
Που επεδείκνυαν μια προσήλωση βυζαντινή
Σε πράξεις ερωτικές,
Καθώς συμβαίνει στους χώρους της αρχαιολογίας,
Σαν βρεθεί κανείς μες στη σωσμένη σιωπή
Των ένδον χώρων.
Στη στήλη των «Διεθνών»,
Εκεί που καταχωρούνται
Οι τρομερές των ανθρώπων ανταποκρίσεις,
Εκεί αναγράφεται η είδηση
Για την ανεύρεση του ταφικού μνημείου
Εκεί που περιγράφονται εν συντομία
τα εγκλήματα,

International

In the International column,
among the reports of strange events,
natural disasters,
there was a reference,
a news item with theological ramifications.
The tomb of Philip the Apostle
had been found, it said,
among the celebrated ruins
of the city of the Phrygians.
Among the stones of the theaters,
the salt pans,
among the stones of other
public buildings
this amazing discovery was made.
But in the rubble
– here the news mentions nothing –
the tangle of bodies
that frequented the baths,
bodies that demonstrated a Byzantine dedication
to the acts of Eros,
won't be identified with any certainty,
as often happens on archeological sites,
in the preserved silence
of interiors.
In the International column
where they record
the awful reports of people,
that's where the news of the discovery
of the memorial tomb
is reported,
there where brief descriptions
of the most appalling

τα πιο επαίσχυντα,
Και τα άλλα, τα όσα συμβαίνουν στις ρωσικές
   τούνδρες,
Στα μέρη που πέφτουν στάλες, σαν κινέζικα στιλέτα,
Στα λυπημένα διαμερίσματα μιας πόλεως επαρχιακής.

crimes are printed,
and the other stuff, what's happening in the Russian
    tundra,
in the places where raindrops fall, like Chinese daggers,
in the sad apartments of a provincial town.

Gail Holst-Warhaft

Αναπόφευκτο

Όταν θα έχουν τελειώσει οι εποχές,
Όταν θα έχουμε γεράσει
Και τα γόνατά μας θα τρέμουν
Μες στους σπασμούς
Θα σταθούμε στις οροφές
Των πατρικών μας σπιτιών.
Θα κοιτάξουμε ο ένας βαθιά τον άλλον,
Θα διαλυθούμε βαθιά ο ένας
Μες στον άλλον,
Θα θυμηθούμε τότε
Που ξεκινήσαμε με τις μεγάλες βάρκες,
Το δρόμο μας φώτιζαν κεριά,
Έπειτα σώθηκε το φιτίλι,
Σκοτείνιασε και ακούγονταν παντού
Κραυγές σφαγμένων,
Εκρήξεις σποραδικές,
Ελάχιστοι κατόρθωσαν να γεράσουν
Από εκείνη τη γενιά.
Όλο ρωγμές πια,
Θα νιώσουμε έκπληξη
Που παραμείναμε ζωντανοί,
Σε πείσμα τόσων απειλών.
Εκείνοι που χαιρετούν από μακριά
Είναι οι παλιοί μας φίλοι,
Ήρθαν να μας συντροφέψουν,
Στα ταξίδια μας.
Εμείς πεθυμήσαμε τη φωνή τους,
Καθώς έβγαινε σαν λιοντάρι
Από τα στόματα.
Ελάτε, κινήστε,
Είναι καιρός,
Θα μας πουν

Unavoidable

When our time is over,
when we've grown old
and our knees tremble
in spasms
we'll stand on the roofs
of our family homes.
We'll look deeply at each other,
we'll dissolve deeply
into one another,
then we'll remember
that we set out in big ships,
candles lighted our way;
later the wick was saved,
darkness fell, everywhere we could hear
the cries of the slaughtered,
occasional outbursts,
very few of that generation
managed to grow old
All full of cracks now;
we'll be surprised
we stayed alive,
under the pressure of so many threats.
Those who greet us from afar
are our old friends,
they came to keep us company,
on our travels.
We longed to hear their voices
emerging like a lion
from their mouths.
Come, move,
it's time,
they'll tell us

Με ύφος παραγγέλματος.
Εγκαταλείψατε τις εστίες σας,
Τις πόλεις σας εγκαταλείψατε,
τα φρουραρχεία,
Τις φυλακές,
Τα καφενεία
Με τις ονομασίες
Των ορεινών εξάρσεων.

as if they were giving orders.
Leave your hearth,
your cities,
garrisons,
prisons,
cafés
named
for mountains.

Gail Holst-Warhaft

DIMOSTHENIS PAPAMARKOS

(Born Malessina, Greece, 1983)

The modern folksong included here by Dimosthenis Papa-markos was read aloud at the Theatre Attis poetry event described in this section's introduction; though a poem, it was originally published in his most recent collection of short stories, published by Antipodes in 2014, which received the 2015 Prize of the Academy of Athens in association with the literary magazine *O Αναγνώστης* (*The Reader*). That collection's title, *Γκιακ* (*Giak*), is a complex Albanian word meaning blood relation, vendetta, and race. Papamarkos is best known for his prose writing, both novels and short stories, and is currently finishing a D.Phil. in Ancient Greek History at Oxford.

από Παραλογή

Περνούσε ο Χάρος μια βολά, βαρύς και φορτωμένος
κι από το δρόμο τον πολύ κι απ' την πολλή τη δίψα
στάθηκε και ξαπόστασε στη βρύσ' του Καλογέρου.
Πιάνει απ' τη σέλα ένα σκοινί, μαύρο σαν την καρδιά
    του
πλεγμένο μια, πλεγμένο δυο, πλεγμένο τρεις και δέκα
από της χήρας 'τα μαλλιά και της μοιρολογίστρας
ν' αντέχει ήλιο και βροχή, ν' αντέχει και τα δάκρυα
κι όταν ακούει τα κλάματα, να σφίγγει, να δαγκάνει
όπως δαγκάνει η δραγκολιά και σφίγγει η
    βουνοχέντρα.
Δένει τους νιους στα έλατα, τις κόρες στα πευκάκια
και τα νιογέννητα μωρά δένει στους ασπαλάθους.
Γυρνάει και λέει στον μαύρο του, τον πλουμιστό τον
    Γρίβα
– Πάω στη βρύση για νερό, να φέρω στο τουλούμι
να πιεις εσύ, να πιώ κι εγώ που 'μαστε αποκαμένοι.
Μα 'ναι η βρύση μακρινή κι είναι γκρεμνός και ρέμα
γι' αυτό πεζός θα κατεβώ, πεζός θα πάω να φέρω.
Μείνε και κοίτα τους νεκρούς μην αρχινούν και κλαίνε
Και σκιάξουνε τον ποταμό και σκιάξουνε το ρέμα
και φοβηθεί και το νερό κι αποστερέψει η βρύση.
– Σύρε και πιες και γέμισε και φέρε μου κι εμένα,
και μην πολλά σκοτίζεσαι, τους σκλάβους θα φυλάξω.
Περνάει στη ζώνη το σπαθί, στη ράχη το δοξάρι
και το τουλούμι το χρυσό κρατεί το και βαδίζει.

from *Paralogue*

It is old Charon passing by,
broken by thirst and road dust.
And at Kalogeros's creek
he stops to rest.

He reaches to his saddle for a rope, black
as his heart, spun once, twice,
three times and ten from the widow's hair
and from the wailer's tress.

Woven safe from sun and rain, hard to tears.
When it hears a whimper,
it bites the way a whip snake bites and tightens
like the round grip of a viper.

It binds youths to cypresses, maidens
to pines and ties babies to calicotomes.
Old Charon turns to Grivas,
his black, bejeweled horse:

'You're beat and I'm parched. I'll fetch water
for us both. But the stream
is far away, the road is steep.
I'll follow it on foot – into the ravine.

'You mind the corpses; stop their screams
Otherwise they'll scare
the water and sap the source or twist
its course and leave the riverbed bare.'

'Go on and drink and bring some to me;
Don't fret – I'll watch the slaves.'
Charon sheaths his sword and shoulders his bow
He carries his golden flask and goes on his way.

Χώνεται μέσα στις πρινιές, λιθάρια δρασκελίζει
κι εκεί στην άκρη του γκρεμνού βγαίνει και
   κοντοστέκει.
Σα θάλασσα ήτανε βαθύς, σαν καλιακούδα μαύρος
λιγοψυχάει ο Χάροντας, μα τον κεντάει η δίψα
τι το νερό το γάργαρο στον πάτο του χτυπούσε.
Βάνει το πόδι το δεξί, που τους ρηγάδες πάτει
και στο δρομάκι το γκρεμνό κινάει και βαδίζει.
Δέκα νοργιές δεν ήκαμε, δέκα νοργιές δεν πάει
όταν γρικά απ' το χάραγμα ανθρωπινή κουβέντα
τραγούδι σαν της πέρδικας, κλάματα σαν του γκιώνη.
Βάζει φωνή στον Γρίβα του, φωνάζει και του λέει:
– Σου 'πα να βλέπεις τους νεκρούς και τους
   αποθαμένους
μη σκιάξουνε τον ποταμό κι έρθει και κόψει η βρύση.
Μα συ αφήνεις τους να κλαιν, αφήνεις τους να λένε.
Κι ο μαύρος του χλιμίντρισε, κι ο μαύρος πηλογάται:
– Άχνα δεν βγάζουν οι νεκροί, κοιμούνται σαν
   παιδάκια.
Κι αν κλάματα συ γρίκησες, φωνές και μοιρολόγια
στο ρέμα κοίτα για να βρεις τον θρήνο ποιος τον κρένει.

He tears through the oak forest,
strides over boulders
and there, at the edge of the cliff,
he stops and lingers.

The gorge is sea-deep, black
like a jackdaw. Charon falters,
but thirst jabs at him, the cliffs teasing
his tongue with sounds of gargling waters.

He reaches out his right foot
a dreaded toe that crushes kings
He walks ten fathoms,
and hears the lifeless as they sing.

He hears their voices rip
through the chasm, human howls:
a song like a maiden's,
cries like an owl's.

He calls out to Grivas,
'I told you to guard the stiffs.
They'll spook the river
and cut the stream from the cliffs.

'Yet you let them babble and whimper.'
And his black horse neighed,
'The dead are soundless;
they are sleeping like babes,

'If you hear laments, cries and moans,
Look into the gorge to see who mourns.'

Chloe Haralambous

ELENA POLYGENI

(Born Patras, Greece, 1979)

Small revelations from the lives of women characterize Elena Polygeni's performance-directed poetry. Based in Athens, she is an actress and musician. Since 2008 she has worked solely with the experimental theater group Mag, who often use her writing in their performances. Her poetry has been translated into Swedish and English.

Γράμματα σε μαυροπίνακα (*Letters on a Blackboard*), Dodoni, 2009; *Η θλίψη μου είναι μια γυναίκα* (*My Sorrow is a Woman*), Poema, 2012; *Η χώρα των παράδοξων πραγμάτων* (*The Land of Paradoxical Things*), To Kendri, 2014.

Για να τελειώνουμε μ' αυτή την υπόθεση

Όχι εμένα, όχι το πρόσωπό
μου, όχι αυτό που κρύβεται κάτω
απ' το πουκάμισο.
Μιλάω κι ας ξέρω ότι η φωνή
θα πνιγεί μες στα ψυγεία που
παγώνουν τα σφαγμένα
ζώα.

Υπάρχει δεν υπάρχει, τι με ενδιαφέρει.

Έτσι στο βρόντο κουνάω τα χέρια προς
τον ουρανό.
Τι όμορφα που είναι τ' αγγελούδια
σκοτωμένα
με τα θλιμμένα μάτια τους, να μας κοιτούν.

To Be Done with the Matter

Not me, not my face
not what's hiding
under my shirt.
I speak up though I know my voice
will drown in the icebox
where frozen animals
hang.

Who cares if it exists or not.

In the racket I raise my hands
to the heavens.
How beautiful the angels are
dead
with their sad eyes watching us.

Karen Van Dyck

V
OUTSIDE ATHENS
Bookshops, Cafés, and Poets in the Provinces

Poetry has always happened outside of Athens as well as in – most notably, where the past century is concerned, in Greece's second city, Thessaloniki, but also in smaller cities, in provincial towns and on islands like Crete and Syros. The thriving literary scene that developed around salons and small presses in the 1970s and 1980s is continued today in a culture of café and bookshop readings; particularly representative are those run by Yiorgos Alisanoglou at his Thessaloniki bookshop Shakespearikon, which, with its own press, is as important as many in Athens. Concerned with their own communities yet also outward-looking, these poets are – aside from the diaspora poets of the final section – the most cosmopolitan of those collected here. Elsa Korneti channels Emily Dickinson; Vassilis Amanatidis's hipster verse could easily have been written in Brooklyn, while he maintains equal allegiance to *Enteftirion*, Thessaloniki's most respected literary magazine, and *Farmakon* in Athens. Olga Papakosta and Chloe Koutsoumbeli write poetry about living on the periphery and at a distance, both geographically and metaphorically. Others inhabit still smaller locales. Angeliki Sigourou writes her ecological verse in Syros. Giannis Palavos, a writer of very short stories with a poetic intensity, divides his time between Athens and his native Velventos. Then, in Ksanthi, there is the ironic, cynical Glykeria Basdeki; in Drama, the sardonic Kiriakos Sifiltzoglou; and, in Cavalla, Georgia Triandafillidou, with her modernist reappraisal of neighborly gossip. The last three particularly pick up on a tradition of provincial Balkan poetry, but also introduce a greater focus on language, as if to suggest that with the influx of migrants and refugees the edges of Greece are becoming more aware of their own melting pot of dialects.

YIORGOS ALISANOGLOU

(Born Kavala, Greece, 1975)

Yiorgos Alisanoglou is at the center of poetry life in northern Greece, known particularly for his book-length series of poems on religion and love, and most recently for *In an Irrational Direction*, an email correspondence with Thessaloniki's most distinguished living author, Dimitris Dimitriadis. Alisanoglou studied Sociology and International Relations at the University of Newcastle upon Tyne, and since 2005 he has run Thessaloniki's gathering place, bookstore and small publishing company, Shakespearikon. He has also translated the work of Charles Bukowski, Jim Morrison, Pink Floyd, Madrugada, Allen Ginsberg, and Joy Division.

Ακάνθινη πόλη (*City of Thorns*), Katsanos, 2007; *Το παντζάρι και ο διάβολος* (*The Beet and the Devil*), Tipothito, 2008; *Jesu Christiana: Μια μελλοντική προσευχή* (*Jesu Christiana: A Prayer for the Future*), Magiko Kouti & Fata Morgana, 2011; *ERO(S): 7 βήματα – 7 λεύγες εντός* (*7 Steps – 7 Leagues Inside*), Shakespearikon, 2011; *Παιχνιδότοπος – τραύμα για 9 μήνες & 3 εποχές* (*Playground – Wound for 9 Months & 3 Seasons*), Kihli, 2016.

Η ζωγραφιά

Πάντα στο ίδιο μέρος
στο ίδιο μέρος σε συναντώ –
γωνία Παύλου Μελά και Ομονοίας
Να περιμένεις στον πολύ ήλιο
με μια πελώρια ζωγραφιά στον ώμο
σαν πόλη
Οι τοίχοι της ασβεστωμένοι πολλάκις
και πάνω τους δαχτυλιές
από φθαρμένη νύχτα και τυπογραφείο
κι η ζωή σου ν' αργοσαλεύει
λίγο παρακεί σαν σημαία
Λέγε· Λέγε –
ποιανής πόλης σημαία είσαι
και πόσος θάνατος σε βρήκε;

The Painting

Always in the same place.
You in the same place –
the corner of Pavlos Mela
and Omonia Square
You wait in the bright sun
a huge painting weighs you down
like a city
its walls whitewashed over and over
with handprint smudges
from the dead night
and the print shop
Your life saunters along slowly
a little off center like a flag
Admit it! Admit it –
Which city's flag are you?
How many deaths
do you stand for?

Karen Van Dyck

GLYKERIA BASDEKI

(Born Larissa, Greece, 1969)

Poet and literary presence extraordinaire Glykeria Basdeki is loved for her work for the online culture magazine *Lifo*, where she writes pop culture posts and articles on esoteric topics like the Dog Collar Museum in Leeds. Having spent some years in Corfu and now living in Ksanthi, always making a living as a high-school teacher, Basdeki came late to the Athens literary scene, and even then gained recognition mostly through her poetic scripts for theater. Translations of some of the titles give a sense of their *Alice in Wonderland*-meets-Sarah Kane aesthetic: *Ramona Travel: The Land of Kindness*; *Donna Abbandonata, or, You Made Me Very Sad, My Dear Mr. George*; and *Ah!: (Re)reading the Wax Doll of Christomanos* (all 2014). Her lyric poetry, though it caught the attention of Jenny Mastoraki early on, has remained at the margins, perhaps because that is where it has its biggest impact; it speaks out about the life of women in small towns, reimagining the folksongs that often have them gagged, buried, and trapped.

Είναι επικίνδυνο ν' ανοίγεις την πόρτα σου σε άγνωστες μικρές (*It's Dangerous to Open Your Door to Young Girls You Don't Know*), Plethron, 1989; *Σύρε καλέ την άλυσον* (*Let Down the Chain*), Endymion, 2012, and Bibliotheque, 2014.

Σύρε καλέ την άλυσον

θα πιάνει κόκαλο
η αλυσίδα
γάλα θα φτύνουν
τα σχοινιά

ούτε να το σκεφτείς
το θαύμα ντάρνλινγκ

δεν έχεις
πιθανότητες
εδώ

τι κι αν
γυναίκα πρωτομάστορα

δεν πιάνουν
οι τίτλοι
στη Δεσμούπολη

GLYKERIA BASDEKI

Let Down the Chain

To drag up
the bones

The ropes
spit
milk

Don't even think
about it darling

No miracles
for you
here

Even if you're
the master builder's
wife

No one's got
pull
in Bondageville

Karen Van Dyck

Η μαμά είναι ποιήτρια

ω, ναι – η μαμά είναι
σπουδαία ποιήτρια
όλη τη μέρα μαγειρεύει κόμματα,
σκουπίζει χρόνους, σιδερώνει
πτώσεις

αντί να δει Δευτέρα βλέπει Τρίτη

λέει το πλυντήριο ωκεανό,
τη χύτρα υπερωκεάνιο

Όταν οι νοσοκόμες
παίρνουν τη ρεβάνς

μένουν
συνήθως
σύριγγες μιας χρήσης
στο
χαλί
κι ο ασθενής
εκλιπαρεί
για
ένα ακόμα
στριπτηζάκι

Mama's a Poet

Oh, yeah – Mama's
an important poet

all day she cooks up commas
sweeps tenses under the rug
irons the genitive

instead of Monday
she gives us Tuesday

for washer, she says ocean
for pressure cooker, ocean-liner

Karen Van Dyck

When the Nurses
Take their Vengeance

usually
disposable syringes
remain
on
the carpet
and the sick man
implores
one more
lap dance

Chloe Haralambous and Moira Egan

Θα 'ρθεις στα λόγια μου

το 'λεγαν θείες, μάνα, γειτονιά – πάντα κυλότα
καθαρή, δεν ξέρεις πότε
θα 'ρθει

το έμφραγμα, το
εγκεφαλικό, μια
απλή λιποθυμία, έστω

σαν έτοιμη από καιρό, εσύ

κυρία, αρχόντισσα

να μη γελάνε
οι γιατροί, να μην
κουτσομπολεύουν
νοσοκόμες

GLYKERIA BASDEKI

You'll Come Around

aunts, mothers, the whole neighborhood said it –
always wear clean knickers, you never know when
it might happen

a heart attack,
a stroke, a simple
fainting even

as one long prepared, you

Madam, Mistress

so the doctors
will not laugh, nor
the nurses
gossip

Chloe Haralambous and Moira Egan

Το τέρας

υπάρχουν κι οι μικρές της χορωδίας

με τις λευκές μάλλινες κάλτσες τους
τα ψύχραιμα λουστρίνια

αυτές μπορεί και να το αγαπήσουν
να το καλέσουν για καφέ ή βόλτα κυριακάτικη
στο Ζάππειο

το τέρας όμως πάντα μαγεμένο
πλην δέσμιο της ασχήμιας του

ξερνάει σε πάλκα βρόμικα

ψαλμούς ανάβει και χορεύει στοιχειωμένα βαλς

The Beast

Then there are the little choir girls

with their white woolen socks
their serene Mary Janes

they might even love it
might even invite it for coffee or a Sunday stroll
in Zappeion

The beast, however, held enchanted
in his ugliness

spews on dirty platforms

lights psalms and dances haunted waltzes.

Chloe Haralambous and Moira Egan

GIANNIS PALAVOS

(Born Velventos, Greece, 1980)

Giannis Palavos, an author of short stories, is widely rec-
ognized as one of Greece's best new writers. Some of his
vignettes, like the one included here, are so short that they
could almost be prose poems – and they are sufficiently
close in their style and intensity to the prose poetry of
Thomas Tsalapatis (p. 215) to make their inclusion in this
anthology instructive. Many take place in the farm town of
Velventos, near Kozani, where he grew up. After studying
journalism at Thessaloniki's Aristotle University, he com-
pleted an Arts Administration degree at Panteion University
in Athens. His short stories have won multiple prizes, includ-
ing the British Council's Best Short Story Award (2005) and
the Greek National Book Award (2014). His translations
from key post-nineteenth-century British and American
writers have appeared in numerous Greek journals and web
publications; among them, it is the understated tones of
Willa Cather and Donald Justice that seem to have affected
his own writing style the most.

Αστείο (*Joke*), Nefeli, 2012.

Password

Δυο καλοκαίρια ολόκληρα, όταν πήγαινα στο χωριό για διακοπές, έκλεβα δίκτυο από τον γείτονα. Στην αρχή το είχε ανοιχτό, χωρίς κωδικό. Όταν κατάλαβε ότι κάποιος τον έκλεβε, έβαλε password. Μια μέρα στο καφενείο τον ρώτησα την ημερομηνία γέννησής του, δήθεν ότι ήθελα να μάθω το ζώδιό του. Γύρισα σπίτι και πληκτρολόγησα τους αριθμούς. Δυο καλοκαίρια έτσι κατέβαζα μουσική. Ώς κι ευχετήρια κάρτα σκέφτηκα να του στείλω στα γενέθλιά του. Σήμερα, 19 Ιουνίου 2009, μόλις πήρα την άδειά μου, μπήκα στο λεωφορείο για το χωριό. Φτάνω και βλέπω απέναντι φέρετρο. Γνέφω στη μάνα μου. «Τον χτύπησε αυτοκίνητο» είπε. «Πήγε άδικα, τόσο νέος». Ανέβηκα στο δωμάτιό μου, άνοιξα το laptop και πληκτρολόγησα το password: δούλευε ρολόι.

Password

For two whole summers, when I'd go to the village on vacation, I'd piggyback internet from the neighbor. In the beginning he had the network open, no password. When he realized someone was stealing, he made one up. Sitting in the *kafeneion* one day I asked him his birthday. To figure out his zodiac, I said. I went home and typed in the date. For two summers that's how I downloaded music. I even considered sending him a birthday card. Today, June 19, 2009, I just got off for the summer and took the bus to the village. I arrive and see a coffin across the way. I turn to my mother. 'Hit by a car,' she said. 'So unjust, so young.' I went up to my room, opened my laptop, and put in the password: like clockwork.

Karen Van Dyck

ELSA KORNETI

(Born Thessaloniki, Greece, 1969)

Active in organizing readings and events with Yiorgos
Alisanoglou and other poets in the north, Elsa Korneti was
born in Munich, Germany, but grew up in Thessaloniki and
still lives there. Appropriately, given the long history of
cosmopolitanism in Greece's second city, there is a clear
glocalism at work in her poetry's interlacing of English and
other languages with Greek. Her career has been similarly
diverse: studies in finance were followed by work as a
journalist; she has published essays, book reviews, transla-
tions, short stories, and eight books of poetry. Her first two
poetry collections, *A Bouquet of Fishbones* and *The Tin Pearl*,
were nominated for the Greek National Poetry Award, and
her third, *Regular People with a Plume and a Brindled Tail*,
received the George Karter Award from the magazine
Porphyras.

Ένα μπουκέτο ψαροκόκαλα (*A Bouquet of Fishbones*), Gavrielides,
2009; *Κονσέρβα μαργαριτάρι* (*The Tin Pearl*), Gavrielides, 2011;
Κανονικοί άνθρωποι με λοφίο και ουρά (*Regular People with a
Plume and a Brindled Tail*), Gavrielides, 2014.

Μια ταλάντευση μόνο

Το κρινολίνο
είναι συμμετρικό
τόσο ζωντανό
Ταλαντεύεται
αιχμάλωτο κι αυτό
της ευπρέπειας
που ο Velasquez
μισούσε
Το υπάκουο παιδί
ελεύθερο
παραληρεί
μόλις η χαριτωμένη
Ινφάντα Μαργαρίτα
με οργή
στροβιλιστεί
σπάζοντας
την περίτεχνη
πορσελάνινη
αλατιέρα

A Slight Hesitation

What symmetry of line
to that crinoline
so rife with life
Such vitality
as it flutters fettered
to the propriety
that Velasquez
loathed
The obedient child
goes wild
without restraint
at the very instant
the delicious
Infanta Margarita
in one vicious
whirl
smashes
the fine
porcelain
salt cellar

Patricia Barbeito

Από σήμερα

Από σήμερα
Ζεις μια υποβρύχια ζωή
Μέσα στο σκοτάδι της αβύσσου
Πασχίζεις να παράγεις
Το δικό σου φως
Κολυμπώντας
Κάπως σαν εκείνα τα φρικαλέα ψάρια της αβύσσου
Με το φωτάκι που κρέμεται σαν έντερο
Εμπρός τους
Κινδυνεύοντας να προσβληθείς
Από τη νόσο του δύτη
Να γεμίσει το αίμα σου νερό
Να γίνεις
Μια φυσαλίδα
Να γκρεμιστείς στο άπειρο
Κυλώντας μέσα σ' ένα
Πελώριο
Συμπαντικό
Δάκρυ

As of Today

As of today
You live your life underwater
In the darkness of the deep
Struggling to emit
Your own light
Swimming
Like those freakish deep-sea fish
With that little lantern dangling gutlike
In front of them
Always in danger of falling prey
To divers' disease
Of having your blood fill with water
Of becoming
An air bubble
Of being extinguished in that immensity
Rolling around in a
Colossal
Cosmic
Tear

Patricia Barbeito

Καλέ μου φίλε

Καλέ μου φίλε ποτέ μην το ξεχνάς
Η σπείρα των ανθρωποειδών
Ελίσσεται με την κομψότητα
Του αλιγάτορα

Κι η φιλοδοξία οφείλει
Να υπερέχει της ηθικής

Τα μαλακά καπέλα των μανιταριών
στροβιλίζονται παρέα με μαύρες ομπρέλες
Ο κόμπος είναι τόσο απρόβλεπτος
όσο και μια αθόρυβη κυτταρική συμπλοκή
κι η κατσαρίδα ατάραχη αφήνει τα ίχνη της
σε άλλη μια εικαστική βόλτα στην ταπετσαρία
τ' Ουρανού εκείνη τη φθαρμένη την κακόγουστη

Ο εκκρεμής άνθρωπος κτισμένος στον τοίχο
ζει με συνέπεια κάτω από το άγρυπνο βλέμμα
του ρολογιού
Κάθε μεσάνυχτα ξεπροβάλλει από
το πορτάκι
Ανακοινώνει το καθήκον του
σαν ένας κούκος
με ξύλινη φωνή

Dear Friend

Dear friend don't ever forget
That the hordes of humanity
Go forth with the delicacy
Of the alligator

And that it is ambition's due
To conquer ethics

The pillowy caps of mushrooms
twirl hand in hand with black umbrellas
A knot is as unpredictable
as the silent collisions of cells
and the cockroach imperturbably leaves her trail
on yet another artful excursion over the worn
    and tacky tapestry of the Heavens.

That half-baked man immured in the wall
leads his life punctually under the sleepless eye
of the clock
At midnight he pops out
of the hatchway
Proclaiming his duty
in the wooden voice
of a cuckoo

Patricia Barbeito

ANGELIKI SIGOUROU

(Born Athens, Greece, 1973)

Though born in the capital, Angeliki Sigourou now lives on the island of Syros; her poetry's deep engagement with nature and the body is very much in keeping with the lifestyle of those who have increasingly come to depart Greece's cities over the past decade, moving back to its islands and villages to establish alternative farms and barter economies. She is the Artistic Director and choreographer of the Akropoditi Dance Theater Company, which is at once a vital part of local island culture and an extremely cosmopolitan enterprise, bringing performers and instructors to Syros from around the world. She graduated from the University of Athens in French Literature, having also studied Arabic, Dance, and Theater. Her poems have been translated into five languages, and her own translations include novels by Mahmoud Darwish and Naguib Mahfouz.

Αράς (*Cursed*), Elektra, 2008; *Χιόνι – χιόνι* (*Snow – Snow*), Nefeli, 2010.

Χρώματα

Κι ήρθαν τα χρώματα. Δεν υπήρχαν. Μα ελπίζαμε σ'
   αυτά
Στο απόλυτο και στο αντίθετό τους
σε όλα τα χρώματα μαζί και σ' ένα ένα χωριστά
ελπίζαμε.
Το χρώμα για το σύννεφο
Τη θάλασσα

Το δέντρο
Το αίμα
Το δέρμα
Τον ήλιο
Τον ουρανό της μέρας
Τον ουρανό της νύχτας
Το ξύλο
Το νερό
Το χώμα
Τη φωτιά

Τίποτα δεν χρωμάτισε καλύτερα ο κόσμος τούτος απ'
   το βάθος
Το χρώμα εκείνο του μεγάλου βάθους
ενώ στην επιφάνεια μόνο γαλάζιο και κόκκινο υπήρχε
            και ίσως κάπου κάπου το πρασινωπό
               χρυσό
Και η βαθιά αμαρτία στο εξής θα αποσιωπείται
για να μπορέσουμε να ονειρευτούμε έναν παράδεισο
   καινούργιο
της γνώσης
της συστολής

Colors

And the colors came. They didn't exist before. And we
    believed in them
In their absoluteness and antithesis
in all colors together and each one separately
we believed

The color of clouds
sea
trees
blood
skin
sun
day sky
night sky
wood
water
earth
fire

This world's success
            was the color it chose for the Deep
That color of the great Deep
        though on the surface only sky blue and red existed
            and perhaps here and there greenish gold
This is why Deep sin will grow silent
so that we can dream a new Paradise
of knowledge
of constraint

και των χρωμάτων των ανόθευτων
των δίχως ενοχές χρωμάτων
Να πάρειΣ σοβαρά τα ψέματά μου
Και με του βάθους χρώμα να χρωματίσειΣ της
  επιφάνειας την αλήθεια

> χρώμα δεν έχει ο ουρανός
> ούτε κι α θάλασσα
> ήταν ψεμα

of unadulterated colors
without guilt
Take my lies seriously
And with the color of Deep
          Color the surface of truth

> *Heaven has no color*
> *nor the sea*
> *It was a lie*

Karen Van Dyck

OLGA PAPAKOSTA

(Born Thessaloniki, Greece, 1966)

There is a maturity to Olga Papakosta's 2013 collection, *Not Carmen Yet*, that makes one forget it is her debut. Although she now lives and works in Athens, as a teacher and translator, it was in Thessaloniki that she was born, and there, at Aristotle University, that she studied Classics as an undergraduate. Her poems, sprinkled with English and pop references, remember her native city with a certain proprietary attitude that lends a wistfulness even to poems such as 'Empty Inbox' which deal with larger global predicaments. Her four collections of Cicero's writings were published by Okeanida in 2003 and 2004.

Όχι ακόμη Κάρμεν (*Not Carmen Yet*), Patakis, 2013.

No New Messages

Κανένα νέο μήνυμα

Όλα ληφθέντα
Αναγνωσθέντα
Διαγραφέντα

Και λίγα, ελάχιστα απ' αυτά
Αλησμόνητα

Οι νέοι φίλοι
Ποτέ δε θα 'ναι
Σαν τους παλιούς

Εκείνους που απλώς χτυπούσαν
Το θυροτηλέφωνο

Empty Inbox

You've not got mail

All messages
opened, read, deleted

Only a very few
unforgettable

The new friends
will never be
like the old ones

Those who just
rang the doorbell
and dropped in

Karen Van Dyck

CHLOE KOUTSOUMBELI

(Born Thessaloniki, Greece, 1962)

Published exclusively by Thessaloniki-based publishers until her most recent collection, Chloe Koutsoumbeli has kept the tradition of the strong poets of the northern provinces (Mihalis Ghanas, Markos Meskos) alive throughout her career, while giving it a feminist spin. Her work puts a spin, likewise, on the rich material of ancient myth; in these poems, stories and figures as familiar as Penelope are reworked until they appear to us in a new and contemporary light. Koutsoumbeli studied Law at Aristotle University and has worked in a bank for the past eighteen years. This last fact places her in yet another tradition: that of the most important woman poet of Greece's post-war generation, and another lifelong bank worker, Kiki Dimoula.

Σχέσεις Σιωπής (*Relations of Silence*), Egnatia, 1984; *Η νύχτα είναι μια φάλαινα* (*The Night is a Whale*), Loxias, 1990; *Η αποχώρηση της λαίδης Κάπα* (*The Departure of Lady Kappa*), Nea Poreia, 2004; *Στον αρχαίο κόσμο βραδιάζει πια νωρίς* (*In the Ancient World By Now It Gets Dark Early*), Gavrielides, 2012.

Το κίτρινο ταξί

Όχι κύριε με μπερδεύετε με κάποια άλλη.
Δεν ήμουνα εγώ
στο κίτρινο ταξί
ούτε καθόμουνα ποτέ στο πίσω κάθισμα μαζί σας.
Ούτε χιόνιζε, είμαι βέβαιη για αυτό
και όχι δεν έπεφταν νιφάδες στα μαλλιά μου.
Δεν έχω άλλωστε μαλλιά.
Δεν με φιλήσατε ποτέ, αλλιώς θα το θυμόμουν.
Και αν με φιλήσατε, εγώ δεν ήμουνα εκεί.
Ούτε ο οδηγός γύρισε καμία φορά πίσω το κεφάλι.
Σιωπηλά διέσχισε τη λίμνη ώς το τέλος
και πού και πού βύθιζε το κουπί
στα μαύρα ολόγυρα νερά.

The Yellow Taxi

No, sir, you are confusing me with someone else
It was not I
in the yellow taxi
nor did I ever sit in the back seat with you
It was not snowing, I am certain about that
and no, flakes did not fall into my hair
On the contrary, I did not have hair
You never kissed me, otherwise I would have
    remembered it
And if you had kissed me, I was, at any rate, not there,
Nor did the driver even once turn back his head
Silently he crossed the lake until the end
and now and then the oar dipped
into the black waters all around

A. E. Stallings

Πηνελόπη III

Γνωρίζει πια η Πηνελόπη
πως δεν είναι οι υπερφίαλες Σειρήνες
που τον καθυστερούν
ούτε η γερασμένη Κίρκη
με τον καταχωνιασμένο πόθο
ούτε κάποια κακομαθημένη Ναυσικά
εγκλωβισμένη σε λάθος ηλικία
με άσπρες κάλτσες και φουστάνια παιδικά.
Δεν είναι οι Λαιστρυγόνες και οι Λωτοί
που τον κρατούν μακριά της.
ούτε οι συντεχνιακοί μικροθυμοί του τάχα Ποσειδώνα
και τα μπλεξίματα με τους παλιούς συντρόφους.

Είναι που στον Αρχαίο κόσμο
βραδιάζει πια νωρίς
η Γη δεν είναι επίπεδη
και οι άνθρωποι κάποτε χάνονται.

Penelope III

Penelope knows by now
that it is not the insolent Sirens
who delay him
nor aging Circe
with her funneled-down longing
nor some spoiled Nausicaa
hemmed into the wrong age
with white socks and school-girl skirts
It is not the Laestrygonians, nor the lotuses
which keep him far from her
and not the trade-union tantrums of, perhaps, Poseidon
and the mix-ups with the old companions

It is that in the ancient world
by now it gets dark early
the earth isn't flat
and men sometimes get lost

A. E. Stallings

VASSILIS AMANATIDIS

(Born Edessa, Greece, 1970)

Vassilis Amanatidis's postmodern, post-feminist work picks up on what is going on in the international art scene and gives it back, transformed, from his standpoint on the edges of Europe. He studied History, Archaeology, and Art History at Aristotle University in Thessaloniki, where he currently lives. He is a poet, prose writer, translator, and performer, and also has a long-running affiliation with the literary magazines *Enteftirion* and *Farmakon*, which publish his poetry and reviews. His poems have been translated into thirteen languages.

> 7: *ποίηση για Video Games* (7: *Poetry for Video Games*),
> Nefeli, 2011; *μ-otherpoem: μόνο λόγος*
> (*m-otherpoem: mono-logos*), Nefeli, 2014.

[υπεροχή: το αίνιγμα]

Η μητέρα διατηρεί όλη την αμφισημία της.
Κατορθώνεται μέσω εκείνου που λέγεται άλεκτον.
Γιατί ναι, είναι και άλεκτη εκτός από αλέξανδρη.
Τούτο της εξασφαλίζει μια υπεροχή.
Θέτει το ον της σε ερμηνεία από τους άλλους.
Κάτι που μας καθιστά όλους ερμηνευτές της
        ερμηνεύτριας.
Είμαστε το κοινό της.

[το σώμα της μητέρας]

Η μητέρα υποθέτει ότι το υλικό μητέρας
        συμπεριλαμβάνει μία αγιότητα.
Σε κάθε περίπτωση, την ευπρόσδεκτη και οικειοθελή
        απομόνωση του μάρτυρα.
Έτσι κάνει τραμπάλα κατά το δοκούν μεταξύ
        μαρτυρίου και έκστασης.
Αυτή την τραμπάλα την κάνει μόνη της.

Μάλλον γίνεται γιατί – ε, το ξανάπαμε – δεν αγαπά το
        σώμα της.

Η μητέρα, στα 18, είναι ανορεξική.
Μετά τρώει σοκολάτες.
Τα σωματικά της υγρά τα απεχθάνεται.
Μάλλον δεν μπορεί να διανοηθεί ότι κάτι θα μπει, κάτι
        θα βγει από μέσα της.
Μέχρι και τις ανάγκες της τις κάνει στο σκοτάδι.

[supremacy: a riddle]

The mother preserves her ambiguity intact
Self-realization by means of what is said to be the unutterable
Indeed, she is both unapproachable and beyond language
This is what secures her supremacy
She lays open her very being to others' readings
And we become the interpreters of the Interpreter
We are her audience.

Patricia Barbeito

[mother's body]

The mother assumes that the stuff of motherhood
   incorporates a measure of saintliness
At the very least, the self-imposed, much desired
   isolation of the martyr
And so, as behooves her, she teeters between torture and
   ecstasy
By herself she teeters.

Possibly this happens because – well, it's already been
   said – she doesn't love her own body

At 18, the mother is anorexic
Later, she scarfs chocolates
She's disgusted by her bodily fluids
Probably she cannot wrap her mind around this fact:
Things both enter and exit from her body
Even when she relieves herself, she does so in the dark.

Patricia Barbeito

KIRIAKOS SIFILTZOGLOU

(Born Drama, Greece, 1983)

After completing degrees in Political Science and Law at Aristotle University in Thessaloniki, Kiriakos Sifiltzoglou returned to his hometown, Drama, where he now lives and works as a lawyer. He was included in Dinos Siotis's 2011 anthology *30 έως 30: Τριάντα ποιητές έως τριάντα ετών* (*30 by 30: Thirty Poets under Thirty*) along with Dimitris Athinakis (p. 7), Eftychia Panayiotou (p. 121), Z. D. Ainalis (p. 221), and Thodoris Rakopoulos (p. 385).

Έκαστος εφ' ω ετάφη (*Each to his Own Grave*), Gavrielides, 2007; *Μισές αλήθειες* (*Half Truths*), Melani, 2012; *Με ύφος Ινδιάνου* (*With the Style of an Indian*), Melani, 2014.

από Μισές Αλήθειες

3.

απ' το ύψος των περιστάσεων
εξαφανίστηκε το ύψος

πλέον έχουμε να κάνουμε
μόνο με περιστάσεις

το κατάλαβαν καλά

οι εναερίτες

    εμφανώς

καψαλισμένοι

14.

αν φερ' ειπείν αν η κακιά στιγμή ήταν
ένας αναπτήρας υγραερίου και έπρεπε
να πας σ' ένα περίπτερο να τον γεμίσεις
και διαπίστωνες έντρομος πως τα πελώρια
βυζιά της περιπτερούς συνέθλιβαν το
Ριζοσπάστη του περασμένου αιώνα
αλλάζοντάς σου τη γνώμη για τον
ισπανικό εμφύλιο

θα ανάβες
και αν ναι
θα το μετάνιωνες;

from *Half Truths*

3.

height has vanished
from the height of circumstances

now we deal only in circumstances

they knew it well: those riggers

who hovered

      seemingly

singed.

14.

say, for instance, as luck would have it,
you had a gas lighter that needed filling
at the corner kiosk and say, for instance,
that you went down there and, terrified,
caught the kiosk-matron's monumental tits
crushing last century's *Daily Worker*,
forcing you to revisit your thoughts
on the Spanish civil war

would you burn up
and, if so,
would you regret it?

26.

αν ένας νταλικέρης κορνάρει χαιρετώντας
τζιτζίκια και γρύλους μεταφέροντας 300
παλέτες ποιητικού υλικού βόρεια της
Δραμαμίνης μπορεί μπορεί και να τον
απασχολεί η δυαδικότητα της δομής μιας
κοινωνίας ή η έννοια της κοινωνικής
δράσης στη δραματουργική κοινωνιολογία

Σκατά   Λάστιχο

26.

truck-drivers who toot
saluting grasshoppers and crickets
as they transfer 300 bales of poetic material
north of Dramamine might – might – be concerned
with the structural duality of a society
or with the concept of social agency
in dramaturgical sociology.

Shit Tires.

Chloe Haralambous

GEORGIA TRIANDAFILLIDOU

(Born Thessaloniki, Greece, 1968)

Georgia Triandafillidou studied Modern Greek Literature in her native Thessaloniki, and since 2000 has lived in Kavalla. Like the Northern Epirot short stories of Sotiris Dimitriou, her poetry takes off from what people say, from conversations overheard in villages, from the mingled idioms of the North (annexed much later than the rest of Greece), and therefore also from Turkish, Vlach, Arvanitika, and other Balkan and regional dialects. She is published by Agra, Greece's most innovative publisher both in content and design; her eclectic work lives up to that reputation.

Ο ποιητής έξω (*The Poet Outside*), Agra, 2004; *Δικαίωμα Προσδοκίας* (*Right of Expectation*), Agra, 2008.

Ξαφνική ιδεοληψία σε συγγενικό σπίτι

Το πιάτο που μας έφερε η γειτόνισσα
γεμάτο ψάρια καθαρισμένα
είναι η χαρά μας.
Το πιάτο που μας έφερε η γειτόνισσα
το πιάτο.
Ψάρια αλατισμένα με πεθαμένα μάτια
μας έφερε η γειτόνισσα
πάει η χαρά μας.
Ψάρια αλατισμένα με πεθαμένα μάτια
τα μάτια.
Το πιάτο που μας έφερε η γειτόνισσα
στάζει στον πάγκο δυο γραμμές ψαρίλα.
Τα φρύδια της γειτόνισσας τρέχουν να ενωθούνε
ο ιδρώτας πια δε στάζει μες στα μάτια της.
Το πιάτο που μας έφερε η γειτόνισσα
φρύδια, σαφρίδια
σμιχτά αλάτια ιδρωμένα λέπια
το πιάτο που μας έφερε η γειτόνισσα
καν' το κομμάτια. Ματιάζει.

Sudden Obsession at a Relative's House

The plate the neighbor lady brought us
full of cleaned fish
is our joy.
The plate the neighbor lady brought us
the plate.
Dead-eyed salted fish
the neighbor lady brought us
gone is our joy.
Dead-eyed salted fish
the eyes.
The plate the neighbor lady brought us
dribbles two fishy lines on the bench.
The neighbor lady's eyebrows race to connect
sweat no longer drips into her eyes.
The plate the neighbor lady brought us
eyebrows, horse mackerel
mixed salted sweaty scales
the plate the neighbor lady brought us
smash it into pieces. It evil-eyes.

George Economou

VI
BORDER ZONES
Poets between Cultures and Languages

Shifting decisively beyond the confines of a single country, this section is necessarily the most varied. What characterizes this group is the central importance of another place to their poetry: these poets came late to the Greek language from other lands and tongues, or – though still writing in Greek – now live or spend considerable time in other countries, speaking other languages. As both immigrants and emigrants, moreover, they share the diasporic multilingualism so often ignored in national accounts of Greek literary history. Many are translators, translating one another or themselves. Often they are in academia, where their subjects are linguistic and cultural difference in a wide range of fields. Their poems address these concerns in form and theme. Mehmet Yashin writes macaronic works, mingling Greek and Turkish on the page. This is a more Balkan, between-worlds perspective which he shares with Stathis Gourgouris – both of them older than the others here and more recognized outside of Greece. Iana Boukova, Moma Radić, and Hiva Panahi bring the influence of Balkan and Middle Eastern languages – Bulgarian, Serbian, and Persian, respectively – to bear on Greek. Dimitris Allos is Greek, but also publishes in Bulgarian, translating Boukova, who translates him in turn. Gazmend Kapllani's early poetry mingles Albanian and Greek. And then there is the European side. Theodoros Chiotis, Christos Angelakos, and Yannis Livadas circulate among them between London, Paris, and Athens, drawing on a wide range of influences from the Beats to recent experimental code poetry. Thodoris Rakopoulos, an anthropologist who lives in Bergen and Athens, reworks the divided life into an experimental poetics. Not surprisingly, these are also the poets whose work has inspired the most experimental translation.

DIMITRIS ALLOS

(Born Athens, Greece, 1963)

The publisher and one of the founding members of *Ah, Maria* (1990–94), the first independent literary magazine in Bulgaria after the fall of Communism, Dimitris Allos lives and works at the intersection of Bulgarian and Greek. His poetry has been translated into Bulgarian and he translates Bulgarian literature into Greek, including that of Iana Boukova (p. 339) before she began writing in Greek herself. Like hers, his poetry is full of animals and plants, but unlike the poets associated with *Farmakon* magazine, nature for him is more worldly, often urban, and sometimes even urbane. He studied Sociology at Sofia University but returned to Athens and has lived there since the mid-1990s. His poems have also been translated into Spanish, French, Italian, and English.

Ψηλός στα άχυρα (*Tall in the Hay*), Kastaniotis, 2000; *Φωνές που δεν γλύτωσαν* (*Unspared Voices*), Arts Foundation, 2002.

ή
Τα άσπρα της σκεύη

«. . . κι εγώ που τρώω μνήμη
σαν κυκλαδίτικο μνημείο . . .»

Δε θυμάμαι πια το όνομά της

το πρόσωπό της ίσως ένα
γκρέμισμα τώρα μετανάστες
κομμένο το ρεύμα

θυμάμαι όμως καλά λιακάδα ήτανε

μεσημέρι

χλωρός ιδρώτας
σκόνη ιδιωτικού δρόμου

χέρι Θεού κατάστηθα θυμάμαι
που μάλαζε τα ψυχικά υλικά

κι εσένα
να αμολάς τους δαλματίνους στο δωμάτιο

γιεπ-γιεπ

να με φιλεύεις το σαββατιανό
να με ταΐζεις το σταφύλι

ρώγα τη ρώγα

or
Her White Utensils

'. . . and I who feed on memory
like a cycladic monument . . .'

I no longer remember her name

her face perhaps
a precipice, now refugees
electricity cut off

but I remember clearly a sun drenched

midday

fresh sweat
dust of a private alley

God's hand right on my chest
I remember kneading my soul's material

and you
letting the dalmatians free in the room

oaou ouaou

treating me to black grapes
feeding me

grape by grape

τα χέρια μου να λερώσω
στον πολιτισμό του κορμιού της

βαθιά

έως το μέσα των σύννεφων

To dirty my hands
with the civilization of her body

deep

down to the innards
of the clouds

Katerina Anghelaki-Rooke

IANA BOUKOVA

(Born Sofia, Bulgaria, 1968)

A bilingual poet, Iana Boukova studied Classics in Bulgaria before moving to Athens in 1994. In Bulgarian, she has published two books of poetry, a collection of short stories and a novel; before she began writing in Greek, a volume of her poetry was also translated by Dimitris Allos (p. 333) and published by Greece's most established poetry publisher, Ikaros. The list of poets whom she has translated into Bulgarian reads like a who's who of important poetic influences for this new generation, among them Giorgos Seferis, Odysseas Elytis, Yannis Ritsos, Katerina Anghelaki-Rooke, and Jenny Mastoraki. She is a member of the online platform *Greek Poetry Now!* (see Further Reading) and has been involved in *Farmakon* magazine since its inception. The crossover with that group is clear in her poetry's themes: dreams, animals, nature. Her poems have also been translated into Spanish, French, Hungarian, Albanian, Serbian, Swedish, and English.

Ο ελάχιστος κήπος (*The Minimal Garden*), Ikaros, 2006.

Ο ελάχιστος κήπος

Άνοιξες την πόρτα
και ήταν που λες μέσα η νύχτα
παγιδευμένη
χωρίς ψωμί για βδομάδες ολόκληρες
Τέτοιος άνθρωπος είσαι
αφήνεις τις βρύσες ανοιχτές
τις πληγές να ματώνουν
φοράς τα γυαλιά σου ανάποδα
και με βλέπεις
με τα παιδικά μου τα παπούτσια
και την κάλτσα κάτω απ' το γόνατο
Ναι αλλά τα γόνατά μου μεγάλωσαν
σαν της Αλίκης
πήρε ο κήπος μας φωτιά απ' το πολύ φεγγάρι
και οι φωνές των καλεσμένων
ακόμα κυνηγάνε το γατάκι
μέσα στο πηγάδι
Τώρα βλέπω το δωμάτιο
κάπου από ψηλά
μικρό στο βάθος το κρεβάτι μου
Άγρια πράγματα αποκρουστικά
προκρούστικα.

The Minimal Garden

You opened the door
and there it was: the night
trapped
for weeks on end with no bread to eat
That's the kind of person you are
you leave taps running
wounds bleeding
you wear your glasses inside out
you see me wearing the shoes I wore as a child
and my stockings up to my knees
But my knees grew like Alice's
our garden caught fire because of too much moonshine
and the voices of our guests are still after the kitten
in the well
Now I see the room
from somewhere high up
in the background my little bed
Wild things
provocatively ugly
Procrustean.

Katerina Anghelaki-Rooke

Μαύρο χαϊκού

«Είδα δύο σκουλήκια να περνούν
δίπλα από ένα κόκαλο»
είπε ο πατέρας μου
Ήταν νεκρός και απλά συζητάγαμε
(Το όνειρο αυτό είναι πραγματικό
και κάθε ομοιότητα με την ποίηση
εντελώς τυχαία)
«Τι λες;» του λέω
«Τίποτα» λέει
«Απλά δυο σκουλήκια
πέρασαν δίπλα από το πόδι σου»
«Αρκετά μαύρο χαϊκού
δε νομίζεις;» του λέω
Γελάσαμε κι αλλάξαμε κουβέντα

Το όνειρο ήταν γεμάτο έντομα
σμήνη από μαύρες μύγες
και κάτι μεγάλα παράξενα μυρμήγκια
που παρατηρούσα από αφύσικα κοντά
χωρίς τον πανικό που με καταβάλλει
στην παρουσία των εντόμων

Υπάρχει μια παγωμένη ησυχία
που κάνει τον φόβο ωραία ανάμνηση

Τρόμαζα μικρή με τα σκουλήκια
άλλαζα πορεία όταν τα συναντούσα
τις μέρες με βροχές
Έμοιαζαν με φλέβες
που σέρνονται στο χώμα
ή με λεπτά ζωντανά εντόσθια
μετά από κάποια περίτεχνη κρεουργία

Black Haiku

'I saw two worms pass
next to a bone'
my father said
He was dead and we were simply talking
(It was a real dream
and any similarity to poetry
purely accidental)
'What do you mean?' I say
'Nothing' he says, 'it was just
that two worms passed next to your foot'
'Quite a dark *haiku*
don't you think?' I tell him
We both laughed and changed the subject

The dream was full of insects
a swarm of black flies
and some large, strange ants
which I watched unnaturally close
without the panic that overwhelms me
in the presence of insects

There's a kind of frozen quiet
that makes the fear a pleasant recollection

I was scared of worms as a child
I changed direction when I came across them
on rainy days
They looked like veins
that crawl over the ground
or like thin, live entrails
after some elaborate massacre

Μαζί κι αυτή η φρικιαστική
κυματοειδής κίνησή τους
όταν όλη η ύπαρξη ορμάει προς τα μπρος
σχεδόν αδειάζοντας ό,τι απομένει

Αργότερα σκέφτηκα ότι έτσι
μετακινείται ο χρόνος

Όπως και οι κάμπιες
Πριν από μέρες είδα στο μπαλκόνι μου
πως τα μυρμήγκια έφαγαν μία ζωντανή
(Είναι σκηνές που συμβαίνουν
ακόμα και στο κέντρο της Αθήνας)
Παρατηρούσα σαν το μάτι από τον Ουρανό
Συλλογιζόμουν – με οργή –
ότι αυτή είναι η στάση του σώματος
που αγαπάνε οι μονοθεϊστικές θρησκείες
Το σώμα με σπασμένη ραχοκοκαλιά
το σερνάμενο
                    το εξευτελισμένο

Η οργή περνάει
Αυτή η κίνηση μένει

Και πάλι σκεπτόμουν – αργότερα –
μήπως αυτές είναι οι στιγμές
που η ψυχή παρακάμπτεται
και το ίδιο το σώμα έχει ανάγκη από Θεό
Μια ανάγκη φυσιολογική
αμετάκλητη
όπως όλες οι υπόλοιπες
ταπεινή εξίσου
στις γλιστερές σωληνώσεις
στη μέσα σφαγή

On top of that there was their freaky
wavelike movement
as if the whole of existence rushes forward
almost emptying out whatever remains

Later I thought
this is how time moves
Or like the caterpillar
On my balcony just a few days ago
I saw the ants eat one alive
(the scenes that take place
even in the center of Athens)
I watched like an eye from the sky
contemplating – with rage –
that this is the shape of the body
that monotheistic religions prefer
The body with a broken spine
crawling
         humiliated

The rage passes
This movement remains

And I was thinking again – later –
maybe these are the moments
when the soul is overcome
and the body itself craves God
A natural need
nonnegotiable like all others
similarly humble
within the slippery conduits
the slaughter inside

Adrianne Kalfopoulou

Στον Μίλτο Σαχτούρη

Να την αγαπάμε την τρέλα μας
που μας χορεύει
με μια μουσική πηχτή
σαν σύννεφο
που κολλάει στα δόντια
την τρέλα μας ν' αγαπάμε
το καμένο φαΐ των αστροναυτών
κοντά κοντά στον απόλυτο ήλιο
κοντά κοντά στον απρόσμενο ήλιο
να τη σεβόμαστε
όταν ξυπνάμε με μάτια ορθάνοιχτα
μεσάνυχτα μαύρα
και βλέπουμε το μαύρο
με όλα του τα χρώματα
να την αγαπάμε
όπως αγαπάει ο βοσκός τη βέργα του
όταν την μπήγει στο χώμα
και λέει εδώ σταματάω
και σπάει στα χέρια του

For Miltos Sachtouris

Let us love our madness
she dances for us
with opaque music
like a cloud
that sticks to our teeth
let us love our madness
the burnt food of astronauts
side by side with the absolute sun
side by side with the unexpected sun
let us respect our madness
when we wake up with wide open eyes
in the middle of the blackest night
and we see all the shades
of black
let us love our madness
the way the shepherd loves his staff
when he thrusts it in the ground
and says: this is where I stop
and it breaks in his hands.

Katerina Anghelaki-Rooke

Fractal

Μερικές φορές το νερό
φτάνει πιο ψηλά από τις μπότες
κι όλα γίνονται στενά
και γεμάτα κραυγές σαν σχολείο

Αλλά εγώ επιμένω
να σου μιλάω στον ενικό
παρόλο που κάθε ύπαρξή σου
έχει την στιγμή της
και το πλήθος τους
θυμίζει πια στρατόπεδο συγκέντρωσης
όπου είμαι αναγκασμένη
να επιβάλλω την τάξη

Πίστεψέ με
εγώ μόνο διαταγές εκτελούσα
Ήμουν σώμα
Παρέλασα κι εγώ
με τα μπαρόκ τάγματα του χάους

Ο χρόνος είναι έγκλημα

Fractal

Sometimes the water
reaches higher than boots
and everything becomes cramped
and full of screams like a school

But I still insist
on speaking to you in the singular
although every one of your existences
has its moment
and their crowds
suggest a concentration camp
where I have no choice but
to enforce measures

Believe me
I was only following orders
I was a body
I marched too
within the baroque units of chaos

Time is crime

Adrianne Kalfopoulou

THEODOROS CHIOTIS

(Born Athens, Greece, 1977)

Theodoros Chiotis is equally at home in Greek and English; it is hard to know which language each poem might have started life in, since they are often developed simultaneously in both. He studied Classics at the University of London and at Oxford and is currently a D.Phil. candidate in Modern and Medieval Languages at Oxford. His research interests include Greek literature and geographies of language. Under his direction the Cavafy Archive at the Onassis Foundation in Athens has focused on multimedia translation, digitalization, and school outreach programs. He has edited an anthology of Greek crisis poetry in English for Penned in the Margins (see Further Reading). His first collection, *Theory of the Machine*, is forthcoming from Farmakon (2016).

Ζώνες διαβίβασης

1.

«Ας ειπωθεί
στον κόσμο του μέλλοντος»:

θα μπορούμε να αναπνέουμε ακόμη κι
    όταν ο αέρας γίνει πυκνότερος.

Μαθαίνουμε από τον Δρ. Μορώ
    τους απαιτούμενους κώδικες για τη σύνθεση νέων
    προσώπων.

2.

Στρατιώτες του θέρους
ζηλωτές του λυκόφωτος
σπίτια που έγιναν στρατώνες.
Όλα αυτά είναι απόηχοι των προηγούμενων χρόνων:

«Δεν χρησιμοποιήσαμε σωστά τον
προηγούμενο χειμώνα,
            μα δεν μπορούσαμε να κάνουμε κι αλλιώς,
για όσο βρισκόμασταν σε καθεστώς υποτέλειας».

3.

Παίξε Grand Theft Auto.
Ξάπλωσε στο χώμα.
Μη δημιουργείς φασαρίες.

Μια εισβολή, περιγεγραμμένη σε μια κάποτε γνωστή
    γλώσσα:

Zones of Frequency

1.

'Let it be told
to the future world':

We will still be able to breathe
    when the air turns thicker.

We are learning from Doctor Moreau
    the codes needed to assemble new faces.

2.

Summer soldiers
twilight zealots
homes turned into barracks.

All these are echoes of previous years:

'We did not make proper use of
last winter,
        neither could we,
while we were in a dependent state'

3.

Play Grand Theft Auto.
Lay on the ground.
Don't cause trouble.

An invasion, described in a once familiar language:

«Αν δεν συνεισφέρεις στο κίνημα
τότε γιατί είσαι εδώ;»

4.

Δώσε (το) σώμα (σου)
σε αυτό που δεν σου μοιάζει.

Μπορεί να το βλέπεις διαφορετικά αλλά
το Ψυχώ δεν αναφερόταν ποτέ στην υγιεινή.

5.

Οδηγίες:

Μείνε ακίνητος.
Σκόρπισε την ιλαρότητα.
Διάλυσε τη μάζωξη.
Κατάλαβε και τα τέσσερα ημισφαίρια.
Επανάλαβε κάτι που δεν υπήρχε ώς τώρα.

6.

Ένας χάρτης για ένα νέο αναπνευστικό σύστημα.
Υποξείδιο του αζώτου αντικατεστημένο από
    δακρυγόνο.
Τα όρια ανάμεσα στο κεφάλι και το πρόσωπο
    καταρρέουν.

    Τώρα: χάραξε κατά μήκος του καμβά.

'If you are not contributing to (the) movement
then why are you here?'

4.

Give (your) body
to what does not resemble you.

You might think otherwise but
Psycho was never about hygiene.

5.

Instructions:

Sit still.
Displace the mirth.
Break the meeting.
Occupy all four hemispheres.
Repeat something that did not exist until now.

6.

A map for a new respiratory system.
Nitrous oxide replaced by tear gas.
Our head and face boundaries collapse.

    Now: cut across the canvas.

                    Self-translated

CHRISTOS ANGELAKOS

(Born Athens, Greece, 1962)

Christos Angelakos is an ardent fan of Amy Winehouse, and listens to music while he writes, often channeling the rhythms directly into his poetry and prose. His macabre imagination is fueled by the gothic strain in both French- and English-language traditions. He studied Byzantine and Modern Greek Studies at the University of Athens and at the Sorbonne with a dissertation on the poet and novelist Aris Alexandrou. He has published two novels and a collection of poetry, and translated Jean Starobinski's essays into Greek. He writes criticism for Greece's best literary magazines and has created a series for the National Radio Station on the poets and prose writers of the Generation of the 1970s.

Τα φώτα απέναντι (*The Lights across the Way*), Ikaros, 2008.

Αν βυθιστείς μες στο κεφάλι σου
κανείς δε θα μπορέσει να σε σώσει

ούτε οι δύτες που πυκνώνουν στο ναυάγιο
ανοίγοντας κιβώτια και βγάζοντας νομίσματα
χτενάκια από φίλντισι και γιορτινούς ταφτάδες

ούτε η γυναίκα που έγραψε τη μοίρα σου
κρατώντας το ράμφος ενός σφαγμένου
κόκορα σαν πένα

ούτε κι εγώ
που απόψε το 'θελα πολύ να μην υπάρχεις

If you dive inside your head
no one can save you

not the divers who fill the shipwreck
opening boxes and removing coins,
ebony combs and party taffetas

nor the woman who wrote your fate
with the beak
of a sacrificial rooster for a pen

nor I
who wish tonight
you didn't exist

Karen Van Dyck

YANNIS LIVADAS

(Born Kalamata, Greece, 1969)

The poetry of Yannis Livadas focuses on opening up poetic forms through the juxtaposition of different languages and traditions. He never fulfilled his Greek military service and refused to participate in formal schooling or attend university because of his individualist and anarchist beliefs. In both his own poetry and his literary criticism he promotes artistic production in which indeterminacy of meaning as well as syntactical and structural innovation, what he calls *organic antimetathesis*, is paramount. Poetry for him is an autonomous creative act, not expressive of anything else. His poems have been translated into English, French, Indian (Bangla), Croatian, Irish, Spanish, Serbian, and Hungarian. He is also an editor, critic, translator, and independent scholar. He lives in Paris, France, and blogs at livadaspoetry. blogspot.fr.

Άπτερος Νίκη/Μπίζνες/Σφιγξ (*Apteral Nike/Business/Sphinx*), Iridanos, 2008; *John Coltrane & 15 Poems for Jazz,* **Marimbo Press, 2008;** *The Margins of a Central Man*, **Graffiti Kolkata,** 2010; *Kelifus,* **Cold Turkey Press, 2011;** *Ravaged by the Hand of Beauty*, **Cold Turkey Press, 2011;** Άτη – Σκόρπια ποιήματα 2001-2009 (*Ati – Scattered Poems 2001–2009*), Kedros, 2011; *La Chope Daguerre + ποιήματα κελύφους* (*La Chope Daguerre + Husk Poems*), Kedros, 2013; Ηχούν οστά (*Sound Bones*), Iolkos, 2014; **Strictly Two, Sea Urchin Editions, 2015;** Το ξίγκι της μύγας (*The Fat of the Fly*), Kedros, 2015; Μοντάρτ (*Modart*), Alloglotta Editions, 2015.

από τις *Μπάσταρδες Ελεγείες*

1.

Μετά από πολλά χειρόγραφα
προτιμώ τις χοντρές μου θείες
που λένε πως είμαι ευγενικός
ό,τι περνάει μέσα μου περνά στον θάνατο
οι χοντρές μου θείες είναι κήρυκες
μιλάνε σε άγνωστα λουλούδια που βαθύνονται
σονέτα αναπολούν τη μουσική τους
αμύθητα αυγά της ύπαρξης σπάνε
μέσα στο καρμικό προθαλάμιο στόμα της έχιδνας
σε έναν κόσμο αναισθητικό βαθύνομαι
με την ασκαυλική μου διάλεκτο
ο παλμογράφος μιας νέας φαντασίας
χωράει στη χάρτινη βαλίτσα μου
αν η ψυχή θελήσει την ψυχή να πυρπολήσει
έχω μια γρήγορη σκέψη ωστόσο αργοκίνητη
ένα προαίσθημα για όραμα της γλώσσας
γράφοντας στο απόβροχο παρελθόν
όλα είναι μια τρομερή αλήθεια
την αυριανή νύχτα.

from *Bastard Elegies*

1.

After so many manuscripts
I like most my fat aunties
Who say I'm gentle.
Whatever passes through me passes through death.
My fat aunties are heralds
Who speak to unknown flowers that deepen.
Sonnets recall their music,
Fabulous eggs of existence break
In the karmic antechamber mouth of the viper.
Into an anaesthetic world I deepen
With my bagpipe dialect;
The pulse meter of a new fantasy
Fits into my paper suitcase.
If soul wishes soul to set fire
I have a swift thought yet slow:
A foreboding vision of language
Writing in the after-the-rain past.
Everything is a ghastly truth
The night after.

Self-translated

Jazz, Λέω

(στο Lee Morgan)

Είναι τόσο υπόγειο αυτό
Το παίξιμο
Όπως μια νυχτερινή φωτιά
Στου άδειου δρόμου τα απομεινάρια
Τόσο ζεστή
Και αναγκαία
Και
Αρχαία που όλοι
Οι άνθρωποι του δρόμου
Πλησιάζουν
Τα χέρια τους
Πάνω της
Γύρω γύρω
Αυτό είναι το
Απόγειο –
Αυτό είναι το παίξιμο.

Jazz, I Say

(*to Lee Morgan*)

It's so subterranean
the playing
       like a nightly fire
on the remains of the empty street
so hot
          and needed
          and
             ancient where all
the street guys
approach
       their hands
          over it
     'round and 'round
    it's the
   tops –
  it's the playing

Jack Hirschman and Dimitri Charalambous

Συγκαιρία

Η σχέση ανάμεσα σε δύο υπάρξεις:
Το κενό που ανάμεσά τους γλιστράει.

Μέσα από τα παράθυρα
βλέπεις των ψυχών τα τζάμια.

Κάθε γενικό σκληραίνει.

Ενώ την αυτοπεποίθησή σου ενισχύω

Βιώνοντας τώρα
μια επιστροφή στον χάρτη,
ή τελικώς βιώνοντας την ορθή διάσταση
ανακαλύπτοντας ενός εαυτού το κυνήγι.
Η ζωή ετούτη ξεμπερδεύτηκε εδώ και χρόνια από τη
φαντασία μου.
Το στομάχι, ένα τασάκι που χωνεύει της ανθρωπότητας
τις γόπες.
Έχω αρχίσει να μισώ τη γραφή, μα όχι ακόμα τον εαυτό
μου ως γράφοντα.
Ο ρόλος που υποδύομαι εξακολουθεί άγνωστος.
Πριν ρίξω όλη ετούτη τη σαβούρα στα σκουπίδια μαζί
με τα απομεινάρια της
μέρας,
σκύβω λιγάκι για να περάσω
κάτω από την αψίδα που η κενότητα τσάκισε τη ράχη
της πριν από αιώνες.

Αυτομεταφρασμένο

Synchronization

The relation between the two existences:
the emptiness that among them is slithering.

Through windows you see
the panes of the souls.

Everything general toughens.

Self-translated

As I Am Boosting Your Confidence

Experiencing now
a comeback on the map,
or finally experiencing the right aspect
discovering the hunt of a self.
This life disentangled years ago from my imagination.
The stomach, an ashtray digesting the butts of humanity.
I have started to hate writing, but not myself as a
writer yet.
The role I play remains unknown.
Before I scrap all this trash along with the
leftovers of the day,
I bend a little to pass
under the arch where emptiness broke its
back centuries ago.

Composed in English

Κάθομαι σ' όλες τις καρέκλες

Κάθομαι σ' όλες τις καρέκλες
Γιατί δεν υπάρχει θέση
Για την τέχνη

Που ξεκίνησε το
2008 το 2011
Ή το 2012

Σταγόνες απ' το πουκάμισό μου
Που στεγνώνει.

Οι καμπανιές της Σεν Ζενεβιέβ

Καθότι οι κλώνοι δεν είναι θεματοφύλακες·
Οι δημοκράτες είναι φτιαγμένοι
Να πέφτουν από τα σύννεφα.

Το αδυσώπητο επικεφαλής.
Μια νύχτα στεφάνι στο απροκάλυπτο.
Τα προβλήματα είναι λύση.

Τα οστά μου σούπα
Μέσα στου τάφου μου
τη λάσπη.

My Bones in the Soup of My Grave

I sit on every chair
because there is no proper place
for the art
established
in 2008, 2011
or 2012;

Water-drops off my drying shirt.

The chimes of St. Genevieve.

My ruthless head granted as a custodian by
the issues of spirit.

What an ordeal;

My bones in the soup
of the mud inside
my grave.

Self-translated

Στο σταντ του *La Manne* στο
90 της *Claude Bernard*

Αυτό είναι αρχείο μέχρι να πάψει να είναι.
Πάρλες.
Λίγο κρύο από τους αγκώνες και κάτω.

Όταν κάθε αποτυχία θα κερνάει βασισμένη
στα στατιστικά που θα τη φέρνουν πρώτη
στην εκτίμηση των πολιτών,
θα αποτελεί δύναμη.
Μας περικλείουν τα αναρριχητικά των ενημερώσεων·
η έγνοια μου μια κόρα
βουτηγμένη στου ήλιου τη σιωπηρή λάμψη.

Ο αέρας παίρνει μια κάρτα με την εικόνα
ενός λιμανιού με φορτωμένα μουλάρια.
Το χρονικό διάστημα που στρέφεται προς το μέρος μου
βρίσκεται αντιμέτωπο με τα ελαττώματά του.

Δυο τρεις στόμφοι.
Η κατευθυνόμενη αφθαρσία βρυχάται για Πλειάδες.

Η σημασία ως ατυχής έννοια
είναι αποκλειστικά
ανθρώπινη.

At the Book Stand of La Manne,
90 Claude Bernard Street

This is an archive until it will cease to be.
Gab.
A little cold under the elbows.
When every failure will pay for drinks based on
The statistics which celebrate its run first
To the public opinion,
It will be a main form of power.
The clinging vines of the newsreel enclose us;
My concern a crust
Dunked in the tacit glare of the sun.
The wind blows away a postcard bearing the image
Of a harbor full of loaded mules.
The temporal timespan that turns towards me
Comes up against its defects.
A couple of rants.
The guided imperishability is growling for Pleiades.

The meaning as an unfortunate sense
Is exclusively
Human.

Self-translated

MOMA RADIĆ

(Born Niš, Serbia, 1969)

For the minimalist writer Moma (Momčilo) Radić, even a single letter might constitute a line of poetry. His first poems were published in Yugoslavia, where, in 1986, he was a member of the literary youth. After studying Classics in Belgrade and French Literature in Paris, he moved to Athens on a tourist visa in 1993; war came to his homeland, and he never returned. He has written in Greek while teaching French and Serbo-Croatian ever since. Radić has translated the poetry of the surrealist poet Nikos Engonopoulos, as well as poets from the Generation of the 1970s such as Antonis Fostieris and Maria Laina. He has also translated the poetry of Yannis Livadas in this section (p. 361). He published his first book in Greek, *Serbian Folktales,* in 2004. His first Greek poetry collection followed in 2010.

Πόρτα (Door), Apopeira, 2010.

Μεσημέρι

Περιμένεις
τη βροχή σα δάχτυλο
καλείς τα σύννεφα
που φέρνουν χάδια
κενά

Η όψη της καρδιάς σου
γλιστρά σαν σαλιγκάρι

Κι όσα λάμπουν
πόδια φιδιών μπράτσα σώματα
ιδρωμένα

πίσω τους
αφήνουν σημάδι

Noon

You await
the rain like a finger
you invite the clouds
bearing vacant
caresses

The face of your heart
slips like a snail

And all things that glow
feet of snakes arms bodies
in sweat

leave traces
behind.

Chloe Haralambous and Moira Egan

Αλήθεια;

Άκουσες τα μυρμήγκια
να φτερνίζονται
αλλεργικά
σε θραύσματα
αναλλοίωτα;

Πώς να μαζέψουν ύστερα
από τόσους πολιτισμούς
τις νεκρές λέξεις
που μου έμαθες
φεύγοντας;

Τραυλός ψαράς

στη σιωπή του σπαρταρούν ψάρια

τραγουδάει καλύτερα
τη θάλασσα που τελειώνει
στα ανοιχτά τους στόματα

Ν

Really?

Did you hear the ants
sneezing
allergically
in fixed
shards?

After so many civilizations
how can they gather
the dead words
you taught me
as you left?

Chloe Haralambous and Moira Egan

Stammering Fisherman

fish writhe in his silence

he sings it better:
the sea that finishes
in their open mouths

N

Chloe Haralambous and Moira Egan

GAZMEND KAPLLANI

(Born Lushnje, Albania, 1967)

Best known for his novels exploring totalitarianism, immigration, borders, and Balkan history, Gazmend Kapllani is a Greek-Albanian writer and recent émigré to the US. His novels, published by Livanis, include *A Short Border Handbook* (2009), *My Name is Europe* (2010), and *The Last Page* (2012), and have been translated into Danish, English, French, Italian, and Polish. The poem included here is from an early poetry collection written originally in Albanian and self-translated into Greek. Through his work as an author and a columnist for leading Greek newspapers, Kapllani is an advocate for human rights. He has held fellowships at Harvard and Brown Universities and is currently at The Susan and Donald Newhouse Center for the Humanities at Wellesley College. He teaches History and Creative Writing at Emerson College.

Μέδουσες και κοράλλια
(ή το τραγούδι του ξένου)

Οι μέδουσες και τα κοράλλια
μακριά από δω
κατοικούν.
Και η λιλιπούτεια
Η μοίρα μας
Πάνω στην παλάμη
Φυλάγει
Ελάχιστο νερό.
Ούτε βάρκα
Πέρασε από δω
Ούτε λευκό πανί, μονάχα λίγος ζέφυρος
Καθώς τον επινόησαν
Τα μαλλιά σου
Επάνω στη φυγή.
Οι μέδουσες και τα κοράλλια
Μακριά από δω
Κατοικούν. Και τα βραχιόλια
Των ονείρων μας
Έμειναν κρεμασμένα
Σε φθαρμένους τοίχους.
Πόσα χρόνια που δε μας επισκέφθηκε κάποιος χτύπος.
Η μοίρα μας
Η λιλιπούτεια
Ελάχιστο νερό
Χωράει.
Ένα πηγάδι
Σκάβουμε
Τα βράδια
Δουλεύουμε με βάρδια

Thus Spoke
the Stranger

Medusas and coral
live far
from here.
Our Liliputian fate
guards
the last vestiges
of water
in the palm
of our hand.
No boat
passes by here
no white sail, just the slightest
Zephyr
caught in your hair
as you flee.
Medusas and coral
live far
from here. Our dream
bracelets
grasp
crumbling walls.
How many years since
someone knocked?
Our Liliputian fate
leaves room
for the last vestiges
of water.
At night
we dig a well
taking turns

– Muzë muzikë muzg –
Μείναμε ξένοι, μου λες,
Τις μέδουσες και τα κοράλλια
Που μου έταξες, το παρθένο νερό
Δεν θα τα δω.
Θεέ μου πόσο καιρό
Κρεμασμένα βραχιόλια ονείρων
Και ο φθαρμένος τοίχος,
Πόσο καιρό που δεν επισκέφθηκε ούτε ένας χτύπος
Και η αυλαία κλείνει σαν μύθος.
Αυτό το σπίτι
δεν του ανήκω
δεν μου ανήκει . . .

– Muzë muzikë muzg –
we mutter
Always strangers, you say
the medusas and coral
you promised me,
the virgin water,
I'll never see them.
Oh God, how many years
of bracelets grasping
crumbling walls?
How many years without a single knock?
The curtain closes like myth
That house
I do not belong to
that does not belong to me . . .

Karen Van Dyck

THODORIS RAKOPOULOS

(Born Amyntaio, near Florina, Greece, 1981)

As a writer of poetry, short stories, social commentary, and anthropology, Thodoris Rakopoulos is extremely prolific. With Thomas Tsalapatis (p. 215), he is also one of the most engaged and engaging critics of life post-crisis. His poetry, however, tends to avoid linear accounts of current events, focusing instead on representing the visual synchronicity inherent in a life lived between cultures and languages; he reserves his skill as a storyteller for his short stories as well as his anthropological work based on ethnographic field-work, most recently on the anti-mafia movement in Sicily. Rakopoulos studied Law and Anthropology in Thessaloniki and London, and now has a research fellowship at the University of Bergen in Norway. He received the Greek National Poetry Prize and the Book Center Prize for his first collection. He publishes essays and translations for journals and newspapers, as well as a blog, *Africa by any other name* (thodorisrakopoulos.blogspot.gr). His most recent book, *Bat in a Pocket* (Nefeli, 2015), is a collection of twenty prose pieces.

Φαγιούμ (*Fayum*), Mandragoras, 2010; *Ορυκτό Δάσος* (*Mineral Forest*), Nefeli, 2013; *Η συνωμοσία της πυρίτιδας* (*The Gunpowder Plot*), Nefeli, 2014.

Επιφάνια

Στάθηκε λοιπόν μπροστά
με το πνευμόνι του διαμπερές
κι ένα μπουκάλι χωρίς πώμα
ή μέσα μήνυμα

με την αμηχανία του ακάλεστου
στο κατώφλι κυριακάτικα
όταν όλες οι κάβες έχουν κλείσει

«ρε Πάνο» του είπα, «από το χώμα έρχεσαι και μου
   μυρίζεις
σαν όταν έσκαβες χωράφια· ο ίδιος· κόπιασε».

Εκείνος δεν απάντησε· ούτε καν φαίνονταν
να έχει καταλάβει· με κοίταζε αργά στο στήθος
σαν να ψάχνει τους υπότιτλους
κι έβγαζε ένα μαντίλι συνέχεια κόκκινο
σκουπίζοντας την ευφυΐα στάλα στάλα από το μέτωπο.

Δεν ήτανε γλώσσα ο Πάνος.
Δεν «το 'χε» που λεν οι γλωσσοπλάστες.
Σε μια μαύρη φωτογραφία ήτανε, χωμένος στο παλιό
   του ρούχο.

Σημ.: αυτό το ποίημα βγήκε με αναμμένο το αλάρμ
μόλις προσπέρασα έναν που σου έμοιαζε ρε Πάνο
ακίνητος στο αεράκι του αμπελώνα
με το πουκάμισό του καπνισμένο
λογάριαζε την αριθμητική των πουλιών.

Epiphany

So he stood in front
with a punctured lung
and a capless bottle
no message inside
the dysfunctional intruder
at the doorstep of a Sunday
when all the watering holes have closed

'Hey Pete,' I said, 'you're coming from the earth and smell
like your digging days in the fields – the same guy – get
   to work.'

He didn't answer – didn't even seem
to understand me, stared long at my chest
as if looking for subtitles
pulling out a continuous red hankie
to wipe away the wits from his forehead drop by drop.

Pete wasn't good with words.
'Didn't have it,' as the wordsmiths say.
He was in a darkened photograph, stuffed in his old
   clothes.

NB: this poem came out with the alarm on
just as I was passing someone who looked like you old
   Pete
standing still in the vineyard breeze
in his fumigated shirt
thinking about the arithmetic of birds.

George Economou

Σχισμένο

Υπάρχει	ένας
πολύ περι	γραφικός
τρόπος να	μου δείξεις
πόσο πολύ	με περιφρονείς
γιατί λοιπόν	διαλέγεις
αλληλο	γραφία
όταν μπορείς	να φτύσεις
κατά	μουτρα
γιατί απλώς	σαλιώνεις
το γραμ	ματόσημο;
Μία	σμα
εργο	δότη
σχίζεις τη	φωνή μου
στα	δύο
σαν	ένα
γράμ	μα

Torn

Is there	any
highly des	criptive
way you can	show me
how deeply	you detest me
why then	opt for
corres	pondence
when you	can spit
into	faces
because you	simply drool on
the post	age stamp?
Con	tamination
big	boss
you tear	my voice
in	two
like	one
let	ter

George Economou

389

STATHIS GOURGOURIS

(Born Los Angeles, USA, 1958)

Stathis Gourgouris's presence on the Greek poetry scene began early on when he wrote reviews for *Planodion*, Yannis Patilis's influential (yet offbeat) literary magazine. Having grown up in Athens, he returned to the US for university. Now a Professor of Comparative Literature at Columbia University, he is the author of the influential study *Dream Nation: Enlightenment, Colonization, and the Institution of Modern Greece* (Stanford University Press, 1996), as well as more obviously political works, most recently *Lessons in Secular Criticism* (Fordham University Press, 2013). His poetry, often self-translated, is hard to place; always standing in relation to the Ancient Greek tradition in terms of its attention to myth, it also places Modern Greece in the context of the Balkans through an emphasis on orality and song. Not coincidentally, his critical work and his poetry have found an audience in the Balkans and the Middle East, and have been translated into Turkish, Serbian, Hebrew, French, and Italian.

Myrtle Trenches (Hoarse Transcontinental Cats Press, 1985; *Πτώσεις* (*Falls*), Plethron, 1988; *Αυτοχθονίες* (*Identicide*), Planodion, 1993; *Εισαγωγή στη Φυσική* (*Introduction to Physics*), Melani, 2005.

Με τον τρόπο του Γ.Σ.

Οι αρχαίοι Αιγύπτιοι πίστευαν
σε εφτά ψυχές σφενδόνες.
Ατένιζαν την κάθε τους τροχιά
όχι σαν μελλοθάνατοι
μα σαν Ολυμπιονίκες.
Ανόητοι καμιά φορά που ήσαν.
Όμως ό,τι αφήναν πίσω τους το άφηναν
κι ας σπάραζε κάπου το κορμί τους.
Κέρδιζαν νέα ψυχή κάθε φορά
μόνο αυτό τους ένοιαζε.
Τον χωρισμό έτσι δεν γνώρισαν, ούτε τον γυρισμό
και την ψυχή την τελευταία τους που πέταξε
ούτε που την κατάλαβαν.

Οι πεθαμένοι άλλων λαών στον Άλλο Κόσμο
φθονούσαν τους Αιγύπτιους.

In the Manner of S.G.

The Ancient Egyptians believed
in seven souls, slingshots.
They embraced the orbit of every soul
not like prisoners who were about to die
but like winners in the Olympic Games.
How foolish they were sometimes!
But whatever they left behind
they really left it,
no matter how much it hurt inside.
With each flight, they gained new soul –
only this mattered.
So they could never understand return
nor rupture,
and when exactly their last soul
was flung into the darkness,
they couldn't quite tell you.

The other dead in the Other World
envied the Egyptians.

Self-translated

Η νύφη με τις σφαίρες

Στο τέλος ξυρίζουν τον νεκρό
έλεγε παλιά μια παροιμία,
η οποία όμως τώρα έχει ξεχαστεί
ίσως γιατί το τέλος μάς τρομάζει,
αν κι οι παροιμίες προφανώς
δεν γίνεται ποτέ να συζευχθούν
σε μια ολόκληρη ζωή
μια μόνο φράση.
Έτσι, λοιπόν, ο κάποτε αξύριστος
υπήρξε κάποτε γαμπρός
πλανήτης στη τροχιά μιας άλλης σφαίρας
(παρότι ο άμοιρος καμάρωνε σαν ήλιος)
και εραστής παροιμιών –
το Μέγα Λάθος –
γιατί ποτέ του δεν εννόησε να κρύψει
από τη γλώσσα μυστικά
ξεχνώντας, ως γαμπρός παροιμιώδης,
ότι κι οι πιο μικρές παρεκτροπές
αλλάζουν την τροπή μιας σφαίρας
και συνεπώς του χρόνου τις πτυχές,
ώστε, όλως αίφνης, να βρεθεί
με πλάτη στη σιδερένια πόρτα
μπροστά σε κάποιο απόσπασμα
μιας νύφης, σε άλλο κόσμο ακέραιης
σ' αυτόν αδικημένης –
αφού κι οι παροιμίες διαλαλούν
ότι ουδέποτε υπήρξε θεία δίκη
κι η γλώσσα από το τέλος της αντλεί
την κάθε περιτύλιξη, μεταίχμιο, ιστορία.
Σαν το συμβάν που ξάφνου δίνει
στη ζωή μας μια τελεία,

The Bride with the Bullets

In the end they shave the dead
says an old folk proverb
now long forgotten
perhaps because the end induces fear
even if proverbs never adhere
to a single phrase
for a whole life.
And so the once unshaven man
groom and planet
to an orbit from another sphere
(even if he thought he was the sun)
lover of proverbs –
Enormous Error –
because he never thought to hide
secrets from his tongue
forgetting, proverbial groom,
how the smallest deviations
shift the turning of a sphere
hence the folds of time,
so that suddenly he finds himself
his back against the steel door
facing the shrapnel of a trigger-happy bride
in another world fully intact
but in this one unjustly treated
since even proverbs claim
there never was a goddess of the just
and language draws its every twist,
threshold, and tale from its own end.
Like the event that suddenly gives
a full stop to our life

η νύφη με τις σφαίρες
τον κόσμο ολόκληρο θα έθετε ως στόχο
αφού, χωρίς θεό, ανέκαθεν ο κόσμος της
σε ένα γαμπρό είχε δεόντως χρεωθεί
κι έπρεπε τώρα να τελειώσει
πριν την προλάβει η ηχώ μιας σφαίρας
που αργεί να καταλήξει
κι έτσι περάσει ακάλυπτη,
μια νύφη δίχως πέπλο,
την άλλη πόρτα που σιωπά,
που είναι δίνη.
Κι αν κύλαγε ευθύς αμέσως τώρα
σε κόσμο άλλο, ξένο, σκοτεινό
θα ήξερε, ο στόχος είχε επιτευχθεί
παρότι ζούσε μόνο με μια σκέψη
μια παροιμία που τώρα έχει ξεχαστεί,
ίσως γιατί το τέλος μάς τρομάζει –
μια νύφη αστόχαστη της μνήμης
αδιάβατη να πλάθει πεπρωμένα σφαιρικά
κι ένας γαμπρός ακίνητος στο τέλος
να περιμένει το πρωί
το ξύρισμα.

the bride with her bullets
makes the whole world her target
since, without god, her own world had always
been duly indebted to a groom
and now this had to end
before the echo of a bullet
slow to come to a conclusion
would catch her unprotected,
a bride without a veil,
slipping through the other door
of silence like a vortex.
And if just now she would slip
into a sphere, foreign, dark, not here
she'd know her target had been hit
even if she lived for a single phrase
a proverb now long forgotten –
perhaps because the end induces fear –
a bride without a thought for memory
intractable, carving bullet spheres of fate,
and a groom immobile in the end
waiting for his morning shave.

Stathis Gourgouris and Karen Van Dyck

Το όνειρο της Αθηνάς

Αύγουστος μεσημέρι.
Μελτέμι στη Βερανζέρου.
Ο Αλβανός τρώγεται να μάθει
τα μυστικά του αναπτήρα.
Στα σκληρά πεζοδρόμια
κάμπτονται τα ψηλά τακούνια.
Τιμωρούνται οι παραβάτες των διακοπών
λουόμενοι στο σκονισμένο
Αστικόν φώς.
Τον Αλβανό τον λένε Edison.
Μαζί του βαπτίστηκε
το Τρίτο Εργοστάσιο Ηλεκτρισμού.
Τώρα φλερτάρει τη φωτιά
σαν νέος Προμηθέας,
δέσμιος πάλι μιας ξένης χειρονομίας.
Κι όλα μαυρίζουν εδώ τριγύρω
(μόνο η Ακρόπολη ολοένα ασπρίζει).
Στις μαύρες αίθουσες εκκλησιάζονται
οι εξ Ανατολών νέοι πολίτες
θυσιάζουν πατρίδες, οικογένειες
καθώς στη λάμψη του βωμού
πάνω από κάτι πελώρια μυστικά
της Άγριας Δύσης
σαρκοβατεί η ιεράρχις
Annie Sprinkle.

Athena's Dream

Cool afternoon in August.
North wind on Béranger St.
An Albanian pondering desperately
the secrets of a lighter.
A hard sidewalk bending
the high heels.
Punishing the violators
of summer-leave who bathe
in the dusty city light.
The Albanian's name is Edison.
His name marks the lightning birth
of the nation's First Electrical Plant.
But now he flirts with fire,
a new Prometheus
bound again by a foreign gesture
in a world that suddenly goes black
so that the dark Acropolis looms now
whiter than ever
and in black cinema-parishes
new citizens from the East
sacrifice their patrimony
to the luminous screen, where high
over enormous mysteries
of the Wild West
rides the white priestess
Annie Sprinkle.

Self-translated

Ανώνυμη βροχή

Τό όνομα του Θεού ξεχάστηκε
γιατί κανείς δεν πρόλαβε
να το γράψει στα σύννεφα.
Κάθε μέρα που βρέχει
στάζει επάνω μας το απειρο-
ελάχιστο κρίμα
της ανωνύμου θεάσεως.
Γι' αυτό οι άνθρωποι εφηύραν
τίς μαύρες ομπρέλες.
Για να κρατήσουν αδιάβροχο
το αθέατο όνομά τους.

Nameless Rain

The name of God was forgotten
because no one bothered
to write it on the clouds.
Every time it rains
upon us falls
the infinitesimal sin
of nameless vision.
Hence humans invented
black umbrellas
to keep their invisible name
waterproof.

Stathis Gourgouris and Karen Van Dyck

MEHMET YASHIN

(Born Nicosia, Cyprus, 1958)

Mehmet Yashin is one of Cyprus's most internationally acclaimed poets. He has been at the vanguard of multilingual literature since his landmark critical study of Cypriot, Greek, and Turkish literature, *Step-Mothertongue* (Middlesex University Press, 2000). His own writing draws on the multilingual Levantine tradition he remembers from his grandmother, who mingled the Turkish and Greek alphabets, languages, and cultures in everyday life. Though his work has only recently begun to be read in Greece, he has won many awards in Turkey and the UK, and his poetry and novels have been translated into more than twenty languages; the first selection of his poetry, *Don't Go Back to Kyrenia*, was chosen for translation by the British Centre for Literary Translation. He lives and teaches in Nicosia, crossing the green line daily.

Don't Go Back to Kyrenia, **Middlesex University Press, 2001;** *Wartime*, **The Happy Dragons' Press, 2007;** *Άγγελοι Εκδικητές* (*Revenge Angels*), Vakxikon.gr, 2015.

Acı kayıp

Kaybetmesem bulamayacaktım
Ωλμεγεν πιρ Ο

Annem zamansız ölmese gerekmeyecekti onu
   canlandırmam
ve babamı fark bile etmeyecektim hayatımdan
   çıkmasa . . .
(Yokedilmek istendiği için varolabilen bir eve doğdum ben
böylece Kutsal Topraklarımız oldu işgal altındaki o
   lanet yer.)
Hiçbirşey kaybetmeyen bunu da başka türlü okuyacak
ve anladığʼnı sanacak, kalpten okunmadıkça
   anlaşılabilirmiş gibi şiir.
Uçan kuşların kanat çırpması devam ettikçe
   bakışlarınızda
boş kalan dallara her baktığınızda, devam eder şiir de.
Ama kendi sınırlarımı belki hiç aşamayacaktım
ilk şiir cennetimden zorla sınırdışı edilmemiş olsaydım.
Şimdi anlıyorum ki, şairler çok iyiliğini görürmüş
   kötülüklerin,
dilsizliğin bir de ve ellerinden alınmış bütün o şeylerin –
Sonsuza dek kaybedilmiş . . . bir şiir olarak bulunsun diye

πυραδα.

The Bitter Loss

If I had not lost it I would not have found it
Ωλμεγεν πιρ Ο

If my mother hadn't died so young, I wouldn't have to call
   her back to life,
and I wouldn't even have noticed my father, if he hadn't
   gone away . . .
I was born to a house which was there only to be
   ransacked later,
and thus, under occupation, that accursed abode became
   our Holy Land.
He who never lost anything will give this a different
   interpretation,
believing he grasps it all, as if you could comprehend poetry
without hearing it read from the depths of the heart.

As the flapping wings of birds in their flight persist in
   your eyes,
so does a poem whenever you gaze at the bare branches
   of trees.
But perhaps I would never have crossed the bounds of my
   inner self,
if I hadn't been exiled from that primordial paradise of
   poetry.
I now realize that poets glean much goodness from evil
   deeds,
from being dumb, from watching their possessions being
   pillaged –
lost for good, for ever, only to be recovered a lot later, as
   a poem.

Πυραδα.

Taner Baybars

De-composition

You can tell by the way she moves her curly hair
whether she is in a good mood or not –
Not. Yapabileceğin birşey de yok.
Aya'ucunda yürü, dokunma bir yere,
eşyalar kırılmak için sıraya girmiş. You too
have to be brave now, no, you don't need to be . . .
Call your double to play
this role. Ezberleyemedin gitti,
ciddiye alıyorsun üstelik oyundaki her sözü –
Ayağın kaymayagörsün. Behind the plastic curtains
two shadows showering, shrinking bellies,
hearts, legs . . . Şekillerin ani değişimi
gölge-oyunundaki gibi shivering giant shapes
all of a sudden kesik kesik su sesi . . . Susss
sözcükler haz'r'olda yaylımateş için sana –
Bodies are wet but the soul
dried up boşaltılmış bir evde. Cıvıltısı uçmuş
kuş, y ı l a n ı n y u t t u ğ u d i l . . .

Yatağa uzanırken delik deşik iniltiyle,
kemiklerimmm τι κούραση θεε μου, diyorsun.
Kimse yanıtlamıyor: Έλα ψυχή μου, geçmiş zaman
ruhu. Çürüyen beden.

Çürüme

Dalgalı saçlarını savuruşundan anlarsın
keyfi yerinde mi değil mi-
Değil. And there is nothing you can do.
Tiptoe . . . Don't touch anything,
the objects form an orderly queue
to be broken. Sen de cesur ol o halde
yok şart değil,
dublörünü çağır o oynasın bu rolü. You still
have not learned your lines by heart
and still take every single word so seriously.
A slip of your feet. Plastik perdenin arkasında
iki gölge, duş yapıyorlar, büzüşmüş karınları
kalpleri, bacakları . . . An instant change of figures
like in a shadow-play titreyen dev şekiller
ve birden stuttering sound of water . . . Shhhh . . .
The word-squad in attention to shoot you
Gövdeler ıslak ama ruh
kupkuru in a forsaken house. The bird staring as
the song flies away, the tongue
swallowed by the snake . . .

As you lay yourself on bed, with a pierced moan
my boooones. Gott, was ist das für eine müdigkeit,
   you mutter
No one answers: Komm, meine Seele, mein hertz.
   The soul of
time begone. Body de-composing.

Bariş Pirhasan

HIVA PANAHI

(Born Sina, Kurdistan [now Iran], 1980)

The Kurdish-Greek writer and poet Hiva Panahi often employs
the imagery of the Persian and Arabic poetry she grew up
with in her efforts to tackle her people's struggles in her
work. She was forced to leave Iran in 1997 when she and
three others witnessed the stoning of their schoolmate by
religious fundamentalists. After a period in jail, she made
her way to Iraq, and eventually to Greece on a scholarship.
There, she studied the Greek language at the University of
Athens and received her Ph.D. in Political Science from
Panteion University. Her poetry is written in Kurdish and
Greek, and has been translated into other languages includ-
ing Filipino, English, Arabic, German, and French.

Τα μυστικά του χιονιού (*The Secrets of Snow*), Maistros, 2008.

Η ανάσα της ελιάς

Εμείς οι περιπλανώμενοι
Εμείς οι ξυπόλυτοι
Εμείς χωρίς χώρο και χώρα
Εμείς οι καμένοι και αναμμένοι άνεμοι
Σε είδαμε, με τις τελευταίες ανάσες
Που κάψανε ένα κομμάτι της θάλασσας.

The Breath of the Olive Tree

We the wandering
We the barefoot
We without space or country
We the burnt and fiery winds
We saw you, with those final breaths
That burned a piece of the sea.

Karen Emmerich

Σύντροφος

Ο ιδρώτας ενός ποιήματος
Στους μυστηριώδεις λόφους
Στη βαλίτσα κουβαλάω το ύψος μου
Μαζί μ' ένα χρωματισμένο υπονοούμενο ταξιδεύω
Λες ακόμη να περιμένω
Να με κοροϊδεύει ο Αριμάν;
Ή να ερωτευτώ τον ήλιο αμαρτωλό κορίτσι;
Λες να κατάγομαι
Απ' τη χώρα των κυττάρων
Λες μια πειθαρχική βροντή
Να με κάνει βροχή του έρωτα
Λες εκεί στα βάθη του χωραφιού
Στον νοθευμένο πόνο του δειλινού
Εκεί το χαμόγελό μου λες ακόμη να είναι μια μίμηση
Στον χαρούμενο καθρέφτη;
Το ψεύτικο λεπτό της μέρας
Μέσα στην ανάσα της ύπαρξής μας
Απ' το φάντασμα με το μαύρο φόρεμα
Μου λες πώς να ξεφύγω;
Η σκιά του πάντως με φοβίζει
Έψαχνα στα παραμύθια
Στους θρύλους των παλιών εποχών
Τη μέρα που δεν θα ξημερώσει
από τις φημισμένες χίλιες νύχτες
Ένα γκρι τραγούδι
του καταραμένου έρωτα
Από πού έχει έρθει;
Στη βαλίτσα κουβαλώ το ύψος μου
Το παραμυθένιο παλικάρι της βροχής
χίλιες νύχτες το λένε
Πως ταξιδεύω.

Companion

The sweat of a poem
In the mysterious hills
I carry my height in the suitcase
I travel along with a painted insinuation
You think I'm still waiting
To be fooled by Ariman?
Or to fall in love with the sun, sinful girl?
You think I come
From the land of celluloid?
You think a well-disciplined thunder
Might turn me into the rain of love?
You think there in the depths of a field
In the falsified ache of dusk
You think my smile there might still be an imitation
Inside the happy mirror?
The fraudulent minute of the day
Inside the breath of our existence?
Can you tell me how to escape
From the ghost with the black dress?
In any case its mere shadow scares me
I've been searching in fairytales
In the legends of old times
For the day that will not dawn
One of the famous thousand nights
A gray song
Of accursed love
Where has it come from?
I carry my height in the suitcase
The fairytale hero of the rain
A thousand nights tell about
How I travel.

Angelos Sakkis

Ένας άνθρωπος από στάχτη

Τα όνειρα έρχονται από μακρινά μέρη
Η πέτρα, τα πουλιά, και εγώ παίρνουμε νέα μορφή ζωής
Τα όνειρα έχουν τον δικό τους δρόμο
Και εμείς σαν όνειρα μακρινά ζούμε πια

Ash Person

Dreams come from far away places
The stones, the birds and I take on new forms of life
Dreams have their own road
And we live far away these days, like dreams.

Maria Margaronis

ACKNOWLEDGEMENTS

Numerous people have helped me with this book, notable among them many of the poets and translators whose work is included in it; especial gratitude is owed to Peter Constantine, who got the project off the ground, and Maria Margaronis, who kept me up to date with the news. Katerina Anghelaki-Rooke, Titika Dimitroulia, Jenny Mastoraki, and Haris Vlavianos have also been important interlocutors. Without Lawrence Venuti's insistence that translation matters – and without the inspiration of his own translations of Antonia Pozzi and Ernest Farrés, which make new things possible in English – this book would have been a less exciting and experimental enterprise. I owe particular thanks to my editor Donald Futers for his patience, writerly insight, and idea to look to the Penguin anthology *British Poetry since 1945* (1970) for ways of mapping an emerging poetry scene. The fact that Nikos Stangos was the commissioning editor of that volume, himself a Greek poet and champion of Greek artists and the between-world existence that makes one culture available to another, made the fit all the more compelling.

FURTHER READING

The brief lists of poetry collections, blogs, and translations in the biographical notes as well as the articles and anthologies included here are intended to help the reader find their way if they are interested in reading more, but are in no way exhaustive.

POETRY COLLECTIONS AND ANTHOLOGIES

Anghelaki-Rooke, Katerina, *The Scattered Papers of Penelope: New and Selected Poems*, ed. Karen Van Dyck (Greenwich: Anvil, 2008; Minneapolis: Graywolf, 2009).

Bien, Peter, et al., eds., *A Century of Greek Poetry: 1900–2000*, bilingual edition (River Vale, NJ: Cosmos, 2004).

Chiotis, Theodoros, ed., *Futures: Poetry of the Greek Crisis* (London: Penned in the Margins, 2015).

Constantine, Peter, et al., eds., *The Greek Poets: Homer to the Present* (New York: Norton, 2010).

Hirschman, Jack, ed., *Cross-Section: An Anthology of Contemporary Greek Poetry* (San Francisco: Erato Press, 2015).

Kabouropoulos, Socrates, 'Contemporary Greek Poets', portfolio, *The Poetry Review*, 102:1 (2012).

Manoussakis, Vassilis, 'Beware of Greeks Bearing Poetry', introduction and portfolio of 15 poets, *Drunken Boat*, 19 (August 2014) <http://www.drunkenboat.com/db19/greek-poets>.

Sachtouris, Miltos, *Poems (1945–1971)*, trans. Karen Emmerich (Brooklyn: Archipelago, 2006).

Siotis, Dinos, ed., *Crisis: 30 Greek Poets on the Current Crisis* (Smokestack Books, 2014).

Tsvetanka, Elenkova, ed., *Poems of Greek Texture: An Anthology of Ten Poets* (Rhodes: International Writers & Translators' Centre, 2008).

Van Dyck, Karen, ed., *The Rehearsal of Misunderstanding: Three Collections of Poetry by Contemporary Greek Women Poets*, bilingual edition including Rhea Galanaki's *Cake*, Maria Laina's *Hers*, and Jenny Mastoraki's *Tales of the Deep* (Middletown, CT: Wesleyan, 1998).

——, 'Austerity Measures: New Greek Poetry', introduction and portfolio of 11 translations, *Mantis*, 13 (Spring 2015).

Vlavianos, Haris, ed., *Αφιέρωμα στη νεότερη ελληνική ποίηση I + II*, special issues on new poetry, *Ποιητική* (*Poetics*), 9–10 (2012).

Ziras, Alexis, ed., *Hellenica: το καινούριο εντός ή πέραν της γλώσσας: Ανθολογία νέων Ελλήνων Ποιητών* (*Hellenica: Novelty Within or Beyond Language: Anthology of Young Greek Poets*) (Athens: Gavrielides, 2009).

ARTICLES AND INTERVIEWS

Barley, Joshua, 'Greece and the Poetics of Crisis', *The White Review* (February 2015) <http://www.thewhitereview.org/features/greece-and-the-poetics-of-crisis/>.

Constantine, Peter, 'A Conversation with Jazra Khaleed', *World Literature Today* (March 2010) <http://www.worldliteraturetoday.org/conversation-jazra-khaleed-peter-constantine>.

Dimitroulia, Titika, 'Les jeunes poètes grecs: un phénomène poétique particulier', *Revue Desmos / Le Lien*, 44 (2015).

Papadopoulos, Stephanos, 'Hurt into Poetry: On Poetry and Greece', *Los Angeles Review of Books* (10 May 2013) <http://lareviewofbooks.org/essay/hurt-into-poetry-on-poetry-and-greece>.

Ritvo, Max, '"Smashing Fascist Heads": Jazra Khaleed on
    Political and Poetic Crisis in Greece', *Los Angeles Review
    of Books* (1 March 2015) <http://lareviewofbooks.org/
    interview/smashing-fascist-heads-jazra-khaleed-
    political-poetic-crisis-greece>.

Stallings, A. E., 'Austerity Measures. A Letter from Greece',
    Poetry (4 September 2012) <http://www.poetryfounda
    tion.org/poetrymagazine/article/244460>.

——, 'Freelance', *The Times Literary Supplement* (5 December
    2014).

——, 'Letter from Athens', *The Poetry Review*, 103:3 (2013).

WEBSITES

e-poema www.e-poema.eu
Farmakon www.frmk.gr
Greek Poetry Now! www.greekpoetrynow.com
(de) kata (n^th) degree Koinonia ton (de)katon www.dekata.gr
Poiein www.poiein.gr
Ta poiitika (The Poetical) tapoiitika.wordpress.com
Teflon teflon.wordpress.com
Me ta logia [ginetai] (Words [can] do it) metalogiaginetai.
    blogspot.gr

NOTES ON THE POEMS

by poets (P), translators (T), and the editor (E)

p. 21 9/11 OR FALLING MAN

This translation rewrites the collection's title *27 ή o ἄνθρωπος που πέφτει* (*27 or the man who falls*) as *9/11 or Falling Man*, and the poet's 27-syllable line into one of twenty syllables, placing a caesura after every ninth or eleventh syllable to inscribe the titular date into the translation. (T)

p. 27 O SAY CAN YOU SEE

The title in Greek, *Πατρείδα*, plays on the words for 'Fatherland' or 'Homeland' (*Πατρίδα*) and 'I saw' (*είδα*), creating a neologism that means 'what I see of my country'. The translation refers to the first line of the American national anthem. (T)

p. 35 ARMED WITH TENDERNESS

'For Katerina Anghelaki-Rooke': See her entry in the Translators' biographies. Also see Further Reading for Karen Van Dyck's translation of her poetry. (E)

p. 37 MY BROTHER PAUL, THE DIGGER OF THE SEINE

'O you dig and I dig / and I dig inside myself towards you': From the collection *Die Niemandsrose* by the poet Paul Celan (1920–70), dedicated to the Russian poet Osip Mandelstam (1891–1938). (E)

p. 57 THE CHILDREN OF ABEL

This poem references both the shipwreck of the MV *Danny F II*, which was carrying a load of almost a thousand cows and sheep, on 17 December 2009, and the death by asphyxiation, five days later, of a lioness and eight tigers on the circus truck transporting them to Yakutsk, Siberia. (P)

p. 67 HEAD OF A SATYR

In the winter of 1877–8, the sculptor Giannoulis Chalepas, as yet unknown and misunderstood, suffered a severe nervous breakdown; he destroyed his studies and works – mainly heads of Satyrs, of which only one, which he had given to his young nephew, survives – and he repeatedly attempted suicide. He was placed 'under observation' and, as his condition worsened, his family sent him to Italy to recuperate. Soon thereafter he returned to Greece with the aim of studying the sculptures of the Acropolis, but he ended up in the Psychiatric Hospital of Corfu. (P)

p. 81 PENTHESILEA

Penthesilea is an Amazon queen in Greek mythology, and the heroine of Heinrich von Kleist's eponymous tragedy (1808). (E)

p. 115 (PENELOPE – ΕΧΩ ΠΑΘΟΣ ΓΙΑ ΣΕΝΑ)

Penelope is the wife of Odysseus, who keeps her suitors at bay during her husband's absence by promising to choose one when she finishes her weaving. What they don't know is that she undoes her day's work every night. (E)

This translation, like Bariş Pirhasan's 'Çürüme' and George Economou's 'Torn', relies on the reader comparing the language patterns and shape of the original and the translation, and filling in the missing English. (E)

p. 117 (THETIS)

Thetis is the Ancient Greek goddess of water and one of the fifty Nereids, the daughters of the sea god Nereus. The name in Greek is a cognate of τίθεται – the one who is positioned, placed, but also who posits. (E)

p. 119 (LOTUS EATERS II)

The inhabitants of one of the islands Odysseus visits on his journey are said to live in a drugged indolent state induced by eating lotus flowers. (E)

p. 123 THE GREAT GARDENER

'For Miltos': A reference to the poet Miltos Sachtouris (1919–2005). See Further Reading for Karen Emmerich's translation of his poetry. (E)

p. 137 NATIONAL ANTHEM, 2008, REDUX

'For Eva Stefani': For Stefani's own poetry, see p. 129. (E)

p. 147 KLEINE NACHTMUSIK

Eine kleine Nachtmusik (Serenade No. 13 for strings in G major), a chamber music composition by Wolfgang Amadeus Mozart. (E)

p. 151 THE LOTUS EATERS

See note to p. 119. (E)

p. 156 WORDS

Wörter: As a teenager Jazra Khaleed lived in Germany for a few years before settling in Greece. (E)

p. 173 RE: LOTUS EATERS

This is a response to Kyoko Kishida's poem on p. 151. See also note to p. 119. (E)

p. 219 WORD MONDAY

In this poem, Greek letters are what they look like: Π
and T have flat roofs, while ζ and ξ have roots that
dangle down. In Greek, to be homeless is to be roofless
(ἀστεγής) and, as in English, the verb 'to uproot' is
used for plants and people. (T)

p. 223 TELEMACHUS

This is the final poem of a triptych, coming after 'Odys-
seus' and 'Penelope'. Telemachus, son of Odysseus, helped
his father defeat his mother's suitors at home in Ithaca,
but never went to war. His name means 'far from war'.
Neoptolemos, son of Achilles, was known as a brutal
warrior and fought with Odysseus in Troy. His name
means 'new war'. (E)

p. 225 SEPTEMBER 3rd 1843

On this date an uprising against the rule of the Bavar-
ian King Otto led to the establishment of a constitution,
for which Syntagma Square in Athens is named. (T)

p. 231 POETRY DOES NOT SUFFICE

'Let him write as many sonnets as he wants about
Faliro': Faliro, now a seaside suburb near Piraeus, was
the subject of a rather whimsical love poem by Lorentzos
Mavilis (1860–1912) involving an heiress with a new-
fangled automobile. (T)

p. 233 POETRY 2048

The title refers to the poem written in 1948 by Nikos
Engonopoulos called 'Poetry 1948'.

'from the treason of Ploumbides': Nikos Ploumbides
was a member of the anti-Nazi resistance and a lead-
ing Communist. He later fell afoul of the KKE (the
Communist Party of Greece) and resigned from

their politburo. After he was arrested and executed by the right-wing Papagos government in 1954, left-wing newspapers insisted that he was alive and well, spending money earned from his treason (allegedly as a secret police spy). In 1958, the KKE exonerated him. (T)

p. 255 INTERNATIONAL
'Philip the Apostle': One of the Twelve Apostles of Jesus. Known as the apostle who preached in Greece, Syria, and Phrygia. (E)

p. 265 PARALOGUE
Οι παραλογές (the paralogues) are a category of Greek folksong, composed in ballad form, which focuses on ancient myth, often about the Underworld. The word also literally refers to a lack of logic (paralogic), and has been used by Greek poets to explain an indigenous form of surrealism which emerged under the Colonels (1967–74) and has recently resurfaced.

'Charon': Charon is the ferryman in Hades who carries the souls of the newly dead across the river Styx, which divides the living from the dead. (E)

p. 281 LET DOWN THE CHAIN
'Σύρε καλέ την άλυσον': In Greek the reference is to the folksong 'The Bridge of Arta', in English, to the Rapunzel story. (T)

p. 287 THE BEAST
'Zappeion': The Zappeion, an important neoclassical building in the center of Athens near Syndagma Square, which has lent its name to the National Garden that surrounds it. (E)

p. 315 PENELOPE III
See note to p. 115. (E)

p. 347 FOR MILTOS SACHTOURIS
See note to p. 123. (E)

p. 369 MY BONES IN THE SOUP OF MY GRAVE
The English translation is from another version of the Greek poem that is untitled. (P)

p. 383 THUS SPOKE THE STRANGER
'*Muzë muzikë muzg*' means 'Muse music dusk' in Albanian. (P)

p. 393 IN THE MANNER OF S. G.
The title refers to the poem 'In the Manner of G. S.' by the Nobel Laureate poet George (Giorgos) Seferis (1900–1971), which begins with his famous line about exile: 'Wherever I travel Greece wounds me.' (E)

p. 405 THE BITTER LOSS
'Ωλμεγεν πιρ Ο': 'He who never lost anything.' He who never dies (alluding to Allah).

'Πυραδα': 'Here he rests.' The orthography used in these epitaphs is called Karamanlidika (Greek) or Karamanlıca (Turkish), in which Greek characters were employed in writing Turkish. This system had gone out of use by the 1930s following the population exchanges between Turkey and Greece. The adoption of the Roman alphabet in Turkey no doubt played a part in this, but the practice continued in Cyprus until 1933. (T)

BIOGRAPHIES OF THE TRANSLATORS

KATERINA ANGHELAKI-ROOKE is one of Greece's best-known and most-loved poets. A Ford Foundation grant enabled her to visit the International Writing Program at the University of Iowa in 1972, and she was a Fulbright Visiting Lecturer at Harvard in 1980-81. Her facility with English has made her a most sought-out translator among younger poets. Her own translations have focused on bringing Russian and American poetry into Greek, often showcasing the points where two languages meet or are irreducibly at odds. The importance of inflection for Russian and Greek poetry is the motor behind her masterful recreation of Russian rhyme and meter in her translations of Pushkin; its lesser prominence in English, meanwhile, has led her to imprint her English versions of her own work with Greek linguistic forms.

Translations: Σύγχρονοι αμερικανοί ποιητές (*Contemporary American Poets*), Ipsilon, 1983; *Beings and Things on their Own*, BOA Editions, 1986; *From Purple into Night*, Shoestring Press, 1998; Aleksandr Sergeevič Puškin, Ευγένιος Ονέγκιν (*Eugene Onegin*), Kastaniotis, 2000; *Translating Life's End into Love*, Shoestring Press, 2005.

In this book: DIMITRIS ALLOS 'or Her White Utensils' (p. 335); IANA BOUKOVA 'For Miltos Sachtouris' (p. 347); 'The Minimal Garden' (p. 341); YANNIS STIGGAS 'Breathing Exercises' (p. 33), 'Simple Math' (p. 31).

PATRICIA BARBEITO teaches courses on race and ethnicity in American literature and culture at Rhode Island School of Design. Her articles have appeared in such publications as *American Literature* and the *Journal of American Culture*. Her translations draw on her understanding of the American vernacular, deploying African-American dialect to capture the mixed idioms in Sotiris Dimitriou's short stories or cultivating a range of different registers – from hard-boiled noir to spoken-word poetry – with Elias Maglinis's experimental novel. Her translations have appeared in *Words Without Borders* and *Asymptote*. In 2013 she won the Elizabeth Constantinides Prize for best translation from the Modern Greek Studies Association.

Translations: Menis Koumandareas, *Their Smell Makes Me Want to Cry* (with Vangelis Calotychos), University of Birmingham, 2004; Elias Maglinis, *The Interrogation*, University of Birmingham, 2013.

In this book: VASSILIS AMANATIDIS '[mother's body]' (p. 319), '[supremacy: a riddle]' (p. 319); ELSA KORNETI 'As of Today' (p. 297), 'Dear Friend' (p. 299); 'A Slight Hesitation' (p. 295).

TANER BAYBARS (1936–2010) is a poet and translator who worked for the British Council until his retirement in 1988. He then lived in the South of France, where he was Corresponding Editor for the London avant-garde magazine *Ambit*. He is best known as the English translator of Nâzim Hikmet. His own poetry includes the collections *Narcissus in a Dry Pool* (1978) and *Pregnant Shadows* (1981).

Translations: Selected Poems of Nâzim Hikmet, Cape, 1967; Mehmet Yashin, *Don't Go Back to Kyrenia: Poems 1977–1997*, Middlesex University Press, 2001.

In this book: MEHMET YASHIN 'The Bitter Loss' (p. 405).

DIMITRI CHARALAMBOUS is a poet who writes in both Greek and English. In the early 1980s he worked with Jack Hirschman and other San Francisco Beat-influenced poets to create the journal *Compages* with its focus on multilingual and revolutionary poetry. More recently he teamed up again with Hirschman to translate the poetry of Yannis Livadas and co-edit the anthology of contemporary Greek poetry *Cross-Currents* (see Further Reading). He has also translated Pablo Neruda's poetry into Greek. He holds a BA and MA in History with an emphasis on Latin America and is a member of the Modern Greek Studies Foundation at San Francisco State University.

Translations: John Coltrane and 15 Poems for Jazz (with Jack Hirschman), C. C. Marimbo, 2008.

In this book: YANNIS LIVADAS 'Jazz, I Say' (p. 365).

PETER CONSTANTINE has introduced a new generation of Greek online poets to American readers in publications such as *Words Without Borders* and *World Literature Today*. He tends to choose poems with broad appeal over those with specialized historical or literary allusions. He is a co-editor of *The Greek Poets:*

Homer to the Present and *A Century of Greek Poetry: 1900–2000*. His translations from Arvantika, a Greek minority language, have appeared in *Modern Poetry in Translation*. A Guggenheim Fellow, he was awarded the PEN Translation Prize, the National Translation Award (USA), and the Koret Jewish Literature Award. Besides his translations from Greek he has also translated works by Babel, Chekhov, Machiavelli, Rousseau, Tolstoy, and Voltaire.

Translations: A Century of Greek Poetry: 1900–2000 (with Peter Bien, Edmund Keeley, and Karen Van Dyck), Cosmos, 2004; *The Complete Works of Isaac Babel*, Norton, 2005; *The Essential Writings of Machiavelli*, Modern Library, 2007; Sophocles, *Three Theban Plays*, Barnes & Noble Classics, 2008; *The Greek Poets: Homer to the Present* (with Rachel Hadas, Edmund Keeley, and Karen Van Dyck), Norton, 2010; Leo Tolstoy, *The Cossacks*, Modern Library, 2010; *The Essential Writings of Rousseau*, Modern Library, 2013; Anton Chekhov, *Little Apples: And Other Early Stories*, Seven Stories, 2016.

In this book: DIMITRIS ATHINAKIS 'A Semblance of Order' (p. 9); STATHIS BAROUTSOS 'Speed Dating' (p. 179), 'Txt Message' (p. 183); JAZRA KHALEED 'Black Lips' (p. 161), 'Death Tonight' (p. 167), 'Re: Lotus-Eaters' (p. 173), 'Words' (p. 157); YANNIS MOUNDELAS 'Hermes in Retrograde' (p. 199), 'Truncated Clouds' (p. 201).

GEORGE ECONOMOU has published fifteen books of poetry and translations. He established a reputation as a Greek-American experimental poet with early books published by Black Sparrow Press as well as his collection *Ameriki: Book One, and Selected Earlier Poems* (Sun,

1977). He edited two of Paul Blackburn's translations, *Proensa: An Anthology of Troubadour Poetry* (University of California Press, 1978), and *Poem of Cid* (University of Oklahoma Press, 1998). His translations from the Greek focus on lesser-known Ancient writers such as Philodemos as well as hitherto untranslated works like the recently discovered fragments of Sappho. His *Ananios of Kleitor* (Shearsman, 2009) is an invented translation. He has also translated C. P. Cavafy. In his writing about translation he highlights the differences between languages, such as the lack of gender specificity in Greek that often renders the object of love poems ambiguous.

Translations: William Langland, *Piers Plowman*, University of Pennsylvania, 1996; *Acts of Love: Ancient Greek Poetry from Aphrodite's Garden*, Random House, 2006; *Complete Plus: The Poems of C. P. Cavafy in English*, Shearsman, 2013; *Unfinished & Uncollected: Finishing the Unfinished Poems of C. P. Cavafy* and *Uncollected Poems & Translations*, Shearsman, 2015.

In this book: KYOKO KISHIDA 'Degenerate Girls Were My Girlfriends' (p. 145); THODORIS RAKOPOULOS 'Epiphany' (p. 387), 'Torn' (p. 389); GEORGIA TRIANDA-FILLIDOU 'Sudden Obsession at a Relative's House' (p. 329).

MOIRA EGAN earned a BA from Bryn Mawr College, an MA from the Johns Hopkins University Writing Seminars, and an MFA from Columbia University. Her *Bar Napkin Sonnets* (Ledge Press, 2009) won the 2008 Ledge Poetry Chapbook Competition. Other collections include *Cleave* (Washington Writers' Publishing House,

2004), *La Seta della Cravatta / The Silk of the Tie* (bilingual; Edizioni l'Obliquo, 2009) and *Spin* (Entasis Press, 2010). She lives in Italy where she writes and translates into both English and Italian. This collaboration with Chloe Haralambous is her first venture into translating Greek.

Translations: John Ashbery, *Un mondo che non può essere migliore: Poesie Scelte 1956–2007* (*A World Which Could Not Be Better: Selected Poems 1956–2007*; with Damiano Abeni), Luca Sossella Editore, 2008.

In this book: GLYKERIA BASDEKI 'The Beast' (p. 287), 'When the Nurses Take their Vengeance' (p. 283), 'You'll Come Around' (p. 285); YIANNIS DOUKAS 'The Children of Abel' (p. 57), 'On the Constellation of Cancer' (p. 59); MOMA RADIĆ 'Noon' (p. 375), 'Really?' (p. 377), 'Stammering Fisherman' (p. 377).

KAREN EMMERICH teaches Translation Studies and Modern Greek Literature in the Department of Comparative Literature at Princeton University. A recipient of translation grants and awards from the NEA, PEN American Center, and the Modern Greek Studies Association, she has translated a range of poetry and prose, including established writers such as Yannis Ritsos and Margarita Karapanou, those less known abroad such as Miltos Sachtouris and Eleni Vakalo, and members of the younger generation such as Amanda Michalopoulou, Sophia Nikolaidou, and Christos Ikonomou. She is that rare breed of translator who builds resonant contexts for her readers, sketching a history of recent Greek literature, but always attuned to the literary effects of her own writing in English.

Translations: Vassilis Vassilikos, *The Few Things I Know About Glafkos Thrassakis,* Seven Stories Press, 2002; Miltos Sachtouris, *Poems (1945–1971),* Archipelago, 2006; Amanda Michalopoulou, *I'd Like,* Dalkey Archive Press, 2008; Ersi Sotiropoulos, *Landscape with Dog and Other Stories,* Clockroot Books, 2009; Margarita Karapanou, *Rien ne va plus,* Clockroot Books, 2009; Margarita Karapanou, *The Sleepwalker,* Clockroot Books, 2010; Yannis Ritsos, *Diaries of Exile* (with Edmund Keeley), Archipelago Books, 2013; Amanda Michalopouou, *Why I Killed My Best Friend,* Open Letter, 2014; Sofia Nikolaidou, *The Scapegoat,* Melville House, 2015; Christos Ikonomou, *Something Will Happen, You'll See,* Archipelago, 2016.

In this book: DIMITRIS ATHINAKIS 'Delirium for the Four Legs of a Love' (p. 11), 'Weakness' (p. 13); PAVLINA MARVIN 'The Perfect Outcast' (p. 205), 'The Weeds' (p. 205); HIVA PANAHI 'The Breath of the Olive Tree' (p. 411); EFTYCHIA PANAYIOTOU 'The Great Gardener' (p. 123), 'Your Justice My Justice' (p. 127); YANNIS STIGGAS *from* 'The Vagrancy of Blood' (p. 47).

STATHIS GOURGOURIS, see poet biography, p. 391.

KRYSTALLI GLYNIADAKIS, see poet biography, p. 135.

RACHEL HADAS, author of more than twenty books of poetry, translations, and essays, studied Classics at Harvard, poetry at Johns Hopkins, and Comparative Literature at Princeton. Since 1981 she has taught in the English Department at Rutgers University. She has received a Guggenheim Fellowship and an award from the American Academy and Institute of Arts and Letters. Her most recent poetry collection is *Questions in the Vestibule* (2016), published by Northwestern University Press. She writes often on Greek poetry in the *The Times Literary Supplement*. Her translations from the Greek focus on poems about Ancient Greece and myth, and like her friend and mentor, the poet and translator James Merrill, view the Ancient and Modern traditions as a continuum.

Translations: A Century of Greek Poetry: 1900–2000 (with Peter Bien, Edmund Keeley, and Karen Van Dyck), Cosmos, 2004; *The Greek Poets: From Homer to the Present* (with Peter Constantine, Edmund Keeley, and Karen Van Dyck), Norton, 2010.

In this book: KYOKO KISHIDA 'Kleine Nachtmusik' (p. 147), 'The Lotus Eaters' (p. 151), 'Sirocco or Soldiery' (p. 153); DANAE SIOZIOU 'Around the House' (p. 193), 'Heaviness' (p. 191), 'Mapping the Geography of the Symptoms of a Footstep' (p. 195).

CHLOE HARALAMBOUS studied Modern Greek at Columbia and Oxford. Her research focuses on the nexus between literature and politics in the history of the Greek and Italian Left. She has been particularly interested in grassroots cultural responses to the crisis and the ways in which they mark a transition in Greek and Italian conceptions of the state. In 2015 she moved to Lesvos in order to work with refugees. Her essay on the present situation (with Katerina Stefatos and Dimitris Papadopoulos) can be found at https://www.press.jhu.

edu/journals/journal_of_modern_greek_studies/Stefatos_Papadopoulos_Haralambous.pdf.

In this book: GLYKERIA BASDEKI 'The Beast' (p. 287), 'When the Nurses Take their Vengeance' (p. 283), 'You'll Come Around' (p. 285); YIANNIS DOUKAS 'The Children of Abel' (p. 57), 'On the Constellation of Cancer' (p. 59); KRYSTALLI GLYNIADAKIS 'National Anthem, 2008, Redux' (p. 137); DIMOSTHENIS PAPAMARKOS *from* 'Paralogue' (p. 265); MOMA RADIĆ 'Noon' (p. 375), 'Really?' (p. 377), 'Stammering Fisherman' (p. 377); KIRIAKOS SIFILTZOGLOU *from* 'Half Truths' (p. 323); EVA STEFANI 'Back' (p. 131), 'Depths' (p. 131), 'Family' (p. 133), 'New Year's Eve' (p. 133).

JACK HIRSCHMAN has translated more than fifty books of poetry from nine different languages. His authors include Paul Celan, Pier Paolo Pasolini, Pablo Neruda, and Roque Dalton. From Greek he has translated Dorou Leftheria, Katerina Gogou and, with Dimitri Charalambous, Yannis Livadas. Charalambous is also his collaborator on *Cross-Section*, an anthology of contemporary Greek poetry (see Further Reading). Hirschman's 1,000-page magnum opus, *The Arcanes*, was published in Italy by Multimedia Edizioni in 2006. He has also edited *Art on the Line: Essays by Artists about the Point Where Their Art and Activism Intersect* (Curbstone Books, 2001), with writing by Amiri Baraka, Vladimir Mayakovsky, James Scully, and César Vallejo, among others. He is a former Poet Laureate of San Francisco.

Translations: Artaud Anthology, City Lights, 1965; *Open Gate: An Anthology of Haitian Creole Poetry,* Curbstone

Books, 2001; *John Coltrane and 15 Poems for Jazz* (with Dimitri Charalambous), C. C. Marimbo, 2008.

In this book: YANNIS LIVADAS 'Jazz, I Say' (p. 365).

GAIL HOLST-WARHAFT is a poet, translator, musician, and literary scholar. She has published translations from Ancient and Modern Greek, French, and Anglo-Saxon in journals and anthologies. Her nonfiction book *Road to Rembetika: Music of a Greek Subculture* (Hakkert, 1980) has become a classic. Other important critical books include *Dangerous Voices: Women's Laments and Greek Literature* (Routledge, 1995) and *The Cue for Passion: Grief and its Political Uses* (Harvard, 2000). Her own poetry has been translated into Greek by Katerina Anghelaki-Rooke and the Cypriot poet Kiriakos Charalambides.

Translations: I Had Three Lives: Selected Poems of Mikis Theodorakis, Livani, 2004; *The Collected Poems of Nikos Kavadias*, Cosmos, 2006.

In this book: APOSTOLOS THIVAIOS 'International' (p. 255), 'Reality' (p. 251), 'Unavoidable' (p. 259).

ADRIANNE KALFOPOULOU teaches at the American College of Greece – Deree, as well as in Regis College's low-residency MFA program. Red Hen has published two collections of her poems, *Wild Greens* (2002) and *Passion Maps* (2009), as well as a work of nonfiction, *Ruin: Essays in Exilic Living* (2014). Her work has appeared in the *Harvard Review*, *Hotel Amerika*, and *The Beloit Poetry Journal*, among other journals. Her poems have been translated into Greek by the poet Katerina Iliopoulou and published by Melani (2014).

In this book: IANA BOUKOVA 'Black *Haiku*' (p. 343), 'Fractal' (p. 349).

SOCRATES KAMBOUROPOULOS has held positions at the General Secretariat for Research and Technology, the University of Crete, and the National Book Center, while also writing poetry, essays and translating the works of poets such as Fiona Sampson, Theo Dorgan, Paula Meehan, and Andrew Maxwell. His work has been featured in *Poetics, Teflon, Poema, New American Writing,* and the *Poetry Review* (see Further Reading).

In this book: DIMITRA KOTOULA 'The Poet' (p. 71).

MARIA MARGARONIS is a bilingual writer, journalist, and broadcaster based in London. Her work has appeared in *The Nation* (where she is a contributing editor), *The Guardian, The Times Literary Supplement,* the *London Review of Books* and many other publications. She also writes and presents documentaries for BBC Radio. She has taught at the New School for Social Research, King's College, London, and Birkbeck, University of London. Currently, she is a research fellow in Modern Greek in the Faculty of Modern and Medieval Languages, Oxford University. She views her reporting on Greece as an ongoing process of translation and interpretation.

In this book: Z. D. AINALIS 'September 3rd 1843' (p. 225); ANNA GRIVA 'The Ants' Lesson' (p. 105), 'Attempt'

(p. 97), 'Triumphal Ode' (p. 109), 'The War with My Animals' (p. 103), 'Ways to Avoid Sadness' (p. 101); THOMAS IOANNOU 'Honourable Compromise' (p. 209); HIVA PANAHI 'Ash Person' (p. 415).

SARAH KATHERINE McCANN graduated from Princeton University (BA, English) and the University of Iowa (MFA, Poetry). A Fulbright Scholar to Greece in 2001, she continues to translate Modern Greek poetry and to write her own. Her work has been published in many journals including *MARGIE, New Voices, Broken Bridge Review, South Dakota Review,* and *Hangin' Loose,* as well as in an anthology of poetry reflecting on the life and work of Robert Frost, *Visiting Frost* (University of Iowa Press, 2005). She was the editor of *Tertium Quid* (Stride Books, 2005), a book of poetry by the late American poet and Grecophile Robert Lax.

In this book: STATHIS BAROUTSOS 'Birdsong' (p. 185); JAZRA KHALEED 'Somewhere in Athens' (p. 159), 'Still Life' (p. 165).

JACOB MOE is an American-born translator and film producer based in Athens. He is a founder and organizer of the annual Syros International Film Festival. After studying literature and political theory at Pomona College, he studied translation theory and practice at the Academy of Athens. He has served as the main translator and interpreter for the Thessaloniki Museum of Photography. Currently he is translating the short stories of Maria Mitsora for Yale University Press, a project for which he was awarded a grant from the PEN/HEIM Translation Fund.

In this book: THOMAS TSALAPATIS 'The Box' (p. 217).

STEPHANOS PAPADOPOULOS was born in North Carolina in 1976 and raised in Paris and Athens. He is the editor and, with Katerina Anghelaki-Rooke, the co-translator of the Greek version of Derek Walcott's *Selected Poems*, published by Kastaniotis Press in 2007. He was awarded a 2010 Civitella Ranieri Fellowship for his third collection of English-language poetry, *The Black Sea* (Sheep Meadow Press, 2012), which was also selected by Mark Strand as the recipient of the 2014 Jeannette Haien Ballard Writer's Prize. Katerina Anghelaki-Rooke's Greek translation of *The Black Sea* was published in 2015 by Kastaniotis. His previous two collections of poetry are *Lost Days* (Rattapallax Press, 2001) and *Hôtel-Dieu* (Sheep Meadow Press, 2009).

In this book: Z. D. AINALIS 'Telemachus' (p. 223); YANNIS STIGGAS 'Armed with Tenderness' (p. 35), 'The Labyrinth's Perfect Acoustics' (p. 43), 'My Brother Paul, the Digger of the Seine' (p. 37), 'Self-Winding' (p. 41).

RICHARD PIERCE is a translator, editor, and sculptor from the San Francisco Bay Area. In his early twenties he lived in Athens for four years, where he was a teacher and journalist. Since then he has lived in Verona, working initially as a teacher, then as an editor at Mondadori, and currently as a freelance translator. A participant in the annual Paros Poetry Translation Symposium and Workshop, he translated the work of Iana Boukova, Krystalli Glyniadakis, Phoebe Giannisi, Socrates Kabouropoulos, Dimitra Kotoula, Angelos Parthenis, and Stamatis Polenakis. His translations have appeared in *The Poetry Review*, *Ars Poetica*, and the online magazine *Greek Poetry Now*.

In this book: STAMATIS POLENAKIS 'Elegy' (p. 235), 'The Great Enigma' (p. 233).

BARIŞ PIRHASAN studied English Language and Literature at Boğaziçi University and Film and Television Directing at the National Film and Television School in England. He is the well-known screenwriter of several Turkish feature films. He has translated Karl Marx, Lewis Carroll, C. P. Cavafy, Walter Scott, E. E. Cummings, and Leonard Cohen into Turkish. In his view, he does not so much translate Yashin Mehmet's multilingual poems as 'process' them in order to expose the intricate power relations between languages. In the case of his contribution to this anthology, for instance, he performs this exposure by substituting English for Turkish and German for Greek.

In this book: MEHMET YASHIN 'Çürüme' (p. 407).

MAX RITVO is a poet living in Manhattan. He was awarded a 2014 Poetry Society of America Fellowship for his chapbook, *Aeons*. His poetry has appeared in *Boston Review*, *The Los Angeles Review of Books*, and as a Poem-a-Day for Poets.org. He is a poetry editor at *Parnassus* and a teaching fellow at Columbia University. His prose and interviews have appeared in *Parnassus*, *Huffington Post*, *Boston Review*, and *The Los Angeles Review of Books*. He is a sketch comic in the NYC-based troupe His Majesty, the Baby.

In this book: JAZRA KHALEED 'Fuck Armageddon' (p. 171).

ANGELOS SAKKIS studied design in Athens and painting at the San Francisco Art Institute. He now lives in Oakland. He has published two chapbooks of poetry, *Memory of* and *Fictional Character*, both with Zarax in 2012. With John Sakkis he has translated four poetry collections by Demosthenes Agrafiotis, an important experimental Athens-based poet active in the international visual arts and poetry scene.

Translations: Demosthenes Agrafiotis, *Chinese Notebook* (with John Sakkis), Post-Apollo Press, 2010; *Maribor* (with John Sakkis), Post-Apollo Press, 2015.

In this book: PHOEBE GIANNISI '(Lotus Eaters II' (p. 119); HIVA PANAHI 'Companion' (p. 413).

FIONA SAMPSON is a poet, essayist, and translator. A specialist in the literatures of Eastern Europe, she co-edited *A Fine Line*, an anthology of young poets from Central and South-Eastern Europe, and founded and edited *Orient Express* (2002–5), a magazine of contemporary writing from that region. In 2005 she became the editor of *Poetry Review*. As a critic, she contributes regularly to *The Guardian*, *The Irish Times*, *The Independent*, *TLS*, and other publications.

Translations: Jaan Kaplinski, *Evening Brings Everything Back*, Bloodaxe Books, 2004, (with Jaan Kaplinski); Amir Or, *Day*, Dedalus Press, 2006, (with Amir Or).

In this book: DIMITRA KOTOULA 'The Poet' (p. 71).

A. E. STALLINGS is a poet and translator who writes from Greece about the Greek situation and literary scene (see Further Reading for her letters from Athens for *Poetry* and *The Poetry Review*). She studied Classics at the University of Georgia and at Oxford and has lived in Athens since 1999. Her verse translation of Lucretius in rhyming fourteeners was heralded by Peter Stothard at *The Times Literary Supplement* as among the most extraordinary classical translations of recent times. Her own poetry works between languages, imagining in *Olives* (TriQuarterly, 2012), for example, that hands (*heria*) and knives (*maheria*) can rhyme in English, though this rhyme is possible only in Greek. Her other poetry collections are *Archaic Smile* (University of Evansville Press, 1999) and *Hapax* (TriQuarterly, 2006). She is the recipient of fellowships from the Guggenheim and MacArthur Foundations.

Translations: The Nature of Things, Penguin Classics, 2007; 'From *Erotokritos*', in *The Greek Poets: From Homer to the Present*, Norton, 2010, pp. 368–76.

In this book: 'Austerity Measures' (p. xxii); KATERINA ILIOPOULOU 'The Fox' (p. 79), 'Mister Tau in a Seascape' (p. 85), 'The Siren' (p. 87); PANAYOTIS IOANNIDIS 'Mosquito' (p. 5), 'The Poet in the Hallway' (p. 5); DIMITRA KOTOULA 'Head of a Satyr' (p. 67); CHLOE KOUTSOUMBELI 'Penelope III' (p. 315), 'The Yellow Taxi' (p. 313); STAMATIS POLENAKIS 'Poetry 2048' (p. 233), 'Poetry Does Not Suffice' (p. 231).

KAREN VAN DYCK directs the Program in Hellenic Studies in the Classics Department at Columbia University. She is the author of *Kassandra and the Censors*

(Cornell, 1998) as well as articles on Greek and Greek Diaspora literature published in journals such as *PMLA*, the *Los Angeles Review of Books*, and the *Journal of Modern Greek Studies*. She has translated the work of the Generation of the 1970s, most notably Katerina Anghelaki-Rooke, Rhea Galanaki, Maria Laina, and Jenny Mastoraki, and collaborated with Eleni Sikelianos on translations of the multilingual nineteenth-century poet Dionysis Solomos. Her translations devise formal experiments which construct connections between the Greek texts and poetry in English. Katerina Anghelaki-Rooke and Haris Vlavianos have translated a selection of her poems into Greek for the journal *Poetics*.

Translations: The Rehearsal of Misunderstanding: Three Collections by Contemporary Greek Women Poets, Wesleyan, 1998; *A Century of Greek Poetry* (with Peter Bien, Peter Constantine, and Edmund Keeley), Cosmos, 2004; *The Scattered Papers of Penelope: New and Selected Poems by Katerina Anghelaki-Rooke*, Anvil Press Poetry, 2008 and Graywolf, 2009; *The Greek Poets: Homer to the Present* (with Peter Constantine, Rachel Hadas, and Edmund Keeley), Norton, 2010.

In this book: YIORGOS ALISANOGLOU 'The Painting' (p. 277); CHRISTOS ANGELAKOS ['If you dive inside your head'] (p. 359); STATHIS ANTONIOU 'The Dogs' (p. 91); STATHIS BAROUTSOS 'My Children' (p. 177, in collaboration with Diamanda Galas); GLYKERIA BASDEKI 'Let Down the Chain' (p. 281), 'Mama's a Poet' (p. 283); YIANNIS EFTHYMIADES *from 9/11 or Falling Man* (p. 21), *from* 'New Division' (p. 21), *from O Say Can You See* (p. 27); PHOEBE GIANNISI '(Penelope – Ἔχω πάθος για σένα)' (p. 115); STATHIS GOURGOURIS 'The Bride with the Bullets'

(p. 395), 'Nameless Rain' (p. 401); ANNA GRIVA *from* 'Depths' (p. 99); DOUKAS KAPANTAÏS 'Country Houses in Winter' (p. 63); GAZMEND KAPLLANI 'Thus Spoke the Stranger' (p. 381); JAZRA KHALEED 'Refrain' (p. 159); KYOKO KISHIDA 'The Violin' (p. 149); GIANNIS PALAVOS 'Password' (p. 291); EFTYCHIA PANAYIOTOU 'Just Before You Stood Up' (p. 127), 'The Outside of My Mind' (p. 125); OLGA PAPAKOSTA 'Empty Inbox' (p. 309); ELENA PENGA 'Fish' (p. 243), 'Heads' (p. 241), 'Nightmare Pink' (p. 247), 'Passages' (p. 239), 'Skin' (p. 245); ELENA POLYGENI 'To be Done with the Matter' (p. 271); ANGELIKI SIGOUROU 'Colors' (p. 303); DANAE SIOZIOU 'The Guards' (p. 189); THOMAS TSALAPATIS 'Word Monday' (p. 219).

RYAN VAN WINKLE is a poet, artist, and critic living in Edinburgh. He writes and produces podcasts for the Scottish Poetry Library and the Scottish Book Trust. His own poetry has appeared in *The American Poetry Review*, *AGNI*, *Poetry New Zealand*, *Poetry Scotland*, and Carcanet's 2010 *Oxford Anthology of New Poets*. He has two collections: *Tomorrow, We Will Live Here* (Salt, 2010) and *The Good Dark* (Penned in the Margins, 2015).

In this book: KATERINA ILIOPOULOU, 'Penthesilea' (p. 81).

INDEX OF POEMS IN ENGLISH

INDEX OF POEMS IN GREEK